Michael Biggins
Janet Crayne
Editors

Publishing in Yugoslavia's Successor States

Publishing in Yugoslavia's Successor States has been co-published simultaneously as *Slavic & East European Information Resources*, Volume 1, Numbers 2/3 2000.

Pre-publication
REVIEWS,
COMMENTARIES,
EVALUATIONS . . .

"Summarizes the topics of the Slavic librarians' electronic discussion list "Slavlibs" in a scholarly way with immediate practical use for a broader audience. . . . A truly international forum for information specialists from both West and East."

Dr. Gottfried Kratz, MA
Slavic Librarian
Muenster University Library, Germany

More pre-publication
REVIEWS, COMMENTARIES, EVALUATIONS . . .

"**A** notable characteristic of this impressive new journal is its wealth of information for librarians and other professionals who work in the Slavic and East European Field. It highlights current developments in publishing, including the latest Internet and electronic resources. Included are articles of a high standard by well-informed and distinguished librarians who have had years of experience in the field and can discuss, for example, "A ten-year history of the Hungarian press" as well as "Recent publishing trends in Poland" and the "Russian book trade in '98 and '99." An extra dimension is the international coverage of reference materials and bibliographic tools in the reviews by a variety of specialists. The journal is of enormous practical benefit and provides an exceptional service. . . . It will clearly be the principal journal that Slavic librarians will consult in the future as it is a rich source of valuable and relevant information for their needs and can be considered a major contribution to the field."

Mary Stevens
Slavic Selector
University of Toronto Library

"**T**he contributors to this erudite collection offer fascinating glimpses into the history of publishing in the South Slav area, from the fifteenth and sixteenth centuries to the present. Regional comparisons are telling: in Bosnia-Herzegovina, for example, only 50 books were published during the entire Ottoman period (1463-1878), while Viennese publisher Josef Kurzbeck alone printed 151 books in Serbian in the last decades of the eighteenth century. The book's focus, however, is on the 1990s, a decade of war, economic chaos, and impoverishment. Here, the authors show how the recent Bosnian War of 1991-95 impacted publishing not only in Bosnia, but also in Serbia, where, under the pressures of the war, readership shrank, print runs declined, and scholarly and publishing standards were impaired. Publishing in Kosovo was also impacted by Milosevic's nationalist agenda; already in the mid-1990s, as this book shows, Serbian authorities pulped Albanian-language books from the Pristina National Library, in an effort to erase the cultural memory.

Taken in sum, this volume makes an important contribution to our understanding of the social and political history of the region."

Sabrina P. Ramet, PhD
Professor of International Studies
University of Washington

"These collected essays go beyond compilation and illuminate the rapidly changing character of pivotal cultural institutions in the lands of the former Yugoslavia. The authors survey the history of publishing from its late medieval inception as a producer of religious catechisms and scriptures, through the 19th century era of "national awakenings," into the state-controlled and ideologically driven socialist era, through decentralized Republican autonomy, and finally in the past two decades characterized by the explosive growth of privately owned presses. Among other valuable insights, the authors show that the major trends of the 1990s had their origins in the previous decade, when ideological rigor gradually gave way to greater diversity and publishers became bolder in producing works by social and political critics. Usable as a reference source, this book also provides a valuable institutional perspective on the major transformations in the lands of the former Yugoslavia over the past half Century."

Robert J. Donia, PhD
Research Associate
Center for Russian and East European Studies
University of Michigan

"The editors of *Publishing in Yugoslavia's Successor States* should be commended for putting a valuable tool into the hands of Slavic librarians and scholars, one which has been sorely lacking. All regions of the area are covered including those which have received little attention in the literature to date: Bosnia, Macedonia, Montenegro, and Kosovo. . . .

Of practical value to librarians and scholars are the final three sections of each essay. There one finds an annotated list of publishing houses, providing details of the kinds of literature in which they specialize. A list of vendors, most with contact information that includes web sites, will certainly be of service to those charged with acquiring these publications for their institutions. Rounding out each essay is a categorized listing of the important newspapers and scholarly and popular journals, each with descriptive comments. This volume will become an indispensable resource for anyone needing access to the publications of this region."

Allan Urbanic, PhD, MLIS
Librarian for Slavic Collections
University of California, Berkeley

Publishing in Yugoslavia's Successor States

Publishing in Yugoslavia's Successor States has been co-published simultaneously as *Slavic & East European Information Resources,* Volume 1, Numbers 2/3 2000.

Map 1: Yugoslavia within its 1991 boundaries, showing the six republics and two autonomous regions. (Source: *Former Yugoslavia*. Scale ca. I:4,800,000. Washington, DC: Central Intelligence Agency, 1996).

Publishing in Yugoslavia's Successor States

Michael Biggins
Janet Crayne
Editors

Publishing in Yugoslavia's Successor States has been co-published simultaneously as *Slavic & East European Information Resources,* Volume 1, Numbers 2/3 2000.

The Haworth Information Press
An Imprint of
The Haworth Press, Inc.
New York • London • Oxford

Published by

The Haworth Information Press, 10 Alice Street, Binghamton, NY 13904-1580 USA

The Haworth Information Press is an imprint of the Haworth Press, Inc., 10 Alice Street, Binghamton, NY 13904-1580 USA.

Publishing in Yugoslavia's Successor States has been co-published simultaneously as *Slavic & East European Information Resources,* Volume 1, Numbers 2/3 2000.

The development, preparation, and publication of this work has been undertaken with great care. However, the publisher, employees, editors, and agents of The Haworth Press and all imprints of The Haworth Press, Inc., including The Haworth Medical Press® and The Pharmaceutical Products Press®, are not responsible for any errors contained herein or for consequences that may ensue from use of materials or information contained in this work. Opinions expressed by the author(s) are not necessarily those of The Haworth Press, Inc.

The Haworth Press, Inc., 10 Alice Street, Binghamton, NY 13904-1580 USA

Cover design by Thomas J. Mayshock Jr.

Library of Congress Cataloging-in-Publication Data

Publishing in Yugoslavia's successor states / Michael Biggins, Janet Crayne, editors.
     p. cm.
     "Co-published simultaneously as Slavic & East European information resources, volume 1, numbers 2/3 2000."
     Includes bibliographical references and index.
     ISBN 0-7890-1045-3 (alk. paper)–ISBN 0-7890-1046-1 (pbk. : alk. paper)
     1. Publishers and publishing–Former Yugoslav republics. 2. Periodicals–Publishing–Former Yugoslav republics. I. Biggins, Michael. II. Crayne, Janet. III. Slavic & East European information resources.
  Z443 .P83 2001
  070.5′09497–dc21
                                                        00-067349

Indexing, Abstracting & Website/Internet Coverage

This section provides you with a list of major indexing & abstracting services. That is to say, each service began covering this periodical during the year noted in the right column. Most Websites which are listed below have indicated that they will either post, disseminate, compile, archive, cite or alert their own Website users with research-based content from this work. (This list is as current as the copyright date of this publication.)

(continued)

*Special Bibliographic Notes related to special journal issues
(separates) and indexing/abstracting:*

- indexing/abstracting services in this list will also cover material in any "separate" that is co-published simultaneously with Haworth's special thematic journal issue or DocuSerial. Indexing/abstracting usually covers material at the article/chapter level.
- monographic co-editions are intended for either non-subscribers or libraries which intend to purchase a second copy for their circulating collections.
- monographic co-editions are reported to all jobbers/wholesalers/approval plans. The source journal is listed as the "series" to assist the prevention of duplicate purchasing in the same manner utilized for books-in-series.
- to facilitate user/access services all indexing/abstracting services are encouraged to utilize the co-indexing entry note indicated at the bottom of the first page of each article/chapter/contribution.
- this is intended to assist a library user of any reference tool (whether print, electronic, online, or CD-ROM) to locate the monographic version if the library has purchased this version but not a subscription to the source journal.
- individual articles/chapters in any Haworth publication are also available through the Haworth Document Delivery Service (HDDS).

Publishing in Yugoslavia's Successor States

CONTENTS

ABOUT THE EDITORS

Michael Biggins, PhD, MS, has served as Head of the Slavic and East European Section at the University of Washington Libraries, Seattle, since 1994. He is also an affiliate faculty member in UW's Department of Slavic Languages and Literatures. He holds an MS in library and information science from the University of Illinois/Urbana-Champaign, and a PhD in Slavic languages and literatures from the University of Kansas. His previous publications include several studies of collection development and acquisitions from Southeastern Europe. He is also a widely published translator of contemporary Slovenian literature (prose fiction, essays, and poetry) into English.

Janet Crayne, MLIS, MA, received her BA in Russian from the University of Wisconsin in 1971, graduating Phi Beta Kappa and with honors. She also holds an MA in Slavic language and literatures and a certificate in Russian area studies. She worked in the Slavic Division of the Harvard College Library from 1982 to 1987, during which time she earned an MLIS degree from the University of Rhode Island. From 1987 to 1993 she worked as Slavic Cataloger at the University of Virginia. She is currently one of two Slavic librarians at the University of Michigan, where she serves as Southeast European Specialist and supervises technical services in the Slavic Division.

Preface

Without any doubt, the 1990s will be remembered as the decade of Yugoslavia's prolonged disintegration. At the time of this writing, it appears equally possible that the 2000s will see either a continuation of this process or the gradual rebuilding of new, smaller societies and nations as they emerge from ten years of conflict, isolation, and authoritarian rule. In North America and Europe, where the decade's most common reaction to the debacle has been a pitying headshake and befuddled exasperation at what is dismissively portrayed as an age-old Balkan internecine feud, it is clear now, in retrospect, that the extent and quality of information about the Yugoslav crisis circulated by governments and mass media was sorely, and often wantonly, inadequate.

In point of fact, since the late 1980s a virtual blueprint of the conflict lay accessible to anyone in a position to track the independent print media that were then emerging in Yugoslavia's various republics. Weekly independent news magazines such as *Mladina* in Slovenia, *Danas* in Croatia, and, later, *Vreme* in Serbia courageously documented the centrifugal political forces at work in Yugoslavia in the years following the death in 1980 of the country's authoritarian leader, Josip Broz Tito. Independent daily newspapers, often located in provincial cities away from the centers of political control, pursued similar policies, adhering to high standards of objective political coverage. The periodical press also weighed in over time with more reflective assessments of the country's evolving political crisis and recommendations for managing it. Finally, as Yugoslavia's old communist paradigm of information management gradually lost control, the market

[Haworth co-indexing entry note]: "Preface." Biggins, Michael, and Janet Crayne. Co-published simultaneously in *Slavic & East European Information Resources* (The Haworth Information Press, an imprint of The Haworth Press, Inc.) Vol. 1, No. 2/3, 2000, pp. xiii-xvi; and: *Publishing in Yugoslavia's Successor States* (ed: Michael Biggins, and Janet Crayne) The Haworth Information Press, an imprint of The Haworth Press, Inc., 2000, pp. xi-xiv. Single or multiple copies of this article are available for a fee from The Haworth Document Delivery Service [1-800-342-9678, 9:00 a.m. - 5:00 p.m. (EST). E-mail address: getinfo@haworthpressinc.com].

xi

also gave rise to numerous tabloid weeklies and dailies that banked on nationalism and fear, serving as handmaidens to media-savvy demagogues and helping to rekindle past rivalries.

Library research collections around the world that emphasize the former Yugoslavia have documented this process in detail and will continue to be an important resource for years to come, as the political and social history of the century's final, most contentious Balkan War is written and rewritten. The political miscalculations and blunders of the 1990s, and the tragedies that have resulted, confirm the importance of maintaining reliable information resources about this and other sensitive and complex areas of the world, which tend otherwise to be obscured by the broad gestures of great power politics or the inattention of America's isolationist mass media. The year 2000 is almost certainly not the end of history in the Balkans as the world has known it for the past decade. The uneasy Bosnian confederation, the emergence of an independent Montenegro, the maintenance of stability in a multi-ethnic Macedonia, and the eventual democratization of authoritarian Serbia and Croatia are all major challenges which, if not successfully resolved, could trigger further crises. Throughout the next decade it will be critically important not just to maintain, but to broaden the flow of reliable information from and about the region, both for purposes of current analysis and for later historical research.

In view of the radical changes in the political and intellectual map of the former Yugoslavia over the past decade, the authors and editors of this volume offer a survey of the publishing landscape there as one step toward ensuring that libraries stay informed about regional information resources and continue to anticipate and meet the needs of researchers and the general public. Six contributors, each with extensive professional expertise in a particular country or region of the former Yugoslavia, have written articles that both sketch the historical context of the region's publishing industry and provide an overview of the publishing houses, authors and titles of greatest potential interest to research libraries today.

The articles reflect the varying degrees to which each republic or region has been impacted by the war. Even in the most disruptive circumstances, the societies of the former Yugoslavia have continued to support native publishing industries. Under a devastating siege from 1992 to 1995, the Bosnian capital city of Sarajevo still managed to produce a daily newspaper, *Oslobodjenje* (Liberation), which was one of the most important civilizing institutions holding the city's shredded social fabric together and is certainly the single most valuable historical document of the siege. If publishers could eke out an existence even in Bosnia in the mid-1990s, then there was no question of their viability in any of the other former Yugoslav republics, where, by comparison, warfare was limited and the economic and social disruptions were held in check.

While the publishing industries in Bosnia and Kosovo have been razed and rebuilt, the industry in Slovenia–which saw only brief hostilities in the summer of 1991, and was then free to realign its market toward neighboring Italy and Austria–has changed incrementally. Ranging somewhere between these extremes are Croatia, Serbia, Montenegro and Macedonia, each of which has suffered variously from isolation, economic sanctions, authoritarian rule, or civil unrest throughout the 1990s. One is impressed by the inefficiency of the region's authoritarian regimes in limiting their populations' access to information, particularly to print media offering objective news coverage, critical analysis of current events, and new creative literature subversive of state ideologies. Perhaps, however, this has happened not out of negligence, but from a cynical acknowledgment on the part of governments that control of the airwaves is enough to ensure control of the masses. In the late-twentieth-century's television landscape, serious, intellectually taxing print media circulating among a minority of a given country's educated class do not provoke the kind of mass demonstrations that topple regimes.

What role the Internet may eventually play in changing Balkan societies remains, of course, entirely speculative. As the articles in this issue make clear, many newspapers and a few periodicals in the region have launched online editions in the past two to three years. War has slowed development of the region's telecommunications infrastructure, and barely viable economies make ownership of, or even access to, computers possible for only a few. Whether wide deployment of Internet access might someday tip the media balance back in the direction of high-quality, high-density printed information is a question that remains, for now, as unanswered for the Balkans as it is for North America and Europe.

What is clear is that, in the meantime, many bright and courageous idealists in these countries will continue to champion the cause of a free press, making a crucial contribution to the slow transformation of their societies and, indirectly, enabling individuals and institutions abroad to form a fuller, more accurate picture of both the straightforward and the complex realities of the Balkans.

The articles in this issue are presented in rough geographic sequence, from northwest to southeast. Their authors include:

- Michael Biggins (Slovenia), Slavic and East European Librarian at the University of Washington, Seattle;
- Janet Crayne (Bosnia and Hercegovina), Senior Associate Librarian in the Slavic and East European Division at the University of Michigan's Hatcher Graduate Library;
- George Mitrevski (Macedonia), Professor of Russian language and literature in the Department of Modern Languages, Auburn University;
- Ivana Nikolić (Serbia), Acquisitions and Exchange Librarian at the National Library of Serbia, Belgrade;
- Frances Trix (Kosovo), Associate Professor of Anthropology (specializing in linguistic anthropology) at Wayne State University;
- Vesna Vučković (Montenegro), Acquisitions and Exchange Librarian at the Crnojević Central National Library in Cetinje, Montenegro.

English translations of the articles on publishing in Montenegro and Serbia, originally written in Serbo-Croatian, are by Michael Biggins. A contribution on publishing in Croatia was not available by press time, and will appear in a future issue of *Slavic & East European Information Resources*.

Michael Biggins
Janet Crayne
Editors
January 24, 2000

Editors' note: Throughout this volume, the lower-case barred d has been typeset as dj.

SLOVENIA

MAP 2. Slovenia

Source: *Former Yugoslavia*. Scale 1:1,750,000. Washington, DC: Central Intelligence Agency, 1992

Publishing in Slovenia

Michael Biggins

SUMMARY. The author traces the history of vernacular publishing and printing in Slovenia from their beginnings in the late sixteenth century, concentrating on the period after 1945 and especially on 1990 to the present. Nearly all the major publishers survived the transition to a market economy, although many of the newest ventures did not. The country's small size has always meant a limited market for material in Slovenian, and publications have become quite expensive relative to income. Still, the Slovenian publishing industry is now strong, streamlined and ready for entry into the European Union. The author discusses current publishers of interest for research libraries and their profiles, then lists important serials by format and subject. A list of suppliers of Slovenian books and serials to Western libraries (vendors and a Slovenian library with active exchanges) is included, along with contact information and descriptions. *[Article copies available for a fee from The Haworth Document Delivery Service: 1-800-342-9678. E-mail address: <getinfo@haworthpressinc.com> Website: <http://www.HaworthPress.com> © 2000 by The Haworth Press, Inc. All rights reserved.]*

KEYWORDS. Slovenia, Slovenian, Publishers and Publishing, Acquisitions

HISTORICAL ROOTS, 1550-1945

Publishing and printing in Slovenia have a venerable but fitful history that begins with late sixteenth-century books printed in the

Michael Biggins, PhD, MLS, is Slavic and East European Librarian, Suzzallo Library, Box 352900, University of Washington, Seattle, WA 98195 (E-mail: mbiggins@u.washington.edu).

[Haworth co-indexing entry note]: "Publishing in Slovenia." Biggins, Michael. Co-published simultaneously in *Slavic & East European Information Resources* (The Haworth Information Press, an imprint of The Haworth Press, Inc.) Vol. 1, No. 2/3, 2000, pp. 3-38; and: *Publishing in Yugoslavia's Successor States* (ed: Michael Biggins, and Janet Crayne) The Haworth Information Press, an imprint of The Haworth Press, Inc., 2000, pp. 3-38. Single or multiple copies of this article are available for a fee from The Haworth Document Delivery Service [1-800-342-9678, 9:00 a.m. - 5:00 p.m. (EST). E-mail address: getinfo@haworthpressinc.com].

vernacular by native Protestant reformers, including catechisms, excerpts of the New Testament, and Slovenian language primers (translated or written by Slovenia's most ardent reformer, Primož Trubar), and culminating in the complete Slovene Bible translated by Jurij Dalmatin (1584). Many early Slovene books bore the imprint of Wittenberg, the center of the Protestant press for most of the German-ruled lands. Like most Habsburg domains that experienced a brief reformation followed by a swift and total counterreformation, use of the printed vernacular in Slovenia was all but snuffed out by the vigorous efforts of the Habsburg crown and Roman Catholic clergy to reassert control over the Slovene-speaking lands. Eclipsed for more than two centuries by the politically and economically dominant German- and Italian-speaking communities that both surrounded and permeated Slovenia from the time of the Counterreformation–from about 1598 until the early 1800s–Slovene literary culture, broadly conceived, passed through a long period of dormancy that corresponds to the *temno* (darkness) of Czech history.

Vernacular publishing revived again in the late 1700s, at the time of the beginnings of a Slovene national rebirth that was fostered by the liberal reforms of Austrian Emperor Joseph II. While the fortunes of Slovene as a medium of printed discourse would rise or fall with the temper of the reigning monarch for decades to come, in the nineteenth century the vernacular charted a steady upward arc as the numbers of Slovene-educated city dwellers and literate peasantry increased, creating a demand for newspapers, periodicals and books printed in their native language.

The end of the 19th and beginning of the twentieth centuries saw a veritable explosion of Slovene-language literature and publications, which can be viewed in retrospect as a central manifestation of an ever-broadening movement toward national self-assertion. The first flourishing of a full-scale Slovene publishing industry coincided with the establishment of Slovenia in 1918 as a constituent element of the newly consolidated Kingdom of Serbs, Croats and Slovenes, and continued for over twenty years, until the invasion and defeat of the first Yugoslavia by Axis forces in 1941. German and Italian forces of occupation closed Slovene publishing houses while obliterating Slovenia as a territorial entity, incorporating its regions into the German Reich, Italy, or Hungary. As elsewhere in Yugoslavia and Eastern Europe, in Slovenia the four years of occupation provided the stage for a civil war that pitted politically conservative, Catholic, or pro-German segments of society against a coalition of Catholic liberals, secular progressives and revolutionary forces dominated by the Communist Partisans. The Partisans maintained active underground presses, both in Ljubljana and the Slovene countryside, producing both newspapers and books that served the cause of their united Liberation Front.

IN TITO'S YUGOSLAVIA

The war years were the most violent in Slovenia's otherwise isolated history, and reinforced many Slovenes' sense of being an endangered nation. The post-war period from 1945 until 1991, during which Slovenia existed as one of six member republics of the Socialist Federated Republic of Yugoslavia, with its capital in Belgrade, brought peace and security for the Slovenes as a nation at the price of civil rights and national sovereignty.

Slovene publishing experienced its next efflorescence when it was reconstituted *ab ovo* in 1945, as Yugoslavia's new Titoist government established several major state-run enterprises to carry the main burden of responsibility for publishing in the republic, which then numbered some 1.5 million mostly Slovene-speaking inhabitants. In the command economy of Titoist Yugoslavia the publishing industry flourished as never before, with generous government subsidies allocated to support the publication of works portraying the new regime in a favorable light. State ideologies that were focused on communism, internationalism, and the glorification of the supranational Partisans' wartime achievements resulted in a plethora of publications on these subjects. Beginning in the 1950s, as Yugoslavia tried to establish a unique identity for itself outside–or between–the Cold War's polarized camps, the government promulgated new state ideologies of political nonalignment and worker self-management. The task of propagandizing and legitimizing these ideologies similarly consumed whole forests of paper.

Within the confines of unitarist Yugoslavia, Slovenia and other republics periodically asserted their own political will against the controls of the federal government based in Belgrade. Brief periods of political and social liberalization, followed each time by renewed imposition of federal strictures, occurred in the early 1960s, late 1960s and early 1970s, and again in the 1980s, until Slovenia and other republics finally seceded from the Federation in 1991. The liberal political climate of those periods fostered spells of more diverse and liberal publishing activity, which continued less intensively even in the following periods of political retrenchment. Non-political works and an enormous amount of material of exceptionally high quality, virtually untouched by ideological formulations–original belles lettres, literary criticism, memoirs, history, philosophy and sociology–enjoyed the benefits of government-subsidized publishing, including large print runs, low retail prices, and wide accessibility to all segments of the population. Except for the party-run Komunist and a few other houses whose missions were ideological, nearly all publishers performed an intricate balancing act of self-censorship, which sought not to commit flagrant violations against political authority, while at the same time providing the Slovene reading public with material sufficiently grounded in reality to sell.

The three main state-sponsored houses that were established soon after 1945–Državna založba Slovenije (State Publishing House of Slovenia), Mladinska knjiga (Youth Books) and Cankarjeva založba (Cankar Publishing House)–actively and productively dominated the Slovene book market for the next 45 years, until the collapse of the unitarist Yugoslav state in 1991 and well into Slovenia's first full decade of independence. Only a handful of pre-war publishers revived after 1945. These included Slovenska matica, which had been founded in 1864 as a publishing arm of the national rebirth and continued to further that mission; the Slovene Academy of Sciences and Arts Publishing House (founded in 1938), which published on all aspects of Slovenia from a non-ideological perspective; and Mohorjeva družba (The Society of St. Hermagoras), a Roman Catholic-sponsored house originally based in Klagenfurt, Austria, which now also opened an autonomous branch in Slovenia. In addition, many smaller, professionally-oriented publishing houses in Ljubljana, university research institutes, learned societies, museums, government agencies, and smaller trade publishers located in the provinces (Obzorja in Maribor, Lipa in Koper, Pomurska založba in Murska Sobota, and others) marketed books and journals to more specialized or regional audiences.

Beginning in the 1960s, the three leading publishing houses in Ljubljana began to develop working relationships with West European publishers, from whom they learned methods of quality book production and marketing strategies. Slovene printers imported Western-manufactured printing and binding equipment and acquired skills that immediately set their product apart from that of the more southern republics. Other Yugoslav publishers began contracting with Slovene printers for the production of their deluxe editions, and over time the quality of Slovene printing was discovered by publishers throughout Eastern Europe. Book clubs, mail-order service, and door-to-door book vending became standard practices in Slovenia in the 1970s, distinguishing its market even more from that of the other Yugoslav republics.

Aside from these incipient market-oriented strategies and standards of production, what made Slovenian publishing unique within the Yugoslav context was the fact that the use of the Slovene language for any practical purpose ended at the Republic's border. Four other Yugoslav republics (Croatia, Serbia, Montenegro, Bosnia) shared a single standard language–Serbo-Croatian, with minor regional variations–and thus materials published in one republic could rely on large potential markets in the other republics, provided the subject matter was of broad interest and distribution networks functioned. Moreover, since Serbo-Croatian served as the lingua franca for all of Yugoslavia, publications from those republics found supplementary, if more marginal, markets in Slovenia and Macedonia.

Slovenia, by contrast, with a total population ranging over the past fifty years from 1.5 to 2 million, and a potential book market much smaller than that, has had to make do with what demand could be generated within the Republic's borders. Complicating this reality is the fact that the Slovene national identity is defined overwhelmingly in terms of language, and that a dynamic market of Slovene-language books and journals is still viewed as one of the most crucially important means of perpetuating that identity. Notwithstanding Yugoslavia's constitutional guarantees to defend national languages within the multi-ethnic state, the harsh lesson in national fragility learned in World War II was now followed by a new, perceived threat of linguistic colonization and eventual assimilation into Yugoslavia's Serbo-Croatian-speaking majority. Almost by inheritance, Slovenes bore a stigma of marginalization, which they used language and the printed word to combat.

Likewise, interest in Slovene publications in the U.S. and Western Europe has always been marginal. Individuals (mostly Slovenes living abroad) and large research libraries could acquire materials through Western distributors, such as Kubon and Sagner in Munich, or directly by contacting one of the three major publishing houses in Ljubljana, each of which usually had one employee assigned part-time to handling overseas retail sales. A few research libraries have maintained book and serial exchange relationships with one or more of three potential partner institutions in Slovenia–the National and University Library, the Library of the Slovene Academy of Sciences and Arts, or the Central Economics Library, all located in Ljubljana.

A high tide of activity in Slovene acquisitions in the U.S. was reached under the federally-sponsored PL-480 program for Yugoslavia, which provided a dozen research libraries with nearly all published material of value from 1967 through 1971. Of those dozen libraries, no more than six continued after PL-480 to develop extensive Slovene collections.[1] A near total lack of formal Slovene language programs in U.S. Slavic studies programs made terra incognita of Slovenia, even among area studies specialists. Yet throughout the 1960s, 1970s and 1980s, Western perceptions of politically unorthodox Yugoslavia as a potentially strategic, ideological wedge in the flank of the Eastern Bloc–perceptions that Tito certainly encouraged, to strengthen his own position–established Yugoslavia as a critically important area for advanced study, according to U.S. government guidelines. Most of the attention in academia focused on the more populous and politically influential Serbo-Croatian-speaking regions. As the short-term, socialist economic miracle that Western credits helped to produce began unraveling in the decade after Tito's death, Slovenia unexpectedly emerged as the Federation's most voluble and weakest link and the earliest catalyst of its disintegration.

THE TRANSFORMATION TO AN INDEPENDENT PRESS
1981-1990

Tito's death in 1980 left wide segments of the Yugoslav population with the sudden, shocked realization of how completely dependent they had become on their leader's charismatic, authoritarian personality as a force for unifying the country's disparate ethnic elements. After the initial shock of loss subsided and federal power devolved on a cumbersome collective presidency consisting of one representative from each of the republics, perceptive constituencies within the republics saw a renewed opportunity to carve out autonomy for themselves, and possibly even independence. Exploiting their position on the linguistic, geographic and political margins of Yugoslavia to take bold steps that would not yet be tolerated in more central parts of the country, Slovene intellectuals accomplished this through a variety of means, including the creation of new, small publishing enterprises in an industry that had been fixed and inflexible since 1945.

The University of Ljubljana's branch of the Socialist Youth League of Slovenia (UK ZSMS) had long been a problem child of the regime, having sponsored for decades the cyclically rebellious student newspaper *Tribuna*. In 1981, the UK ZSMS founded its own publishing house, Knjižnica revolucionarne teorije (Library of Revolutionary Theory–whose acronym, Krt, translates to mole in English). Under a thin guise of Marxist revisionism, Krt from the start published anarchist texts that subverted government orthodoxy and sought to give students and youth a sense of their potential influence. Subjects included the history of the Slovene youth movement, the Prague Spring of 1968, punk as a social phenomenon in Slovenia, and other politically threatening topics that otherwise would never be covered in print. Many of Krt's early authors and editors were faculty and students at the University, although the 10 to 12 titles it published per year also included translated anthologies of Western political and social theorists. Krt's print runs went as high as 2,500 copies and often sold out.[2]

A year later, in 1982, a group of established writers, philosophers, sociologists and others organized an open letter signed by 60 prominent intellectuals and addressed to all of Slovenia's main cultural institutions, declaring the need to establish a new journal of social, political and literary ideas. In this way *Nova revija* (The New Review) came into existence, a journal that sought to highlight Slovene national history and identity, emphasizing the importance of religion, democracy, human rights and civil society. In 1987, *Nova revija's* famous issue no. 57 bore the heading "Contributions toward a Slovene national program," and featured sixteen articles by leading intellectuals on various aspects of Slovenia's past and future, stressing particularly the need to separate from Yugoslavia. At this provocation, the government pronounced itself ready to shut the journal down, as it had other Slovene journals when they had dared to cross the line in earlier decades (*Beseda*, *Revija '57*, and *Perspektive* in the 1950s and 1960s).

As a sign of how radically diminished the government's influence was, it yielded after vigorous objections from Slovene intellectuals.[3] At the height of its popularity in the 1980s, *Nova revija* had a press run of some 3,500 copies, which has since dropped to around 1,500 in the 1990s.

The most radically open, objective, and aggressive news publication in the 1980s was the weekly magazine *Mladina*. Founded in 1943 as the Communist Party's magazine for young people, in the early 1980s it became radicalized, espousing freedom of speech and of the press and pursuing sensitive investigative stories to uncover government corruption. By the late 1980s it developed an iconoclastic, no holds barred style, and was responsible for uncovering plans by the Yugoslav National Army to suppress the Slovene national movement. Its highwater press runs of 65,000 copies in the 1980s dropped to around 25,000 by the mid-1990s.

Creative literature–poetry, prose fiction, and the essay–also attained a last golden age of the century in the late 1980s. Nearly all of the country's writers were involved in one way or another in the drive to independence. A protest event sponsored by the Society of Slovene Writers in 1988 involved dozens of writers in a marathon public reading to express moral support for four Slovenes whom the federal government had arrested and accused of military espionage. New belles lettres, much of it topical and dealing openly with the injustices and traumas of the past 50 years, typically sold in press runs ranging from a low of 800 to as many as 3,000 copies.

Yet amidst the political and intellectual ferment and excitement–paradoxically–the socialist and unitarist state, which Slovene writers were committed to subverting, continued to provide publishers with ample cash subsidies to produce the same writers' works in large, carefully edited press runs, finely printed and bound using high-quality materials.

1990- : THE CHALLENGE OF A SMALL, FREE MARKET

It's easy to write a book, harder to sell it, and hardest of all to Slovenes.

–Slovene saying, quoted by publisher Jaro Mihelač

"We've experienced a cultural upswing that we're simply never going to surpass. Perhaps in the process we've also reached the summit of our national delusion. Books are at a crisis point. Businesses are establishing more stringent economies, and the criteria for measuring quality have been reduced to the lowest common denominator. Those writers are being published who have the best business sense and know how to secure wealthy sponsors."[4] So wrote Vladimir Kavčič, one of the country's most respected novelists, in 1992. The societal transformation that had begun twelve years earlier had seen the country through a series of tense showdowns with Slobodan Milošević, the Serbian Communist party boss and de facto ruler of Yugoslavia as it disintegrated; a ten-day armed engagement with federal forces in 1991, which brought Slovenia its independence; and a steady economic and cultural reorientation away from the Slavic south, back toward the Germanic and Italian Northwest, as before 1918–with the ultimate goal of joining the European Union. Yet most of the transition from a command economy to a free market had taken just two years, with a suddenness that sent much of the publishing industry into shock.

Nearly all major Slovene publishers survived the economic transition. A rare, but predictable exception was Komunist, publishing house of the League of Communists. The three major houses founded after 1945–Državna založba Slovenije, Mladinska knjiga and Cankarjeva založba–fared well in comparison with their state-founded counterparts elsewhere in Eastern Europe, thanks to their de facto adaptation to market standards of production several decades before, facilitated by state-subsidized capital investments. Beginning in 1987, the field opened for new, privately owned publishers in Slovenia. Many of the earliest private publishers specialized in the humanities, especially belles lettres: Amalietti was founded in 1988 by David Tasić, and was a virtual non-starter. Tasić joined with Dušan Cunjak the next year to open Emonica (Emona being the Latin name for Ljubljana), which was slightly more successful and attracted a series of promising young writers, until the firm folded for sheer unprofitability in the early 1990s. In 1988 Tasić also founded Karantanija (a Slovenization of the Latin name for Slovenia), which at first struggled to produce titles pitched toward a nationalist sensibility, until it finally settled into a more realistic and profitable existence as a publisher of popular foreign literature in Slovene translation. One of the most successful new publishing entrepreneurs was Jaro Mihelač, who co-founded the straightforwardly named Slovenska knjiga (Slovenian Book) publishing house in 1987, but then, after minimal success and frustration at his partners' focus on turning quick profits, left and made a second attempt with the new and similarly forthright Mihelač imprint in 1991. Mihelač was Slovenia's first private publishing success story; he gained the respect and loyalty of the country's best authors by paying them competitive honoraria. Mihelač's annual list of new titles went from a high of 50 in 1993 to just 10 in 1995, and by 1997 the company was eking out a living. Mihelač and one other successful new publisher, Vale-Novak, both managed to open bookstores of their own in Ljubljana in the mid-1990s, in order to cope with the fact that most Ljubljana bookstores were the property of the three main pre-1990 publishers and gave low priority to marketing titles published by their competition. Indeed, in 1997 one observer identified two primary causes for the overwhelming tendency of new publishers to fail–one being the retention of all established bookstores in the hands of the three largest publishers, and the other being the Ministry of Culture's slow strangulation through budgetary neglect of public and school libraries, which until 1990 had been one of the main engines of the Slovene book trade.[5]

A third cause, which had become so much a part of common wisdom as to go without mentioning, was the steady decrease in government subsidies for the publishing of original Slovene works. One could speculate on a fourth cause–that the widespread creative enthusiasm of the 1980s had been spent and most or all of Slovenia's long pent-up political taboos had been named, analyzed and defused by the time private publishers were allowed to enter the market, resulting in a drop in demand. Similarly, Slovene authors began to comment on literature's loss of social status since 1990, displaced as it had been in the new market economy by a sudden rush of business opportunities and the new challenge of surviving within a competitive marketplace. A fifth cause–rapidly rising retail book prices–only compounded the problem of decreased demand, leading to the creation of a vicious cycle of ever-decreasing demand causing prices to spiral further upward.

The new overhead costs with which publishers had to contend were, to a significant extent, government-imposed. A new five-percent sales tax was introduced in 1992, from which books were not exempted. Further behind the scenes, the tax on authors' honoraria was increased to twenty-five percent (in the 1980s it had been much lower), driving authors to insist on still higher honoraria in order to compensate for the loss, and another tax of thirty percent was levied against publishers' profits. In addition, many publishers–especially the big three–still retained excessive numbers of editors and support staff from the state-subsidized 1980s. All of these costs were passed on to the retail buyer in the form of higher prices–which, of course, caused consumers to buy fewer books, which led to a vicious cycle of smaller press runs and higher per-unit costs, and consequently still higher retail prices.[6] By the mid-1990s, typical press runs for original Slovene belles lettres ran from 200 to a maximum of 1,000 copies, with a press run of 500 qualifying as good.

The dilemma was and remains acute. Certain categories of publications deemed critical to a small, linguistically isolated nation–contemporary belles lettres, highly specialized textbooks, translations of foreign literature, and most scholarly publications–are marginally profitable in even large markets, and in small markets not at all. In those circumstances, quality publishing requires artificial life support in order to survive.[7]

The first government of independent Slovenia showed little inclination to exempt culture from the pressures of the new market economy. What meager subsidies for publishing were available were awarded only to support meritorious new work, republications of classics, and translations of important foreign works into Slovene; the government made it clear it would not use subsidies to rescue faltering publishers from bankruptcy. From 1990 to 1991 the share of the Slovene government's budget allocated to support cultural activities shrank from 1.02 percent to 0.79 percent (UNESCO actually recommends a minimum of 1.5 percent). By 1993, culture's share of the government's budget was down to 0.53 percent.[8] Out of the Ministry of Culture's budget, even as successive Ministers continued to voice stubborn optimism that support would eventually increase, the amount set aside for publishing subsidies steadily dropped each year, as indicated in Table 1.[9]

Publishing advocates cried foul, particularly that the government's five-percent tax on retail book sales was netting the government twice as much in revenues as the government then allocated back out in the form of publishing subsidies. But the government stood firm: viewing books as yet another taxable commodity among many, its representatives knew that many pre-1990 press runs of two or three thousand copies had been exaggerated and driven by the plan-oriented socialist economy, that inventory often had lain unsold, and that even with significantly smaller press runs and higher taxes, the overall trend in book publication promised continued steady increases in state revenues throughout the decade of the 1990s, as Table 2 suggests.[10]

As the government began taking early measures in the late 1990s to prepare for Slovenia's eventual acceptance into the European Union, a value added tax (or VAT; in Slovene DDV, for *davek na dodano vrednost*) was proposed to replace the former sales tax. When the draft legislation on the VAT turned out to include books at a level of eight percent–even higher than the sales tax–the reaction from the publishing lobby was strong. The director of Mladinska knjiga argued early

TABLE 1. Slovene Ministry of Culture Subsidies to Publishers, 1990-1995

Year	Total amount awarded	No. of titles supported	Amt. per title (average)
1990	5,000,000 DM	210	25,367 DM
1991	4,500,000 DM	202	22,585 DM
1992	2,528,000 DM	153	15,852 DM
1993	2,484,000 DM	142	17,498 DM
1994	1,320,000 DM	145	9,320 DM
1995	1,017,000 DM	120	8,476 DM

TABLE 2. Book Titles Published in Slovenia per Year, 1989-1997

Year	Titles published
1989	1,932
1990	1,853
1991	2,459
1992	2,136
1993	2,440
1994	2,906
1995	3,194
1996	3,441
1997	3,647

on that the requirement that publishers pay the VAT on their stock at the time of production (rather than at the time of sale) imposed an unfair burden, since the typical Slovene press run took an average of two years to sell. He predicted that retail prices would increase by as much as 20 percent, slowing sales and forcing many smaller publishers into bankruptcy.[11] By spring 1998 even the usually sympathetic Minister of Culture claimed to see no reason to exempt the publishing industry from the VAT, arguing that publishers had made eight million dollars in clear profit in 1997, with a total turnover of 200 million dollars, and prospects for continued growth of 10 percent per year. Counterarguments posited by major publishers against the VAT included:

- As a publishing market, Slovenia is handicapped by its small size.
- Great Britain has a zero-level VAT on books. Only five European Union countries tax books at Slovenia's proposed level of eight percent or higher; examples include Denmark, whose government then reallocates a share of the revenues to the country's libraries, which then buy nearly 50 percent of all press runs for their collections. By contrast, the Slovene government's record of reinvesting tax revenues into literacy, libraries, and culture was already less than promising.
- Once the VAT was established, it would be difficult to retract.
- Neighboring Croatia had introduced the VAT on publishing, and sales of books subsequently went down by as much as 50 percent.
- The VAT on publishing works counter to Slovenia's interests, where national identity is based on language.
- That a VAT was required in order to qualify for membership in the EU was a given; yet how, precisely, the VAT was to be implemented was purely an internal matter for Slovenia. The publishers urged the government to apportion the VAT's burden wisely and in the national interest.[12]

Whatever understanding publishers and the government finally achieve regarding the VAT, it is clear that the publishing industry in turn-of-the-century Slovenia remains strong. Slovenes are avid book buyers and appear undeterred by retail prices that have increased disproportionately to the average personal income. School textbooks, practical handbooks on gardening and housekeeping, children's books, affordable reprint editions of established Slovene classics (still meaning, for many people, pre-twentieth century authors), and translations of foreign bestsellers and classics achieve the highest volume in sales. At the same time, most publishers recognize that their ability to attract and market the best Slovene contemporary authors–whether in belles lettres, or on subjects ranging from philosophy to history and economics–remains a crucial measure of their prestige.

CURRENT PUBLISHERS OF INTEREST
FOR RESEARCH-LEVEL COLLECTIONS

Generous estimates in the early 1990s put the total number of registered publishers nationwide at 300, though more selective estimates based on a definition of "publisher" positing a minimum output of five titles per year put the figure at around 150, with only forty-three of those focused on publishing as their primary activity. After several years of harsh market realities and diminished state support, many of the smaller publishers have been winnowed out, leaving the market to the large, established concerns, the most market-savvy newcomers, and those new publishers of quality books that have established supplementary revenue streams. By late 1998, only the largest publishers had made their catalogs of current titles and older stock available on the World Wide Web in databases designed with varying degrees of sophistication and in varying stages of completion. Over the following year–by late 1999–few smaller newcomers had established a Web presence. Each of these publishers' Web sites offers users the option of buying its stock directly over the Internet, but there is–in early 2000–still no comprehensive online Slovene bookstore that transcends the boundaries of individual publishers.

Trade Publishers

Cankarjeva založba (http://www.cankarjeva-z.si/). Rubrics for Slovene belles lettres and humanities provide limited listings of current titles and back stock of interest for research libraries. Most of CZ's stock consists of literature in translation, dictionaries, encyclopedias, and how-to books that enjoy wide demand in Slovenia, but are of marginal use to a research collection outside of Slovenia. Of most interest to libraries here will be CZ's new titles by leading contemporary Slovene authors, and major new works on Slovene or Yugoslav history, politics, economics and culture.

DZS (formerly Državna založba Slovenije: http://www.dzs.si/ang/ index.htm). DZS is publisher of the the ongoing series of complete, annotated variorum editions of major Slovene writers, *Zbrana dela slovenskih pesnikov in pisateljev* (Collected works of Slovene poets and writers), which are a foundation stone of any good Slovene literature collection. Outwardly unprepossessing, the collected works also avoid illustrations, but supply expert annotations that often run to as much as 25 percent of each volume. Some of the larger, ongoing sets have been in publication for over 30 years and are only now reaching completion. Titles listed under the rubrics Leposlovje > Slovensko klasično, Slovensko sodobno (Belles lettres > Slovene classic, Slovene contemporary) will dependably be authored by some of the best past or living Slovene writers. Rubrics for humanities and essays/ monographs also lead to title listings of interest for area studies collections.

Mladinska knjiga (http://www.mkz-lj.si/). As the name suggests, children's books and books for youth have been the company's traditional specialty, but it has also functioned for decades as a respected publisher of belles lettres; titles appearing in its series *Kondor* and *Nova slovenska knjiga* are particularly reliable. MK is also the publisher of the compendious and authoritative *Enciklopedija Slovenije* (Encyclopedia of Slovenia); begun in 1987, the Encyclopedia reached its thirteenth volume in 1999 (covering rubrics beginning with Š and T), and after completion of this first alphabetical sequence is expected to enter into a series of supplements, consisting of addenda and corrections to the earlier volumes, which were still significantly influenced by communist ideology. MK is also a publisher of atlases, dictionaries, facsimiles of Slovene classics, art albums, memoirs, biographies, and historical works.

Obzorja (http://www.založba-obzorja.si/). Of all major commercial publishers, Obzorja–the only one not based in Ljubljana–has the most pronounced orientation toward intellectually demanding topics and the largest stock of original Slovene titles in history, social and political theory, and belles lettres. Its series *Znamenja* (Signals) has made outstanding Slovene work in all genres (fiction and non-fiction) available in an affordable pocket-sized paperback format.

Slovenska knjiga (http://www.slo-knjiga.si/). Founded in the late 1980s, this publisher is best known for its series *Monumenta Slovenica*, consisting of facsimile reprints of rare early printed books, manuscripts, maps and other materials of significance for Slovene cultural history.

Prešernova družba (http://www.prdr.com/home.htm). Founded as a book club and publisher in the 1950s, the Prešeren Society issues and distributes low-cost editions of Slovene and foreign belles lettres to subscribing members by mail. One book, usually by a lesser-known contemporary author, is published and distributed to all members each year, while others are available on a mail-order basis, or in retail stores.

Študentska Organizacija Univerze (ŠOU: http://www.sou.uni-lj.si/ zaloznistvo/). The successor to the UK ZSMS, ŠOU functions as an umbrella organization for a variety of publishing initiatives, ranging from textbooks to original history, criticism and literature. ŠOU favors consistently excellent new work that appeals to a young, educated audience. Aside from textbooks, its most prominent series is Beletrina, which has been publishing prose by outstanding young Slovene writers since 1997. ŠOU has emerged as one of the country's leading smaller publishers. Information about ŠOU and the following three publishers is available at <http://mila.ljudmila.org/index/>.

Krtina. The successor to Krt, it continues to publish new Slovene work in sociology and culture studies, as well as translations of foreign work into Slovene.

*Založba *cf.* A newcomer since 1997, this small publisher specializes in original Slovene work in intertextual theory, Slovene social history, and new belles letters, as well some foreign work translated into Slovene.

Znanstveno in publicistišno središče. A small, yet prolific independent publisher with a relatively long history (since 1990), ZPS specializes in Slovene cultural history.

Nova revija. Since becoming Slovenia's leading monthly journal of literature and ideas, Nova revija has also diversified as a book publisher in its own right, giving preference to work that highlights Slovene national identity. Its series *Samorog* (Unicorn) features original prose and poetry; *Zbirka Interpretacije* issues collections of interviews, studies and documents about leading contemporary authors. Occasional special editions, such as *Temna stran meseca* (The Dark Side of the Moon, 1998–a collection of documents and photographs portraying the victimization of individual Slovenes under the Yugoslav communist government) and *Slovenska kronika XX. stoletja* (Slovene Chronicle of the 20th Century, 1995-1996–a profusely illustrated, oversized, two-volume chronological presentation of Slovene history since 1900) attempt to revise the received version of the Slovene historical record through major publishing events designed to reach a broad readership.

Enotnost: formerly Delavska enotnost (Workers' Unity). It remains an important publisher of contemporary social thought and history.

Pomurska založba (http://www.jasico.si/yellowpage/0/pzalozba/). Located in the far northeastern town of Murska Sobota, it is one of a handful of Slovenia's most prestigious provincial publishing houses, pursuing a broad subject profile ranging from belles lettres to history.

Lipa. The foremost publisher in the Slovene Littoral (Primorsko) region, located in Koper, Lipa is comparable in profile and in the scope of its activities to Pomurska založba.

Založba Capris (http://pina.soros.si/~capris/knjige/). Based in the coastal town of Koper, the stated mission of this new publisher is to document the history, folkways and literature of the Slovene Adriatic region and its unofficial capital.

Didakta (http://www.didakta.si/). A small publisher located in Radovljica since 1992, it specializes in elementary and secondary school textbooks and children's literature, but also issues some original belles lettres, literature in translation, hiking handbooks and guides to Slovenia. By diversifying also as a language school, the company manages to underwrite part of its publishing program.

Institutional Publishers (Universities, Institutes, Societies, Museums, Galleries, Archives)

Slovenska akademija znanosti in umetnosti (SAZU), and Znanstvenoraziskovalni center (ZRC) SAZU. The Academy, founded after World War II, sponsors research in the humanities and social sciences. The Scholarly Research Center (ZRC) is an umbrella organization within SAZU responsible for promoting interdisciplinary collaboration among the Academy's institutes, as well as international collaboration. A prolific publisher, ZRC has information at http://www.zrc-sazu. si/založba/. SAZU itself is publisher of several annual and irregular serials issued by its various subject divisions (or razredi), such as the Division of Historical and Social Sciences, the Division of Philological and Literary Studies, the Division of Natural Sciences, and others.

Slovenska matica. The Slovene publisher with the oldest pedigree, Slovenska matica was established in 1863 as a society for the promotion of Slovene culture. It publishes about a dozen new, Slovene-specific titles in the humanities and social sciences each year, as well as translations of foreign literature and some work in the sciences and technology.

Univerza v Ljubljani (University of Ljubljana) and its various divisions, including Fakulteta za družbene vede, Filozofska fakulteta (and its departments: History, Slavic Languages, etc.), Ekonomska fakulteta, and others, issues dozens of important scholarly titles per year.

Univerza v Mariboru, its colleges and departments: a far less prolific publisher than the University of Ljubljana, the University of Maribor's publishing tends to be limited to textbooks for courses taught there.

Zveza zgodovinskih društev Slovenije (League of Slovene Historical Societies). The historical societies joined in the league are regional societies (such as for Celje, the Southern Littoral, Ljubljana, etc.). Jointly through the League they publish conference proceedings and collections of historical documents of cross-regional significance.

Statistično društvo Slovenij. The Statistical Society is the country's association of professional statisticians and is responsible for publishing discussions of statistical standards and practices.

Narodna in univerzitetna knjižnica (NUK–the National and University Library in Ljubljana) issues catalogs of the Library's major exhibits, and jointly with Narodna galerija or other institutions and occasionally publishes major commemorative works illuminating all aspects of important historical or other documents.

Narodna galerija. The National Gallery, whose major published catalogs are of its permanent, mostly pre-1900 collections and occasional exhibitions of Slovene art from private or other collections.

Moderna galerija is an active publisher of exhibit catalogs, many of them extensive studies of twentieth-century Slovene artists or schools of artists.

Slovenski gledališki in filmski muzej (the Slovene Theatrical and Film Museum) in recent years has been publishing with increasing frequency finding aids to the Museum's film archives and critical studies of Slovene film, as well as histories of theater in Slovenia.

Zgodovinski arhiv, Ljubljana (Historical Archive, Ljubljana). Zgodovinski arhiv, Celje (and other cities) publish thematically unified collections of regionally and nationally significant historical documents.

Government Publishers

Statistični urad Republike Slovenije. The official governmental statistical agency, it publishes statistical monthlies and annuals (see Section VI, under Official and Government Publications), and the prolific monographic series *Rezultati raziskovanj* (Results of investigations), each of which presents an in-depth, thematic statistical survey of a particular socio-economic aspect of contemporary Slovenia.

Uradni list Republike Slovenije. Publisher of the Slovene government's legislative gazette, Uradni list also issues monographic law compilations on a wide range of specific topics.

Ministrstvo za ekonomske dejavnosti, Ministrstvo za obrambo, and other Ministries of the government frequently function as publishers, issuing collections of articles that advance the government's positions on economic reforms, preparations for EU membership, and other subjects, depending on the Ministry's brief.

Urad za žensko politiko, and other government agencies. The Agency for Women's Policy is one of many agencies authorized to sponsor conferences and publish conference proceedings.

Slovene Publishers Outside Slovenia

Through nearly four decades of communist rule in Yugoslavia/Slovenia, Slovene-affiliated publishers abroad provided an important outlet for discussion of topics too sensitive to pass censorship in the home country. At the same time, they were and remain vital to discussion of important topics among the numerically significant, mostly bilingual, but decidedly minority populations of ethnic Slovenes that continue to inhabit the regions of Austria (Carinthia) and Italy (Trieste and the region of Venezia-Friuli) bordering on Slovenia.

Založba tržaškega tiska (ZTT, Trieste, Italy). The leading Slovene publisher in Trieste.

Devin (Trieste). Bearing the Slovene name of the town and castle north of Trieste where Rilke wrote the *Duino Elegies*, Devin publishes new Slovene belles lettres, and documents pertaining to the history of the Slovene population in Italy.

Krožek za družbena vprašanja Virgil Šček (Trieste). This society, named for a leading figure in the pre-War movement for minority rights in the Trieste Region, publishes historical work, in Slovene or Italian, pertaining to the history and culture of ethnic Slovene enclaves in Italy.

Zveza slovenskih kulturnih društev (Trieste, Gorizia, Udine). The League of Slovene Cultural Societies in Italy publishes biographical studies of leaders within the Slovene communities in Italy and works on historical topics of local interest.

Goriška Mohorjeva družba (Gorizia, Italy). A counterpart of Mohorjeva/Hermagoras in Austria and Celje, Slovenia, it is the Catholic-affiliated Slovene publisher in Italy. Less productive than in the past, it still manages to issue at least one significant new book each year, which is distributed by mail to members of the society.

Wieser (Salzburg, Austria). Founded in the 1980s, Wieser has made propagating Central European culture its mission. It brings contemporary writing from all former Habsburg lands, including Slovenia, to the attention of the German-speaking public through translations of belles lettres and other new writing. It also serves as a significant publisher of new Slovene writing in the original language.

Mohorjeva založba (Klagenfurt, Austria). Affiliated with the Catholic Church, and known as Hermagoras in German, Mohorjeva pursues a publishing program that includes Austrian writers whose primary languages are either German or Slovene.

Drava (Klagenfurt). The secular counterpart to Mohorjeva/Hermagoras in Carinthia, it specializes in works by and about the Slovene ethnic minority in the Austrian state of Carinthia, as well as more general works about minority, ethnic, and linguistic issues in Austria.

Slavica/Anton Kovač Buchhandel (Munich). Founded in 1960 by Slovene émigré Rudolf Trofenik, it has functioned for over four decades as both a South Slavic bookstore and an occasional publisher of scholarly monographs on South Slavic or Slovene subjects, usually in one of several long-established topical monographic series. Its series *Litterae Slovenicae* issues facsimile reproductions of historically important works.

CURRENT SERIAL PUBLICATIONS
FOR A RESEARCH-LEVEL COLLECTION

National Bibliography

Currently only two series of the national bibliography continue to be published in printed format. *Slovenska bibliografija: Knjige* is issued four times per year by the National and University Library (NUK) in Ljubljana, and provides a classified listing of all monographs published in Slovenia, by a Slovene author (regardless of imprint) or on a Slovene topic (again, regardless of place of publication). The quarterly issues of *Knjige* are accompanied by an annual index which provides additional access to that year's titles by author, title, or subject phrase. Given the phlegmatic nature of Slovenia's book market, the issues of *Knjige* appear in just enough time (with about a year's delay) still to be somewhat useful for collection development purposes. *Slovenska bibliografija: A, Serijske publikacije*, registering serial publications, is also still published by NUK in printed form, although with considerable delay (the volume listing serials published in 1994/1995 was only issued in 1999). Publication of the third and, arguably, most useful subseries of the national bibliography–C, *Članki in leposlovni prispevki v serijskih publikacijah in zbornikih* (index to articles appearing in serials and edited collections) ceased in 1989 with a single volume covering 1978-1979, after which that facet of bibliographic control became much more difficult (though compensated, to a very limited extent, by such Western indexes as *Historical Abstracts* and the *MLA International Bibliography*).

The corrective for stalled bibliographic control over articles appearing in periodicals was delivered with Internet access to the National Library's (NUK's) online catalog, which provides cataloging for monographs, serials, and articles within serials. A user can search across all types of publications in a single search, or can specify the kind of material to be searched, thus creating an ad hoc serials index as needed. As of late 1999, indexing of serial articles covered imprints from 1990 through early 1999, leaving articles published from 1980 through 1989 a significant blind spot, for the time being. The database's scope extends to all materials published in Slovenia, or anywhere in the world about Slovenia. Indexing records for many periodical articles include extensive abstracts in both Slovene and English (or, occasionally, German). NUK's catalog and index are available as part of Slovenia's online library catalog network, COBISS (Cooperative Online Bibliographic System and Services) and is accessible on the National Library's home pages at http://www.nuk.uni-lj.si/katalogi/index.html (one port of entry among many, since over 200 Slovene libraries currently are a part of COBISS).

Newspapers

Delo. Ljubljana, 1951- . Daily). Since 1991 subtitled "An independent newspaper for independent Slovenia," it is the newspaper of national record and includes regular sections devoted to literature (4 pages every Thursday); science with a Slovene and Central European focus (4 pages on Wednesdays); culture including music, film and art (2 pages on Wednesdays); business and employment trends (several pages on Tuesdays); and sports (six pages on Mondays). A "Saturday supplement" (Sobotna priloga) running up to 16 pages consists of in-depth investigative and feature reporting on all aspects of contemporary Slovenia. *Delo* maintains 24 bureaus throughout Slovenia and retains its own correspondents in major foreign capitals. It is also the publisher of a tabloid daily (Slovenske novice) and several weekly news magazines targeting specific demographic groups or interests.

Dnevnik. Ljubljana, 1991- . Daily). Renamed from *Neodvisni dnevnik* (1990-1991), prior to 1990 again Dnevnik. Slovenia's second most widely read newspaper. Extensive excerpts from each day's issue and a full archive are freely available online at http://www.dnevnik.si/. Its Sunday edition published since 1962, *Nedeljski dnevnik*, has the highest circulation of any newspaper in Slovenia.

Ljubljanske novice. Ljubljana, 1999- . (Daily). Slovenia's most comprehensive, fully Web-based daily news source, with extensive coverage of Slovene domestic, Balkan regional and world news. Includes extensive daily coverage of cultural events. Available at http://www.si-int-news.com/index.html. An archive is available, but consists of only selected stories from past issues.

Primorske novice. Koper, 1963- . Twice per week). An exclusively regional newspaper for the Slovene coastal region. Substantial excerpts from the most recent issue are posted to the paper's web site at http://www.prim-nov.si/.

Republika. Ljubljana and Trieste, 1994- . The only daily with its own Sunday edition, *Republika*'s strength is in its reporting of events affecting the Slovene communities in Italy and Austria, as well as news of metropolitan Slovenia.

Slovenec. Ljubljana, 1991- . Slovenia's most politically conservative daily newspaper.

Slovenske novice. Ljubljana: Delo, 1991- . Daily tabloid, controlled by Delo, focused on Slovene personalities, media and popular culture.

Večer. Maribor, 1953- . vol. 9). (Daily). News coverage is countrywide, with added focus on events in the Maribor region (Northeastern Slovenia). A condensed online version exists at http://www.vecer. com/, including an archive of older issues since 1998.

News Weeklies and News Magazines

Kmečki glas. Ljubljana, 1943- . Weekly magazine intended for rural subscribers. Its focus is Slovenian agriculture within the larger economic and political context, with practical how-to features.

Dolenjski list. Novo mesto, 1950- . A weekly news magazine featuring coverage of the Dolenjsko region (South Central Slovenia). Excerpts of all issues from 1996 to present are accessible online, http:// www.dol-list.si/.

Mladina. Ljubljana, 1943- . The epoch-making weekly news magazine of the 1980s, in the 1990s it continued to be regarded as Slovenia's most independent and critical news outlet.

Naša kronika. Ljubljana: Dnevnik, 1999. Weekly lifestyle magazine, with feature articles mostly on daily life and social conditions in and near Ljubljana.

7D = [Sedem dni]. Maribor: Večer, 1976- .

Tednik. Ptuj: Radio-Tednik, 1948- . The most important weekly newspaper of the region around Ptuj in eastern Slovenia. As a regular feature, it includes the regional official gazette, *Uradni vestnik*.

Vestnik. Murska Sobota, 1949- . Weekly news from and about the Prekmurje Region of far northeastern Slovenia, bordering on Hungary. A complete online version of the latest issue is posted at http://www. p-inf.si/besedila/VES.htm.

Official and Government Publications

Mesečni statistični pregled Republike Slovenije. Ljubljana: Zavod Republike Slovenije za statistiko, 1991- . Monthly statistical compilations, primarily of economic productivity indicators, accompanied by about ten pages of commentary.

Rezultati raziskovanj. Ljubljana: Statistični urad Republike Slovenije, 1991- . A series of specialized statistical publications, each of which focuses on a different social or political aspect of Slovenia. Individual titles published include population censuses, statistical overviews of migration, employment, trade, and other economic statistics, etc.

Slovenija v številkah. Ljubljana: Statistični urad Republike Slovenije, 1994- . The abridged version of the Statistical Yearbook (*Statistični letopis*), also published annually.

Statistični letopis Ljubljane. Ljubljana: Mestni zavod za statistiko, 1968- . An annual compilation of statistical information pertaining specifically to Ljubljana and its environs.

Statistični letopis Republike Slovenije. Ljubljana: Zavod Republike Slovenije za statistiko, 1990- . (Annual) The official statistical yearbook of Slovenia.

Uradni list Republike Slovenije. Ljubljana: Uradni list, 1991- . (60 to 70 issues per year). Provides full text of all Slovene federal and some local legislation. An online version is also available for a yearly subscription fee at http://www.uradni-list.si/.

Economics and Business

Gospodarski vestnik: slovenski poslovni tednik. Ljubljana, 1952- . Weekly magazine reviewing the state of the economy in Slovenia, with analyses of individual companies.

IB revija: za strokovna in metodološka vprašanja gospodarskega, prostorskega in socialnega razvoja Slovenije. Ljubljana: Zavod Republike Slovenije za makroekonomske analize in razvoj, 1991- (vol. 25). Monthly journal devoted to issues of urban and rural development in Slovenia.

Kompass: poslovni imenik Slovenije = Kompass: register of industry and commerce. Ljubljana: Gospodarski vestnik, 1993- .

MM Slovenija: Marketing Magazine for Management, Marketing and Promotion. Ljubljana, 1981- . Monthly magazine designed to promote Slovene business opportunities among foreign entrepreneurs. Also published in Slovene- and Czech-language editions.

Naše gospodarstvo: revija za aktualna gospodarska vprašanja = Our economy. Maribor: Ekonomsko-poslovna fakulteta: Društvo ekonomistov Maribora, 1955- . (Quarterly). Articles pertaining to Slovene economic development.

Razvojna vprašanja statistike. Ljubljana: Zavod Republike Slovenije za statistiko, 1991- . (6 per year). Articles analyzing the macroeconomic situation in Slovenia.

Slovenia Business Weekly. Online at http://www.gzs.si/eng/news/sbw/, no subscription required. Sponsored by the Slovene Chamber of Commerce, it provides news on business developments throughout the country. Older issues also available, from 1998.

Slovenian Business Report. Ljubljana: Gospodarski vestnik, 1991- . (Monthly). Reproduces in English the text of laws affecting commerce and finance; publishes statistical and industry overviews.

Slovenia Weekly. Ljubljana: Vitrum, 1994- . An English-language digest of economic and political news affecting Slovenia, for the non-Slovene businessperson or professional. Available in both print and full-text online versions on a subscription basis. Online at http://www.vitrum.si/sw/.

Slovenska ekonomska revija = Slovene Economic Review. Ljubljana: Ekonomska fakulteta; Zveza ekonomistov Slovenije. A scholarly publication on Slovene macroeconomic conditions.

Working Papers EDP. Maribor: Faculty of Economics and Business Administration, 1990- . (4 per year). In English, each issue consists largely of a monographic study of current topics in Slovene macroeconomics.

Geography and Ecology

Geografski vestnik. Ljubljana: Zveza geografskih društev Slovenije, 1925- .

Geografski zbornik. Ljubljana: Slovenska akademija znanosti in umetnosti, 1952- .

Geographica Slovenica. Ljubljana: Inštitut za geografijo Univerze, 1972- . Published annually, each volume is organized around a specific theme in Slovene geography, such as land use, demographic change, or environmental protection within specific regions of the country.

Varstvo narave = Nature Conservation: A Periodical for Research and Practice of Nature Conservation. Ljubljana: Zavod Republike Slovenije za varstvo naravne in kulturne dediščine, 1962- .

Vestnik. Ljubljana: Ministrstvo za kulturo, Zavod Republike Slovenije za varstvo naravne in kulturne dediščine, 1971- .

Ethnography

Etnolog: glasnik Slovenskega etnografskega muzeja. Ljubljana: Muzej, 1991- . (New series, vol. 1 = vol. 52).

Glasnik Slovenskega etnološkega društva = Bulletin of [the] Slovene Ethnological Society. Tables of contents of recent issues and brief summaries of some articles are available on the Society's home page at http://www.sed-drustvo.si/.

Razprave in gradivo = Treatises and Documents: Journal of Ethnic Studies. Ljubljana: Institute for Ethnic Studies, 1994- (vol. 24-). Annual volumes consist of articles devoted to issues of ethnic relations, both in Slovenia and in countries that are home to Slovene ethnic minorities. Some articles deal with ethnic relations in neighboring countries not involving Slovenes (such as Croat-Italian relations in Croatian Austria after World War II). Much of the research is based on copiously documented statistical analysis, and all articles are equipped with a brief summary in English.

Traditiones. Ljubljana: Slovenska akademija znanosti in umetnosti, Inštitut za slovensko narodopisje, 1972- . The leading scholarly publication of Slovene ethnological and folklore studies.

Religion

Acta ecclesiastica Sloveniae. Ljubljana: Inštitut za zgodovino cerkve pri Teološki fakulteti, 1979- . An annual monographic series devoted to the history of the Roman Catholic church in Slovenia.

Cerkveni dokumenti. Ljubljana: Slovenske rimskokatoliške škofije, 1979- . (2-3 issues per year).

Družina: slovenski katoliški tednik. Ljubljana, 1952- . A weekly magazine about religion and social issues sponsored by the Roman Catholic Church. Excerpts from recent issues are available online at http://www.druzina.si/index.html.

Ognjišče. Koper, 1965- . A Catholic-oriented monthly news and feature magazine focusing on the events in the Slovene coastal region, with attention to Slovene-Italian religious interrelations. Nearly complete issues are also available online at http://www.ognjisce.si/revija/.

History (Mostly of Slovenia) and Auxiliary Disciplines

Acta Histriae. Koper: Milje, 1993- . (Annual). Thematically-focused collections of articles exploring the role of the Istrian peninsula in Slovene history.

Annales: anali Koprskega primorja in bližnjih pokrajin. Koper: Zgodovinsko društvo za južno Primorsko, 1991- . (Irregular). A forum for scholarship on the history, culture and ecology of the Slovene Littoral and surrounding regions.

Arheološki vestnik. Ljubljana: Slovenska akademija znanosti in umetnosti, Znanstvenoraziskovalni center, Inštitut za arheologijo, 1950- .

Arhivi. Ljubljana: Arhivsko društvo Slovenije, 1978- .

Bilten. Ljubljana: Slovenska akademija znanosti in umetnosti, Znanstvenoraziskovalni center, Inštitut za slovensko izseljenstvo, 1990- . Newsletter of the Slovene Academy's Institute for Emigration Studies.

Borec: revija za zgodovino, literaturo in antropologijo. Ljubljana: Mladika, 1949- . (Two to four issues per year).

A journal of Slovene history during and since World War II, *Borec* was initially sponsored by Partisan war veterans. It continues to advocate the achievements of the Liberation Front and its members, and frequently publishes memoirs and eyewitness accounts, though in recent years the journal's advocacy has been tempered by the objectivity of a younger generation of contributors.

Časopis za zgodovino in narodopisje = Review for History and Ethnography. Maribor: Univerza v Mariboru; Obzorja, 1904- (new series, 1965-). The University of Maribor's journal of Slovene history, covering all periods to the present day and with particular emphasis on eastern Slovenia around Maribor.

Dve domovini: razprave o izseljenstvu = Two Homelands: Migration Studies. Ljubljana: Institute for Slovene Emigration Research, 1990- .

Kronika: časopis za slovensko krajevno zgodovino. Ljubljana: Zveza zgodovinskih društev Slovenije, Sekcija za krajevno zgodovino, 1953- . (Three per year). A journal of Slovene local and regional history.

Obvestila Arhiva Republike Slovenije. Ljubljana: Arhiv RS, 1990- (vol. 6-). News bulletin of the Slovene National Archive.

Prispevki za novejšo zgodovino = Contributions to the [sic] Contemporary History. Ljubljana: Inštitut za novejšo zgodovino, 1986-

(vol. 26-). Published by the Institute for Contemporary History, *Prispevki* focuses on Slovene history from the late 19th century through the present day. Extensive summaries in English accompany each article, there are numerous reviews of recently published books in each issue, and every year an overview of the Institute's activities during the previous year is published.

Viri = [Sources]. Ljubljana: Arhivsko društvo Slovenije, 1980- . (Annual). The Slovene Archival Society's annual series of collections of selected archival documents organized around specific topics, such as pre-1929 Slovene political party programs, collections of previously unpublished, historically important letters, etc.

Zgodovina za vse. Ljubljana, 1993- . (Semi-annual). A new historical journal that aims to present Slovene social history in a style which is easily accessible to the general reader, yet which remains true to fact and grounded in original documents.

Zgodovinski časopis = Historical Review. Ljubljana: Zveza zgodovinskih društev Slovenije, 1947- . (Quarterly). Slovenia's leading scholarly historical journal, it covers the full chronological range of Slovene history, from medieval times to the present day.

Art, Music, Performance, Media

Ekran: revija za film in televizijo. Ljubljana: Zveza kulturnih organizacij Slovenije, 1962- . (Six per year). Edited by Marcel Stefančič and, more recently, Simon Popek, two of Slovenia's leading film critics. A serious journal of film theory, more than 50 percent of each issue consists of original work by Slovene critics on domestic and world cinema. Selected articles from the current issue are also available online at http://www.ljudmila.org/ekran/.

M'Ars: časopis Moderne galerije Ljubljana. Ljubljana: Moderna galerija, 1989- . (Quarterly).

Maska: revija za gledališče, ples, opero. Ljubljana: Zveza kulturnih organizacij Slovenije, 1991- . (Quarterly). Journal for theater, dance and opera. Selected articles from the most recent issue are available at http://www.ljudmila.org/maska/.

Mediana: analiza medijev v Sloveniji : branost, gledanost in poslušanost. Ljubljana: Inštitut za raziskovanje medijev, 1992- . (Two per year).

Mediana International: Slovenian Media Guide: Reading, Viewing and Listening. Ljubljana: Media Research Institute, 1993- . An irregular, probably annual survey of the readership of Slovenia's most widely distributed media outlets, including newspapers, magazines, and radio and television stations. Intended to help businesses place their advertising strategically, it provides useful circulation statistics and demographic analysis.

Muzikološki zbornik. Ljubljana: Filozofska fakulteta, Oddelek za muzikologijo, 1965- . (Annual).

Slovenski gledališki almanah = Slovene Theater Annual. Ljubljana: Slovenski gledališki in filmski muzej, 1992/93- .

Literary Journals

Dialogi: revija za kulturo. Maribor: Kulturni forum, 1965- . A literary monthly which had its highpoint in the 1960s and 1970s.

Dva tisoč = 2000: časnik za mišljenje, umetnost, kulturna in religiozna vprašanja. Ljubljana: Društvo 2000, 1969- . Founded by university students during one of Slovenia's periods of tentative liberalization in the 1960s, the ideology of 2000 was originally based on French personalist philosophy, which has had active adherents among liberal Catholics and others in Slovenia since the 1930s. While the journal's contents are heavily oriented toward original and translated prose, poetry, drama excerpts, essays, philosophy and historical studies, it has also assumed a decided role as social critic, which emerges in the polemics that it regularly features. Some information about the journal is available at http://mila.ljudmila.org/2000/

Literatura. Ljubljana: Literarno-umetniško društvo Literatura, 1989- . One of the two most important journals for new Slovene writing, alongside *Nova revija*. Features new prose fiction, poetry, essays and criticism by Slovene authors and translations of contemporary foreign work. Very brief samples from the current issue are accessible online at http://www.kud-fp.si/retina/umetnost/literatura/.

Litterae slovenicae. Ljubljana: Slovene Writers' Association, Slovene PEN, and Association of Slovene Literary Translators, 1991- . A semiannual journal of Slovene literature in translation, designed to raise Slovenia's literary profile among readers abroad. Issues alternate target language, but are usually in German, English, French, Italian or Spanish. Individual issues may be organized around the work of a particular writer, group of writers, period, or genre. The successor to *Le livre Slovène*, which served the same function since the 1960s.

Nova revija. Ljubljana: Cankarjeva založba, 1982- . Since its founding, the most politically important Slovene literary journal. It continues to attract new writing by leading authors and frequently introduces work by promising new writers.

Rast. Novo mesto: Dolenjska založba, 1990- .

Sodobnost. Ljubljana: DZS, 1963- . (Six double issues per year). After *Nova revija* and *Literatura*, one of Slovenia's most prominent literary journals. Includes new prose, poetry and drama excerpts, literary history and criticism, and book reviews.

Srce in oko. Ljubljana: Prešernova družba, 1989- . (Monthly).

Philology (Language and Literature Studies)

Acta neophilologica. Ljubljana: Filozofska fakulteta Univerze v Ljubljani, 1968- . (Annual).

Eseji. Ljubljana: LDS, 1986- .

Jezik in slovstvo. Ljubljana: Slavistično društvo Slovenije, 1955- . (Eight issues per year). One of the two or three most important Slovene philology journals, with studies in both language and literature.

Jezikoslovni zapiski. Ljubljana: Inštitut za slovenski jezik Frana Ramovša, 1991- . (Annual).

Linguistica. Ljubljana: Slovenska akademija znanosti in umetnosti, Inštitut za slovenski jezik, 1955- .

Primerjalna književnost. Ljubljana: Slovensko društvo za primerjalno književnost, 1978- . (Two per year). Studies in comparative literature.

Problemi. Ljubljana: LDS, 1962- . (Eight per year).

Seminar slovenskega jezika, literature in kulture: zbornik predavanj. Ljubljana: Univerza v Ljubljani, Filozofska fakulteta, Oddelek za slovanske jezike in književnosti, 1965?- . An annual collection of lectures on Slovene language, literature, history and other topics, delivered by faculty as part of the University of Ljubljana's summer Slovene language seminar.

Slava: debatni list. Ljubljana: Debatni krožek slavistov Filozofske fakultete Univerze v Ljubljani, 1987- . Publishes essays and research in progress by students and faculty of the Ljubljana University Department of Slavic Languages, primarily on Slovene topics. A very rudimentary informational Web page, with tables of contents of some issues, is available at http://www.ijs.si/lit/slava.html-l2.

Slavistična revija. Ljubljana: Slavistično društvo Slovenije, 1948- . (Four per year). The leading refereed journal of Slavic studies, with primary focus on Slovene language and literature. Tables of contents and subscription information are available online at http://www.ijs.si/lit/sr.html.

Slovenski jezik = Slovene linguistics studies. Ljubljana: ZRC SAZU; Lawrence, KS: University of Kansas, 1997- . (Annual).

General or Other Humanities and Social Sciences

Acta Analytica: Philosophy and Psychology: International Periodical for Philosophy in Analytical Tradition. Ljubljana: Društvo za analitično filozofijo in filozofijo znanosti, 1986- .

Časopis za kritiko znanosti, domišljijo in novo antropologijo. Ljubljana: Študentska organizacija univerze, 1978- . Issued irregularly (about four to six times per year), the journal seeks to keep pace with trends in critical theory, applying them in thematically focused issues to various aspects of contemporary Slovene society and culture.

Dokumenti Slovenskega gledališkega in filmskega muzeja. Ljubljana: Muzej, 1979- .

Družboslovne razprave. Ljubljana: Inštitut za družbene vede Univerze v Ljubljani, 1984- . An important medium for sociological research and commentary relating to Slovenia.

Filozofski vestnik. Ljubljana: Slovenska akademija znanosti in umetnosti, Znanstvenoraziskovalni center, Filozofski inštitut, 1989- (vol. 6). English-language summaries of selected articles from recent issues are presented at http://www.zrc-sazu.si/www/fi/filvest.htm.

Glasnik Slovenske matice. Ljubljana: Slovenska matica, 1954- . Published semiannually, the Glasnik carries news of the Slovenska matica, publishes proceedings of the scholarly conferences that it organizes, mostly on Slovene historical, ethnographic, literary and other topics.

Knjižnica: glasilo Zveze bibliotekarskih društev Slovenije. Ljubljana: Društvo, 1957- . (Quarterly). The official publication of the Union of Slovene Librarians' Associations, *Knjižnica* is the country's primary vehicle for discussion of topics in librarianship.

Pavliha: satirični list za vznemirjenje javnosti Republike Slovenije. Ljubljana, 1944-1992; resumed in 1999- . (Biweekly). Slovenia's leading magazine of satirical social and political commentary.

Pravnik. Ljubljana: Zveza društev pravnikov Republike Slovenije, 1965- . (Monthly). Slovenia's leading legal journal, its articles cover a wide range of contemporary Slovene legal issues, including minority rights and legal implications of planned membership in the European Union.

Primorska srečanja. Koper, 1977- . (Monthly). A general interest magazine with a regional cast, *Primorska srečanja* brings together new Slovene belles lettres and translations from Italian, regional historical studies, and studies in the arts of the Southern Littoral (Koper) region.

Razgledi. Ljubljana: Delo, 1992- . (Two per month, on newsprint). Formerly *Naši razgledi*, it is a forum for discussion of the impact of politics and economics on Slovene cultural life. *Razgledi* is one of Slovenia's most respected magazines of social thought and literary criticism.

Revija Obramba. Ljubljana, 1969- . Monthly magazine covering issues of the military, national defense, civil defense, and police, particularly as they pertain to Slovenia.

Revolver: revija za kulturna in politična vprašanja, revija s homoerotičnim nabojem. Ljubljana: Roza klub, 1990- . (Approximately 3 per year). Slovenia's first gay-oriented magazine; a significant share of each issue is devoted to issues and events of interest to the gay and lesbian community in Slovenia.

Rodna gruda. Ljubljana: Slovenska izseljenska matica, 1954- . Monthly journal addressed to Slovene emigrants abroad.

Slovene studies. New York: Society for Slovene Studies, 1979- . (Two per year). North America's scholarly journal for all aspects of studies pertaining to Slovenia.

Slovenija: quarterly magazine. Ljubljana: Slovenska izseljenska matica, 1987- . In English (despite the Slovenian title), it consists of feature articles on contemporary Slovene culture and politics, designed as outreach to a non-Slovene audience, including émigré communities. Selected articles from recent issues are also available at the magazine's online site, http://www.arctur.si/slovenia/index. html.

Slovenski almanah. Ljubljana: Delo, 1992- . (Annual). Published by Slovenia's leading daily newspaper, the *Almanah* provides an overview of the year's events in Slovenia and the world, based on media coverage.

Slovenski filozofski zvezki. Ljubljana: Društvo za analitično filozofijo in filozofijo znanosti; Filozofska fakulteta Univerze, 1992- . (Irregular).

Svobodna misel. Ljubljana: Svobodna misel, 1992- (Vol. 30-). (Two per month). Edited by novelist Vladimir Kavčič, "Free

Thought" is issued in a visually appealing, illustrated magazine format; it "respects the accomplishments of the National Liberation Struggle [i.e., Tito's Partisans in World War II], yet is able to be critical toward our past and present." Deals with contemporary social, political and environmental issues, as well as historical topics. Information about the magazine is posted at http://www.aks.si/revija_sm/.

Teorija in praksa: revija za družbena vprašanja. Ljubljana: Fakulteta za družbene vede Univerze v Ljubljani, 1964- . (Six per year). *Theory and practice*, a highly respected journal of social theory, is perhaps the most important forum for discussion of Slovenia's reconciliation with its recent past and, as importantly, its rapidly changing present. Contents consist mostly of original Slovene contributions, with some translations of foreign work. Information about the journal, but no access to contents, is available at http://www.ijs.si/lit/sr.html.

Tribuna. Ljubljana: Študentska organizacija Univerze v Ljubljani, 1951-1998. The student newspaper of the University of Ljubljana, *Tribuna* traditionally served as the testing ground for each new generation of Slovene intellectuals, and for its daring was periodically shut down by the pre-1991 government. Since 1991, until its suspension in 1998, it tended away from controversial topics and more closely resembled a typical student newspaper. A Web page with tables of contents of the last issues is still available at http://www.sou.uni-lj.si/tribuna/.

Zbornik za umetnostno zgodovino = Archives d'histoire de l'art. Ljubljana: Slovensko umetnostnozgodovinsko društvo, 1921- . (New series, 1951-).

Sciences and Mathematics

Acta carsologica. Ljubljana: Slovenska akademija znanosti in umetnosti, Inštitut za raziskovanje Krasa, 1955- . Studies on karst formations. Slovene Istria and the Littoral Region are the location of the original karst (Kras in Slovene), a barren upland landscape of limestone formations.

Preprint Series of the Department of Mathematics. Ljubljana: Društvo matematikov, fizikov in astronomov Slovenije, 1977- .

Children's Literature

Ciciban: list za najmlajše. Ljubljana: Mladinska knjiga, 1945- . For beginning readers.

Kekec: literarna revija za učence osnovnih šol. Ljubljana: Mladika, 1991- . For intermediate readers (elementary school).

Publications for Women

Jana: slovenska družinska revija. Ljubljana: Delo, 1972- . A family magazine with focus on women, it includes occasional feature articles on current events and interviews with prominent personalities.

Naša žena. Ljubljana: Delo, 1941- . Slovenia's oldest magazine for women, it primarily provides advice and instructions on home crafts.

Some Suppliers of Slovene Books and Journals

- Knjigarna Konzorcij (Consortium Bookstore), Slovenska 29, p.p. 33, 1117 Ljubljana, Slovenia. Fax: 061 224-057. E-mail: konzorcij@ mk-trgovina.si. Previously the main Ljubljana outlet of Mladinska knjiga, this is the largest bookstore in Ljubljana, stocking titles by all publishers. It is able to provide both in-print books and serial subscriptions to foreign clients. It currently supplies Slovene materials to the Library of Congress. Basic information is at http://www.konzorcij. com/.
- Dr. Anton Kovač, Slavica Verlag, Elizabethstrasse 22, D-80796 Munich, Germany. The best Slovene specialty bookstore outside of Slovenia, Kovač-Slavica Buchhandel maintains an extensive and well-selected stock of current publications tailored to research library interests.
- Kubon & Sagner, D-80328 Munich, Germany. Germany's main Slavic studies book and periodical supplier, it also maintains current Slovenian stock.
- Otto Harrassowitz Verlag, 65174 Wiesbaden, Germany. Serves as a supplier of Austrian imprints, including Slovene-language ones.
- Narodna in univerzitetna knjižnica, Turjaška 1, 1000 Ljubljana, Slovenia. The National and University Library's Acquisitions Department continues to maintain active book and serial exchange ties with a number of major libraries in Europe and North America.

Presently, no good published selection tools exist for new Slovene titles. From 1953 until 1996, *Knjiga*, a monthly review of the Slovene publishing scene sponsored by the Slovene Union of Publishers and Booksellers, provided full listings of newly published books, along with mildly evaluative reviews of a small number of titles in each issue. (Since *Knjiga* was the Publishers' Union's own mouthpiece, there was a predictable reluctance to handicap publications' market-ability with negative press.) The mid-1990s' decline in government subsidies for publishing spelled the end of *Knjiga*, which had been largely dependent on them. As a substitute, book selectors can do occasional searches for all new Slovene imprints in the Slovene online catalogs of COBISS (or in new issues of *Slovenska bibliografija. Knjige*). COBISS searches can also be delimited by subject categories of particular interest, as well as year of publication. Some scholarly journals, such as *Prispevki za novejšo zgodovino* for history, or *Litera-tura* for belles letters and criticism, include extensive and quite current book review sections, which can help to identify well-regarded new publications, most of which will still be in print.

CONCLUSION

A newcomer stepping into the world of Slovene publishing at the turn of the century and looking for signs of ferment might have a sense of arriving ten or fifteen years late–the most significant changes in content having already taken place in the 1980s, and in industry infra-structure in the 1990s. The industry as it exists in 2000 has been groomed and streamlined for entry into the European Union, or at least for survival as a profitable, market-oriented industry that pays its taxes. The traumas that Slovene society incurred from 1945 to 1990, but was forced for decades to suppress, have now been widely aired and assuaged in public discussions, in print, and through the broadcast media. Slovenia's geopolitical significance to the West, as part of the great Yugoslav Balkan transitional zone to the former East Bloc, has passed into history; Slovenia has become, de facto, an integral part of Western Europe, and has rapidly reestablished its historic trade and cultural ties to Austria and Italy as relations with its fellow South Slavic neighbors–Croatia, Bosnia and Serbia–have broken down or stagnated. From its fortunate valleys the turmoil of the Balkans seems thousands of miles away, even if at times it has been no more than a hundred. What is striking is how stable the publishing scene, the range and identity of the main publishers, and the repertory of serial publications has remained throughout the 1990s, especially in comparison with the much greater flux in publishing evident in countries to the south, and in other Central and East European societies in transition.

NOTES

1. Besides the Library of Congress, in the U.S. Harvard and Indiana University continue to develop exceptionally strong Slovene collections. Less comprehensive, but good, collections are currently maintained at the University of California, Berkeley, the University of Chicago, Columbia University, the University of Kansas, New York Public Library, the University of Washington, and elsewhere.

2. Miloš Likar, "Deset let delovanja založbe Krt," *Knjiga*, 1991, no. 12: 468-469.

3. *Slovenska kronika XX. stoletja* (Ljubljana: Nova revija, 1995-1996), 2: 386.

4. Vladimir Kavčič, "Vstopamo v novo obdobje, postajamo del Evrope," *Knjiga*, 1992, no. 6: 82.

5. Peter Kolšek, "Eniživotarijo, drugi živijo, tretjih pa ni : zasebno založništvo deset let pozneje," *Delo*, 22 December 1997: 8.

6. Matjaž Kmecl, "Knjiga, kdo bo te kupil?" *Knjiga*, 1993, no. 1-2: 2.

7. Martin Žnideršič, "Publishing in Countries in Transition and in Slovenia," *ISBN Review* 18 (1997): 148-149.

8. Sergij Pelhan, "Davek bo verjetno še ostal : pogovor z ministrom za kulturo Sergijem Pelhanom," *Knjiga*, 1993, no. 7-8: 189-191.

9. Approximate figures taken from Jaro Mihelač, "Večno ponavljajoča se tema: (naša) država in knjiga: s kongresa Kulturnega foruma," *Delo*, 23 March 1995: 9.

10. *Statistični letopis Republike Slovenije*, 1994-1998 (Ljubljana: Statistični urad Republike Slovenije).

11. Jože Korinšek, "Knjige je vedno več, proda se jih vse manj: pomenek o razmerah v založništvu," *Delo*, 6 November 1997: 16.

12. Matos, Milan, "Kakšne bodo posledice novega davka na knjige?" *Delo*, 7 May 1998: 13.

BOSNIA AND HERCEGOVINA

MAP 3. Bosnia and Hercegovina

Source: *Bosnia and Herzegovina*. Scale 1:2,640,000. Washington, DC: Central Intelligence Agency, 1997

Publishing in Bosnia and Hercegovina

Janet Crayne

SUMMARY. The article contains several sections, the first of which covers publishing in Bosnia and Hercegovina (including the Muslim-Croat Federation and Republika Srpska) throughout history, focusing on the period 1945-1998. The second section is devoted to a review of recent publications, which are broken down into (1) newspapers and periodicals that appear more frequently than monthly, (2) serials analyzed by subject, (3) significant monographic publications, and (4) a brief survey of publishers and collections. *[Article copies available for a fee from The Haworth Document Delivery Service: 1-800-342-9678. E-mail address: <getinfo@ haworthpressinc.com> Website: <http://www.HaworthPress.com> © 2000 by The Haworth Press, Inc. All rights reserved.]*

KEYWORDS. Bosnia, Bosna, Herzegovina, Hercegovina, Bošnjak, Muslim-Croat Federation, Republika Srpska, publishers and publishing

A central historical fact is pertinent to the study of publishing in Bosnia and Hercegovina–namely, that in the modern period Bosnia did not become an independent state until 1995. From the late fifteenth century to 1878, Bosnia was part of the Ottoman Empire. From 1878

Janet Crayne, MA, MLIS, is Senior Associate Librarian, Slavic and East European Division, 111G Hatcher Graduate Library N., University of Michigan, Ann Arbor, MI 48109-1205 (E-mail: jcrayne@umich.edu).

Special thanks for advice on this article go to Snježana Buzov, Kemal Bakaršić, and Michael Biggins. They should receive much of the credit for getting this done, and none of the blame for any errors.

[Haworth co-indexing entry note]: "Publishing in Bosnia and Hercegovina." Crayne, Janet. Co-published simultaneously in *Slavic & East European Information Resources* (The Haworth Information Press, an imprint of The Haworth Press, Inc.) Vol. 1, No. 2/3, 2000, pp. 41-82; and: *Publishing in Yugoslavia's Successor States* (ed: Michael Biggins, and Janet Crayne) The Haworth Information Press, an imprint of The Haworth Press, Inc., 2000, pp. 41-82. Single or multiple copies of this article are available for a fee from The Haworth Document Delivery Service [1-800-342-9678, 9:00 a.m. - 5:00 p.m. (EST). E-mail address: getinfo@haworthpressinc.com].

to the end of World War I it was part of the Austro-Hungarian Empire. Between the two World Wars (1918-1941) it was part of the Kingdom of Serbs, Croats and Slovenes (later the Kingdom of Yugoslavia). During World War II much of Bosnia and Hercegovina became part of the so-called Independent State of Croatia (Nezavisna Država Hrvatska, a satellite state of the German Reich). From 1945 on it was part of Yugoslavia, but seceded along with the other republics in 1992.

During the Ottoman Period there were only four presses in Bosnia: one in Goražde, two in Mostar, and one in Sarajevo. The total publication output in Bosnia during that time was only four newspapers and fifty book titles.[1] The printing of the first Bosnian book was commissioned by Božidar Vuković, who sent two brothers to Venice to study printing and to purchase the equipment necessary for the establishment of a printing press. In 1527 a church missal, or *Služabnik*, was printed there. In 1529 Teodor, one of the brothers, arrived with the printing press in Goražde, where Božidar was Abbot of Hram sv. Đordja (Church of St. George). The press remained there for almost five years. It was subsequently taken to other locations in the region, but remained in Bosnia for a total of fifteen years. After this, what some have termed a brief period of enlightenment, no Bosnian press existed in Bosnia for 337 years, and publishing for that country was done outside Bosnian boundaries. Published materials were either commissioned from outside Bosnia, or they were exported for sale in the country.

In the second half of the nineteenth century, publishing entered a new phase. The first journal for a Bosnian readership was published from 1850-1870 by Ivan Franjo Jukić (pseudonym Slavoljub Bošnjak). *Bosanski prijatelj* was published in Croatia in four issues, and written in the vernacular[2] in the Roman alphabet. The journal covered Bosnian history, culture, and society. From 1861 to 1869 Bosnia was administered by Topal Osman Paša, who recognized that by law he was required to establish and maintain one centrally located publisher in his *vilajet*, or administrative district. This suited his need to document Bosnia and Hercegovina as an entity autonomous enough to publish its own official and educational materials. He therefore summoned Ignjat Sopron to Sarajevo in 1865, who became the city's first publisher-printer. From the start Sopronova pečatnja had two typesetters: one from Belgrade, who set type in Cyrillic and Roman scripts, and another from Constantinople, who set type in Arabic. In

1866 the press became the official property of the Turkish authorities and, as such, became the official vilajet publishing house, staffed by a director, two typesetters, four assistants, translators, and distributors. After the Austro-Hungarian takeover it functioned as a Turkish language press and continued to publish materials in the Arabic alphabet. This no longer private, but state enterprise was known as Vilajetska štamparija, and later, Vilajetska pečatnja.[3] Despite its official ties, the press also published for private individuals, and in several alphabets, including Latin, Cyrillic, Arabic, Greek and Hebrew.

Publishing by the Franciscans in Mostar began in 1872, when the Austrian Consul interceded on their behalf, and permission was granted for them to acquire a press. In that year a press was delivered to Mostar via Trieste and Dubrovnik, but was almost immediately impounded by the Turkish authorities. Then, in 1873 the press was permitted to operate as Tiskara Katoličke misije u Hercegovini (Press of the Catholic Mission in Herzegovina). The press split in 1876, and the larger component renamed itself Tiskara franjevačka (Franciscan Press). It remained in operation until 1896 under the leadership of Don Frane Miličević. In 1898 Nedeljko Radičić took over direction of the press, and replaced it with a new one, which he later sold. Mostar was also the location of the Hercegovina vilajet press, and its paper of record, *Neretva*, which was introduced in 1876, and closed at the end of 1877, when the vilajet was abrogated.

When Austria-Hungary occupied Bosnia and Hercegovina in 1878, it inherited a publishing tradition that was seeded by Ottoman and Franciscan initiatives. Although still in its infancy, publishing in the major cities of Sarajevo and Mostar reflected a linguistic flexibility that was necessary in establishing a large multilingual readership. Languages in common usage were Serbo-Croatian, Ladino (Judaeo-Spanish used by the Sephardic Jews), Turkish and Greek. They were written in various alphabets, including Cyrillic and Roman (for Serbo-Croatian), Arabic (for Turkish and classical Arabic texts), Hebrew (for Ladino), Greek, and others. Typesetters were hired and type was purchased to typeset and print what the communities read.

Sarajevo, for example, had two such religio-ethnic communities: a sizable Sephardic Jewish community and a large Muslim community. Both were very well established. By the beginning of the twentieth century the Sarajevo Jewish community published its first journal in Ladino, *La Alborada*, from 1900 to 1901. At about the same time, the

Muslim community began publishing its journal, *Behar*, which began publication in 1900 and ceased in 1911. This journal was devoted to literary entertainment and instruction for Muslim readers.[4] It was published bi-monthly and chiefly in the Roman-script version of the vernacular, but its contents also included excerpts in Turkish.

The late nineteenth century produced several notable publications originating in both Sarajevo and Mostar. In Sarajevo: *Bosanski vjestnik*, the first newspaper published in Bosnia; *Bosna*, the official vilajet paper of record; and *Sarajevski cvjetnik*, an officially sanctioned but private paper on politics and culture. The Serbian cultural society Prosvjeta began publishing *Bosanska vila* at that time, and the Franciscans began issuing *Glasnik jugoslavenskih franjevaca*. In Mostar Aleksa Šantić's *Zora*, a journal for the arts, began publication. *Hercegovački bosiljak, Kršćanska obitelj*, and *Biser* were all published then by Hrvatska dionička tiskara (Croatian Printing Company).

Under Austro-Hungarian rule publishing remained active and continued to grow.[5] The number of publishers increased to forty (two established under Ottoman rule, and thirty-eight new ones). In Sarajevo there were fifteen publishers–one old and fourteen newcomers. Notable were the titles *Večerni Sarajevski list, Kalendar Bošnjak, Sluzbeni list*, the paper of record, and *Glasnik Zemaljskog Muzeja*, the first scholarly journal published in Bosnia. The first medical journal, *Jahrbuch des bosnisch-herzegovinischen Landesspitales in Sarajevo*, began in 1894 and ran through 1900. It contained scholarly literature that included case studies written by Austrian specialists who practiced at the regional hospital in Sarajevo. With the occupation, the use of German (and also Hungarian) in publishing increased. Similarly with the influx of Ashkenazi Jews from Austria, the Jewish community required materials published in Yiddish (Judaeo-German printed in Hebrew characters). An example of how flexible publications had to be to suit a large readership is the official publication *Der Tourist* (1910-11), which was published in Sarajevo in German, but also contained segments in Serbo-Croatian, Hungarian, Turkish, Ladino and Yiddish.

Some specialized presses developed within Sarajevo, publishing materials of interest to specialized segments of the community. Consequently, Sarajevo had Jewish, Muslim, Serbian and Croatian publishing houses. This was also the time when many of the predecessors of presses in the 1950s came into existence. Srpska dionička štamparija u

Sarajevu began, and eventually became the state-affiliated Svjetlost. Prva hrvatska tiskara, Sarajevo, became Štamparsko preduzeće "Veselin Masleša," Bosnische Post became Štamparija "Oslobodjenje."

After the end of the First World War publishing resumed in much the same way as prior to the war. Restrictions persisted, in that each publisher had to obtain permission to open for business. Although certain requirements had to be fulfilled, permission ultimately depended on the political import of a press and/or its publications. In Sarajevo, as part of the Kingdom of Serbs, Croats and Slovenes, there were twenty-two publishers–nine dating to before the war, and thirteen new ones. Once again they included specialized houses for ethnic and religious groups. As during the Austro-Hungarian period, publishing was also developing in other major cities throughout Bosnia and Hercegovina.

From 1941 and 1945 Bosnia and Hercegovina were incorporated into the fascist Independent State of Croatia. The established publishing houses were either forced to go out of business or became state publishers. There were an additional eleven illegal Bosnian publishers during World War II, supported by the partisans and, of course, not subject to government controls. The Sarajevo partisan press was discovered early in the war and shut down in 1941, but other presses remained open and active. One serial that got its start with the partisans was the newspaper *Oslobodjenje.*

By 1945 few functioning publishing houses remained in Bosnia, so between 1945 and 1948 all the publishing resources in Sarajevo that remained after the war were pooled to provide a small number of active and productive presses.[6] Between 1945 and 1951, 1,750 books were published, compared to fifty during the Ottoman period, 1,600 during the forty years of Austro-Hungarian dominance, and 2,000 during the 23 years under the Kingdom of the Serbs, Croats and Slovenes.[7]

The years 1948 to 1951 marked Yugoslavia's split with Stalin, the Cominform, and Soviet-style Communism. Workers' self-management became the model that all state enterprises followed, and consequently publishing enterprises underwent a phase of restructuring. Državna štamparija, the largest publisher in Bosnia, provides a good example of this. In that year it combined with Oslobodjenje, and the new publishing house took the name of Oslobodjenje.

Between 1945 and 1972 there were three major dailies in Sarajevo:

Oslobodjenje, Sarajevski dnevnik (both established in the mid-to late 1940s), and *Večernje novine* (established in 1964). *Oslobodjenje* and *Večernje novine* were both official publications of the Socialist League of Working People (Socijalistički savez radnog naroda, or SSRN) and they had strong Party ties. Both were published by NP "Oslobodjenje" but had separate editorial staffs. *Večernje novine* was an evening paper and therefore complemented *Oslobodjenje*. Judging from circulation statistics from that period, it is estimated that their combined circulation included between four and six percent of the populace of Yugoslavia as a whole.[8] It is clear that the readership for one paper was not necessarily the readership for the other: when circulation peaked for *Oslobodjenje* in the sixties and early seventies, the circulation of *Večernje novine* plummeted, and when *Oslobodjenje*'s statistics plummeted in the mid-1960s, *Večernje novine*'s peaked. More localized papers came into existence as well, and increased in number–for example, *Front slobode* (Tuzla), *Naša riječ* (Zenica), and *Krajina* (Bihać, Drvar, Velika Kladuša and other cities). A bimonthly Islamic newspaper, *Glasnik Vrhovnog islamskog starješinstva u SFRJ*, began publication once again after a hiatus during the war. By 1973 its circulation had increased almost fivefold. It continues today under the title *Glasnik*. The biweekly *Preporod*, the organ of the Association of Ilmija in Bosnia and Hercegovina and *Islamska misao*, a monthly publication, were also published. One weekly devoted to a young audience was *Male novine*, which began publication under the current name in 1956. The paper was intended to evoke in Yugoslav youth a sense of patriotism. *Svijet*, published by Oslobodjenje as its seventh issue (on Tuesdays), was a weekly illustrated newspaper magazine that reflected the format of *Oslobodjenje*. It contained information on sports and culture, summaries of the news, and reporting on contemporary issues. It began publication in 1958. *Zadrugar* was an annual that began publication in 1945. It became independent in 1954, focusing on economics and agrarian politics.

When Yugoslavia redefined its version of Communism in 1951 in terms of workers' self-management, publishing standards became profit-oriented. Profits were generated by high-volume sales, and that meant the publication of titles that were sure to sell. These included official publications and officially sanctioned publications. Even though Titoist Yugoslavia was more liberal than Stalinist Yugoslavia, publishing practices included a form of censorship designed to keep sales and profits high. In addition, Bosnian publishing had always existed at the discretion of its state sponsor, for which censorship was a way of life. While, outwardly, publishers appeared to have discretion over the titles that they produced, authors pre-censored their work to avoid having it rejected for political reasons.

In Titoist Yugoslavia of the 1960s and 1970s, Bosnia was transformed into a thriving center of heavy industry, particularly of munitions production, and it received a disproportionate share of central support for industrial development.[9] The existence of Bosnia's large Muslim population helped secure Yugoslavia's collaboration with countries among the Non-Aligned Nations which had large Muslim populations. Bosnia's industrial development was its reward for the international role that it had played. As a constitutionally recognized ethnic group within the Yugoslav Federation since 1974, the Muslims' political importance afforded them benefits that other legally recognized ethnic groups received.[10] Thus the Bosnian government functioned successfully as a coalition among Serbs, Croats and Muslims. Tito died in 1980, and ethnic groups gradually strengthened as separate political forces. This coincided with a period of economic decline, and the discovery of corruption in the highest levels of government, industry and banking. The economic decline added to discontent. Despite repressive measures throughout Yugoslavia, nationality issues grew in importance. Probably due to its coalition government, Bosnia was able to maintain the status quo for a longer period of time following Tito's death than some of the other republics. Publishing experienced gradual changes, but it did not undergo a sudden revolution. Many of the publishing houses that had operated out of multiple cities and two or more republics during the Communist period in Yugoslavia, such as Svjetlost, remained, but these were now competing with new publishers that were frequently more republic-based. Some publishing houses also continued to serve specific ethnic and/or religious groups. In certain cases publishers that were formerly known to have close ties with the Yugoslav Communist Party, or with the Bosnian equivalent, no longer maintained them, but all the same kept their old names (such as Oslobodjenje). In other cases the ties remained intact. The same variations held true for the publications themselves.

A case in point was the newspaper, *Oslobodjenje*, which began in 1943 as the official newspaper of the partisans under Marshal Tito. After Liberation it became a Communist paper. Its staff had been multiethnic during the war, and its editorial stand favored pluralism. Both the hiring practice and editorial stand remained intact as the newspaper made the transition to a Communist publication. In the summer of 1988, a new editor had to be appointed to the paper. The appointment was normally made on the basis of a party political decision. Since this appointment could be withdrawn or replaced by another, the editor had to "toe the Party line." This time the editorial staff voted on its own, and recommended two candidates, ensuring their contribution to the decision-making process and challenging the long-established system of Party control. Although the staff-selected candidates were not necessarily those that the Party wanted, the Party nevertheless selected one of the recommended candidates, Kemal Kurspahić.[11] Within a very short time following Kurspahić's appointment, the newspaper developed a reputation for interpretive reporting, and as a forum for a broad cross-section of opinions and commentaries. The paper's editorial policy no longer affiliated itself with the Party (or before 1992, with any party). With the first issue of 1990, *Oslobodjenje* appeared without its oath of loyalty to Tito: without that symbolic phrase the newspaper established its independence from party politics, and set the stage for other papers to follow.[12] It had taken a full ten years from the time of Tito's death for the newspaper to take an active editorial stand independent of Party political ideology.

Throughout the late 1970s and 1980s, publishing thrived in Bosnia and Hercegovina. The number of books and brochures produced per year varied from 688 to 856; the number of newspapers from 200 to 387; and the number of magazines from fifty-four to 114. There were no great fluctuations in titles published over a period of fourteen years. As newspapers lost the habit of self-censorship during this time, their circulation statistics predictably increased.[13] Within this same twenty-year period learned societies and institutions, formerly dominated to a large degree by political interests, began to come into their own. Bosnia's Scientific Society (Naučno društvo) transformed itself into the Akademija nauka i umjetnosti Bosne i Hercegovine (the Bosnian Academy of Sciences and Arts), establishing symbolic parity with the Academies in other Yugoslav republics. The National Library, National Museum and Oriental Institute were viewed as unique institutions with unique holdings, and attracted researchers worldwide.

In 1992, following the secession of several Yugoslav republics, Bosnia and Hercegovina declared its independence. Shortly thereafter

Serbian nationalist paramilitaries and former Yugoslav People's Army units invaded the new nation. The tactics used were called "ethnic cleansing," which referred to the elimination of all evidence of an ethnic group, specifically the Muslim (Bosnian majority) population. In addition to the systematic slaughter of Muslims, all religious structures, including mosques, and all libraries, archives and museums were targeted for destruction. Croatia also attempted to lay claim to parts of Bosnia and Hercegovina by destroying whatever it could not have, and by killing those who would not yield. Within three to four years the trappings of a civil society in Bosnia and Hercegovina had been demolished. Along with most landmarks, the major libraries and archives in the country had been virtually destroyed. When Sarajevo was under siege, many citizens remained determined to sustain an active cultural and intellectual life, albeit without food, water, medicine or shelter. In that sense Sarajevo as a society remained "civil," even though its civil structures were in rubble. *Oslobodjenje*, the Sarajevo daily, published almost every day during the siege, and became a symbol of social and multicultural strength for the city's people.

Following the war in Bosnia, the Dayton Accords (1995) defined the territory of Bosnia-Hercegovina in terms of two so-called Entities: autonomous Republika Srpska, and the Muslim-Croat Federation. Together they make up the Republic of Bosnia and Hercegovina, which currently is occupied by a NATO Stabilization Force designated as SFOR. Put succinctly, "the war in Bosnia-Hercegovina destroyed much of the country's infrastructure and severely disrupted its economic life."[14] As a means of comparison, in 1995 the GDP for Bosnia and Hercegovina was less than one-fourth the 1991 GDP, and per capita income was about one-tenth the 1991 figure. It also had an external debt of 3.2 billion dollars. In 1995 the World Bank committed 5.1 billion dollars to Federation programs, and donations and loans by other organizations and institutions followed close behind. Initial projections by the International Monetary Fund (IMF) looked very good: the growth rate per annum was thirty-five percent, wages had tripled and unemployment had dropped to, at most, sixty percent. But by 1997 taxes were taking half of all wages earned, and unemployment was stable but not declining.

In 1996 Republika Srpska had a growth rate of zero percent, and wages were one-third those in the Federation. The 1997 projected growth was five percent and there was seventy percent unemployment. Analysts have stated that until large, formerly government-owned enterprises, including banks, have been privatized (and not purchased by the government or its representatives), the economy will not be able to recover rapidly, if at all. Real privatization has been made a pre-condition for assistance to both the Federation and to enterprises in the RS which have expressed some interest in outside assistance. If Republika Srpska were to fail economically, it could bring the fragile economy of the Muslim-Croat Federation down with it. Outside financial assistance would also free the populace from the economic grip that the Serbian Entity's de facto leader, Radovan Karadžić, has on it.

The private sector in the Muslim-Croat Federation is growing very slowly and the black market, despite all efforts to keep it under control, is flourishing. In 1998 the IMF reported an annual growth rate of forty percent, and the GDP was reported to stand at 4.1 billion dollars. Despite these minor gains, the country's poverty level places it second only to Albania, which has the lowest per capita rate in Europe. The World Bank projects that the Federation will achieve two-thirds of its prewar GDP in the next decade.[15] That could have little meaning if billions of dollars in loans must be repaid.

Restoration and reconstruction continue to be a very difficult job, since many of the cultural and religious institutions in Bosnia had been targeted for destruction during the war, and few libraries and collections were left intact. The National and University Library in Sarajevo lost ninety percent of its collection, and the building (the ornate, Moorish revival style Vijećnica, or former City Hall, located in central Sarajevo) is unusable. It should be noted that prior to 1992 plans were already being made for a new library, since Vijećnica no longer contained adequate space for the growing collection and library services. The war, of course, forced the revision of those plans to accommodate the Library's new situation.

It is clear that the National Library will require many years to own once again a collection of two million titles and that its main collection will not be housed in Vijećnica. The Austrian government provided winterization funding for Vijećnica, but there has been no news of restoration funding from any sources since then. In the past, the Sabre Foundation provided free shipping for books donated by American university presses, and by American university libraries and academics. Unfortunately that funding was reduced in 1997, and donors must now, for the most part, cover their own shipping costs. Book donations have been tapering off, probably due to mailing costs, which are still quite high. Exchanges, once a staple of academic American libraries and their East European counterparts, have been slow to resume. Some former exchange partners with the National Library no longer maintain any library exchanges. Other libraries have ceased their exchanges with Bosnia, because their academic programs no longer require in-depth collections. On the whole, fewer exchanges have been renewed, and in general, fewer materials are being exchanged. One obstacle in the way of efficient exchanges is the relative lack of Internet communications even in major cities such as Sarajevo, Mostar, Bihać and Tuzla. Without e-mail, one offer of books made to several competing libraries would require almost a year for the list to be sent out, searched by the partner libraries, mailed back, and then fulfilled. Because most of the materials now being offered by Bosnian libraries on exchange are new publications, the libraries are competing with vendors who are offering the same titles. Most vendors use e-mail, and therefore make their offers far in advance of the exchange lists. It is not rare for an exchange library to be offered materials that it has already purchased from a vendor.

In the mid- to late-nineties, many individuals donated their time to assist with Internet projects, library automation, and other endeavors in Bosnia and Hercegovina. The means of support have varied with the credentials of the individual and the nature of the proposed project. In addition, the National and University Library and librarians are receiving assistance from non-governmental organizations, such as the Network Library Program, and the Soros Foundation affiliates. This includes subsidies for trips on professional business, and for providing Internet access to e-mail and the Web. Colleagues in neighboring countries such as Slovenia and Croatia conduct workshops to help librarians learn how to use computers in a library environment. It is hoped that Bosnian libraries will eventually have computers that will link them in a network with Croatian and Slovenian libraries. Slovenia has taken the additional step of offering free tuition to Bosnians who wish to attend Slovenian universities.

Despite the disruption of daily life during almost four years of war in Bosnia-Hercegovina, an estimated four hundred publications were produced and deposited with the National and University Library. Dr. Enes Kujundžić, the Library Director, admits that this is a number, "which due to the war, communication[s] blockade, occupation of some parts of the country, cannot be considered complete."[16] The monographs published during that period are listed in *Bibliografija monografskih publikacija, 1992-1994: popis ratnih izdanja*, which is the National Bibliography for those years. The front cover contains a rendering of Viječnica, the former National Library, and the back cover contains a rendering of the rubble that remained after the building was shelled. Following this wartime publication, new volumes began to appear. In 1997 the national bibliography of serial publications, *Bibliografija serijskih publikacija, 1992-1996* was issued. It contains 331 titles in the body of the publication, and 88 in an addendum. The reader is reminded in the introduction that these totals should be compared to the 511 titles that were published in 1983. It is clear that the severely reduced staff of the National Library is committed to the continued publication of the national bibliography, as well as filling in lacunae retrospectively. In 1997 it issued a retrospective bibliography of serial publications, *Bibliografija bosanskohercegovačkih serijskih publikacija, 1945-1949*, which was intended to be a companion to *Bosanskohercegovačka bibliografija knjiga i brošura 1945-1951* by Đordje Pejanović, but was never published. In 1998 the National and University Library in collaboration with the Business Association of Publishers and Booksellers of Bosnia and Hercegovina published *Books and publishers from Bosnia and Hercegovina* for the Frankfurt Book Fair. The first part, entitled "Bosanskohercegovačka bibliografija knjiga 1992-1996," contains 1,303 monographic entries. Taking into account the estimated 400 monographs published during the war, about 900 monographs were published from 1994 to 1996. Publishing has become quite active once again, and publishers proliferate. That same volume lists about 1,800 publishers in Bosnia and Hercegovina for 1996. The National Library has also begun publication of a new library and information science journal, *Bosniaca*, discussed below. The series *Edicia Memoria Bosniaca* contains reprints of publications salvaged from the rubble of Viječnica.

Publishing has resumed and proliferates in the major cities of Bosnia and Hercegovina, including Banja Luka, Bihać, Mostar, Pale, Sarajevo, Travnik, Tuzla, and Zenica, to name a few. Bosnia has an ISBN number: 9958, and the Bosnian Union of Publishers organized the first annual book fair after the war in 1999. As noted above, *Books and Publishers from Bosnia and Hercegovina* for 1996 lists approximately

1,800 publishers. Prices are considerably higher now, due to a substantial decline in state subsidies for publishing, and to higher production costs. There are also customs clearing charges which, in Bosnia, have been quite high (as much as 150 dollars in 1998), but which may now be decreasing. On occasion, publication subsidies have been and are being provided by non-governmental and government organizations such as UNESCO, USAID, the Open Society Fund and SFOR. There are bookstores in Sarajevo, but because formal distribution networks are only now being established, their inventory is not all of high quality. Both new and second-hand books are sold on the street, as an alternative to newly established storefront businesses and the independent vendors who established themselves during the war. The materials being sold internally are those that are being sold abroad, although this was not the case when certain items had limited circulation in 1994-95. Many of the prewar publishers still exist, such as Svjetlost and Oslobodjenje, but many new ones are giving the established houses heavy competition. Major learned societies and academic institutions have begun publishing once again. As the serial list below indicates, the various sections of the Academy of Sciences and Arts have continued to publish where they left off before the war; serials issued by University departments have done the same. The Oriental Institute, National Museum, and History Institute have also resumed publishing. Paralleling the work of these institutions, a private publishing profile is also emerging which spans a fuller range of formats and subjects. A much broader subject profile is now being established by religiously affiliated publishing houses, such as Biser, El Kalem, and Ljiljan. Recently the publisher and distributor Šahinpašić issued a CD-ROM of war issues of *Oslobodjenje*, an indication that publishing formats could be diversifying. Materials are being microfilmed in Sarajevo, and the focus is on newspaper runs. In short, a publishing profile is emerging in Bosnia which promises to span the full range of subjects and formats.

As of 1995 the National Library is the ISSN and ISBN agency and the CIP provider for Bosnia, but sadly, not all the postwar publications from Bosnia are represented in the National and University Library's collection. In 1995 the "Law on Library Activity" required the deposit of ten copies of printed or reproduced material, and fifteen copies of official publications, in the National and University Library.[17] According to Dr. Kujundžić, ". . . due to the new political environment in

Bosnia and Hercegovina, since 1991 many publishers' . . . understanding of legal deposit regulations was not so strict as it was required . . . [This has] had negative implications on the number of books received by our library."[18] Although the system is in place, it is not being uniformly observed by publishers. Since the Library serves both the general public and the academic community, the absence of deposit copies has a major impact on collection quality and quantity. Moreover the Library does not have deposit copies for exchange with other libraries, and is thus deprived of other titles received on exchange.

Given the slow start that exchanges have had following the war, American libraries have initiated methods of acquiring and/or sharing hard-to-obtain but important materials. When one item is needed by many libraries, such as a run from the wartime European edition of *Oslobodjenje*, libraries can apply to have it filmed by the Slavic and East European Microfilming Project. The Slavcopy consortium provides photocopies of brittle books and serials considered necessary to the participant libraries. With the exception of individual gifts, vendors serve as the major source of Bosnian materials. Among them Slavica Verlag, in Munich (Elisabethstrasse 22, D-80796 Munich, Germany) prides itself in offering publications of excellent quality. Although it specializes in selling Slovenian publications, it has a separate, highly selective list in its catalog for Bosnian materials. The prices are high (German shipping costs and taxes account for this), but the quality is excellent. Slavica will establish standing or continuation orders, and those orders can be relied on. Slavica Verlag also functions as a publisher of materials of excellent quality. Srbica Book Store (2238 Dundas Street West, Toronto, Ontario, M6R 3AP Canada) mainly offers Serbian materials, but it also lists some Bosnian publications. Its prices are lower than Slavica's, but it does not market materials as quickly. Its provision of Republika Srpska publications, including serial subscriptions, has been excellent. It provides firm orders and approval plans. It has a Web site at http://www.srbica.com. Isis (Semsibey Sok., 10/2, Beylerbeyi, 81210, Istanbul, Turkey) can be contacted by e-mail address at isis@turk.net. It provides extensive, and arguably the best coverage of publishing throughout the Muslim-Croat Federation and Republika Srpska. It has lower prices than either of the other two vendors, but more selection is required of the bibliographer. Although this vendor provides subscriptions to serial publications as well as multi-volume sets, coverage can be problematic, and expenditures can therefore yield low returns. The owner is willing to establish approval plans, and accepts firm orders, as well as standing orders and continuations. (After this article was written, the owner of Isis began referring customers to Dragan Marković of University Press, Sarajevo, fax + 387 71 46-82-60, for Bosnian materials.) All three vendors provide coverage of the humanities and the social sciences, while the natural sciences do not receive the same level of attention. All three vendors respond well to requests for specific subjects, titles, authors and/or publishers. Norman Ross Publishing, Inc. (http://www.nross. com) provides the best microfilm coverage of Bosnian materials. The company not only distributes, but creates microfilms of preservation quality, and has proven attentive to the needs and ideas of librarians.

REVIEW OF PUBLICATIONS

Newspapers and Weekly or Biweekly Periodicals in Bosnia and Hercegovina

The following titles are arranged by frequency and, within each frequency, alphabetically. Serials published monthly or less frequently are arranged by subject in a subsequent section.

Daily Newspapers and News Services

Alternativna Informativna Mreža (AIM) (Daily) is a joint operation of the European Civic Forum and former Yugoslav journalists. It began in 1992 in response to the repression and displacement of reporters in former Yugoslavia. As it describes itself, "The main objective of AIM is penetration through the information blockade and offering unbiased high-quality professional information." AIM also promotes the development of independent media in the region. Its strength lies in presenting in-depth coverage of specific issues from within the region. Networks of local reporters send their articles to editorial offices throughout Southeastern Europe, and those offices forward the articles on to the Paris office. It sends out daily reports over e-mail. There are several different services offered by AIM. Aim Press provides daily reports, which come in the form of individual e-mail texts. There are also specialized reports on Kosovo via *BalkanPress*, and on Bosnia-

Hercegovina via *IzborBiH*. An English-language monthly selection/ summary is available in print as *AIM Review*, and a French language selection/summary is available in *Le Courrier des Balkans*. The online version contains current coverage, archives, a browser, and links to other sites. Contact information is available at: http://www.aimpress. ch/, or via e-mail at admin@aimpress.org.

BOSNET. This news service got its start during the war in Bosnia. It collects news reports from selected sources, then delivers them in various forms: (1) Bosnet is the regular mailing list with sequential postings; (2) Bosnet-digest is a digest in one posting per day; (3) Bosnet-b provides news in the vernacular; (4) Bosnet-www summarizes daily news and provides hypertext links to the full stories. Contact information is available at http://www.bosnet.org/, or via e-mail at majordomo@ bosnet.org.

Dnevni avaz (Daily). Founded in 1995 in Sarajevo by Fahrudin Radončić, this paper has strong ties to the Stranka demokratičke akcije (Party of Democratic Action, or SDA, the Muslim ruling party), which gives it an edge over *Oslobodjenje* or *Večernje novine* in reporting on party politics. This newspaper had a daily circulation of 23,000 in 1998, and today has the largest readership among the dailies. According to the Freespeech website, it "received generous funding at the launch, which helped it to raid [the] best journalists from its rival Sarajevo daily *Večernje novine.*" It has a conservative editorial stand, and is distributed in the Federation, as well as abroad. Contact information: Editor, Mensur Osmović. Fax: (387) (71) 65 90 64. Web access via http://www.freespeech.org/ex-yupress/musbos.html, or directly at http://www.dnevni-avaz.com/.

Front Slobode (Daily). A news magazine published in Tuzla. It began as a regional partisan newspaper and, like *Oslobodjenje*, retained its political ties after the war. In 1993 it severed those ties and became an independent publication. It has managed to remain independent of party affiliations, and therefore serves a watchdog function. Today it supports multiculturalism, and usually expresses liberal points of view. It is distributed in the Tuzla-Podrinje Canton, but can be purchased elsewhere. Contact information: Editor, Sinan Alić. Fax: (387) (75) 25 15 21. Web access via http://www.freespeech.org/ex-yupress/musbos.html.

Glas Srpski (Daily). Published in Banja Luka, this conservative newspaper serves Banja Luka and other areas of Republika Srpska. Contact information: Editor: Tomo Marić. Fax: (387) (58) 11 759. Web access via http://www.freespeech.org/ex-yupress/ bossrb.html, or at http://www. bl.ac.yu/banjaluka/novosti.html.

ONASA [Oslobodjenje News Agency]. Founded in April 1994, during the war, *ONASA* now provides up-to-date Web access to news that can be selected by date and time, or by service. The services are all news, business news, election news, or general news. Each, some, or all services can be purchased at rates scaled to the number of end users. Contact information: Fax: (387) (71) 2765 90. E-mail: marketing@onasa. com.ba. Web access at http://www.onasa. com.ba/.

Oslobodjenje (Daily). Published in Sarajevo, it has an international distribution, and has an on-line version, or did, until the summer of 1999. Its political stand varies with the issues, since it is not affiliated with the party in power, but it tends to be very liberal. Its staff was and is multiethnic, and it still takes a multiethnic political stand in its publishing practices and political views. The oldest daily newspaper in Bosnia, *Oslobodjenje* began as the official newspaper of Marshal Tito's Partisans in 1943. In 1988 Kemal Kurspahić became the new editor, and shortly thereafter the newspaper became known for its interpretive reporting, and as a forum for varied opinions and commentaries. At the same time *Oslobodjenje* maintained a pluralistic stance, publishing in the vernacular in both Cyrillic and Roman alphabets. As nationalism in the Yugoslav republics gained strength, and the republics moved towards secession, *Oslobodjenje* would not yield in its determination to uphold multiethnicity, and refused to favor one ethnic group over another. During the war, the paper aligned itself with the Bosnian government against Serbian aggression. *Oslobodjenje* was the only newspaper that continued to publish throughout the hostilities in Bosnia and the siege of Sarajevo, missing only one issue. It served the people of Sarajevo and unoccupied Bosnia by providing the news and serving as a symbol of solidarity. It established another office in Ljubljana, which published a weekly "European" edition for consumption beyond Bosnian borders. The Slovenian office was able to support the Sarajevo daily by sending in supplies in an armored truck. Surplus newsprint was given to other publishers in Sarajevo, for their use. The editorship is now in the very capable hands of Mehmed Halilović. The Sarajevo daily along with its weekly magazine supplement, *Nedelja,* is again being published for a broader readership. Contact information: Editor, Mehmed Halilović. Fax: (387) (71) 664

977. E-mail: info@ Oslobodjenje.net. Web access via http://www. freespeech.org/ex-yupress/musbos.html, or directly at http://www. oslobodjenje.com.ba/.

Slobodna BiH (Daily). This is the Bosnian edition of *Slobodna Dalmacija*, published in Split and Mostar. Contact Information: Editor, Ivica Profaca. Fax: (021) 383 102, (021) 383 108. E-mail: info@ slobodnadalmacija. hr. Web access via: http://www.slobodnadalmacija. hr/.

Večernje novine (Daily). One of three dailies that were published in Bosnia before the dissolution of Yugoslavia, *Večernje novine* was the evening paper, while *Oslobodjenje* was the morning paper. Both were published by Oslobodjenje, and both were official publications of the Communist Party. *Večernje novine* now has a liberal orientation, and publishes five regional editions daily. All editions are identical, except for the section "Local Chronicle," which varies with the locale within Bosnia where the edition is published, namely Tuzla, Zenica, Mostar, Bihać, or Sarajevo. *Večernje novine* was the first newspaper available in Banja Luka, but it is also distributed within the Muslim-Croat Federation. Contact information: Editor, Sead Demirović. Fax: (387) (71) 664 977. Web access via http://www.vecernjenovine.ba/.

Weekly News Magazines

AS: nezavisna informativno-politička revija (Weekly). Review of news and politics. Distributed in Sarajevo.

Azra (Weekly). A women's family-oriented magazine, formerly called *Una*, distributed in Sarajevo, Zenica and Tuzla and published by Avaz. Contact information: Editor, Nadja Marići. Fax: (387) (71) 658 940. Web access via *Dnevni Avaz* at http://www.freespeech.org/ ex-yupress/musbos.html.

Behar: nezavisni sedmičnik za politiku i kulturu (Weekly). Covers politics, society and culture and is distributed in Sarajevo.

Bošnjak (Weekly). Covers journalists and journalism and is published in Travnik.

Ekonomist: bosansko-hercegovački nedjeljnik za poslovne ljude (Weekly). Published by the Futura Group in Sarajevo, it covers the Bosnian economy and economics.

Horizont: informativno politički tjednik (Weekly). A political periodical published in Mostar.

Hrvatska Riječ (Weekly). This paper has a conservative orientation.

The Sarajevo branch of the Croatian Democratic Union (Hrvatska demokratička zajednica or HDZ, Croatia's conservative and national-istic ruling party) established it in 1995, and still plays a role in its staffing and financing. It is published in Sarajevo, and is distributed in Sarajevo and Croat sectors of the Federation. Contact information: Editor, Zlatko Tulić. Phone/Fax: (387) (71) 65 09 09, or (71) 44 46 21. Web access at http://hrvrijec.hic.hr/.

Hrvatski list (Weekly). Official publication of the Croatian Repub-lic of Herceg-Bosna.

Image: prvi BiH tabloid (Weekly). A tabloid publication devoted to light entertainment, such as games and humor. It is published by Avaz.

Ljiljan (Weekly). Founded in 1990, it is heir to *Muslimanski glas*, the official publication of the SDA, the Federation's Muslim ruling party. When it changed its name to the present one, it became an independent publication, although it still generally reflects conserva-tive SDA political positions. *Ljiljan* is oriented to a Muslim reader-ship. It is published in Sarajevo and is distributed in the Federation, as well as abroad. It has an online site containing articles from the printed version, in Bosnian. Contact information: Editor, Ismet Veladžić. Fax: (387) (71) 664 549. E-mail: ljiljan@bih.net.ba, or nljiljan@aol.com. Web access via http://www.freespeech. org/ex-yupress/musbos.html and also at http://www.nippljiljan.com/politika/.

Ma-Ma: informativno edukativni magazin (Weekly). A magazine published in Bihać that covers the economy and business.

Nezavisne novine (Weekly). This moderate publication began in Banja Luka after the war. It is unique in that it is gaining popularity in both Entities. It is regularly available in Republika Srpska, and at times available in Tuzla or Sarajevo. Contact information: Editor, Zelj-ko Kopanja (who remains editor, despite being seriously injured when a bomb exploded under his car in 1999). Fax: (387) (58) 60 676. Web access via: http://www.nnbl.co.yu/ and also at http://www.freespeech. org/ex-yupress/bossrb.html.

Oslobodjenje Ratno (Weekly). Also known as *Srpsko Oslobodjenje*. Founded in 1992 during the Sarajevo siege, it is published in Pale, the Bosnian Serb capital situated in the highlands above Sarajevo. Al-though editorial information makes a claim that it is the heir to the Sarajevo daily, *Oslobodjenje*, it is the Republika Srpska counterpart and is conservative within that frame of reference as well. It is distributed in

Republika Srpska, as well as outside of Bosnia. Contact information: Ranko Preradović. Phone/Fax (387) (51) 786 813; 783 357; 783 413.

Prijedorsko ogledalo: informativno politički list (Weekly). A political periodical with a moderate to liberal stand on issues, it is published in the north-central town of Prijedor. Contact information: Director, Edin Ramulić. E-mail: editor@bih.net.ba. Web access at http://novo-ogledalo. prijedor.ba/.

Reporter (Weekly). A moderate to left-of-center newspaper, published in Banja Luka, that is funded by the Open Society Fund and the Swedish Helsinki Committee. In October 1999 its distribution was forbidden in Serbia. In an act of defiance it resorted to its Web version to disseminate subsequent issues. Contact information: Editor, Perica Vučinić. Fax: (381) (78) 315 792. E-mail: rep@inecco.net. Web access at http://www.reporter.co.yu/.

Slobodna Bosna (Weekly). A liberal publication from Sarajevo, it is aimed at an intellectual audience with a pop culture orientation. It began publication shortly before the war, and then revived in 1994. It is distributed in the Federation and around Banja Luka. At the time this article was written, Mr. Avdić was in prison, but he continues to function as editor of this periodical. Contact information: Editor, Senad Avdić. Fax: (387) (71) 444 895. Web access via http://www. freespeech.org/ex-yupress/musbos.html.

Svijet; also known as *Sarajevski svijet* (Weekly). In 1996 the Ljubljana edition of *Oslobodjenje* became the weekly news magazine *Sarajevski Svijet*, which had been published before the war. It is now published in Sarajevo. Some staff of the earlier weekly newspaper have continued as staff of the current weekly magazine. The editorial policies of both seem to be about the same. It is distributed throughout Bosnia (Federation and Republika Srpska). Contact information: Editor, Zlatko Dizdarević. Fax: (387) (71) 456 142. E-mail: svijet@bih. net.ba. Web access at http://www.freespeech.org/ex-yupress/musbos.html.

Sport: prvi BiH sportska revija (Weekly). Published by Avaz, it reviews the week's sports.

Zetel oglasnik: informativno oglasni list (Weekly). An advertising periodical that focuses on trade and international relations, published in Zenica.

Bi-Weekly Magazines

[Avazov] fokus (Biweekly). A magazine that covers politics. It is published by Avaz and distributed in Sarajevo.

Azra (Biweekly). A magazine for women and their families, published by Avaz.

BiH Perspektive: informativno politički časopis (Biweekly). A political periodical.

[Bosna i Hercegovina] Dani (Biweekly). This news magazine is the heir to *Naši dani*, a Communist youth-run and -oriented magazine from the 1980s. It was revived under its current name during the war as a monthly, and began publishing more often after the war. It was one of the first of the published media to interpret news for itself, particularly when it focused on the Party structure. As Kemal Kurspahić explained, during a Party attempt at removing *Naši dani*'s editor, "They had set standards which we in the big media would do well to emulate . . . openness with which one can approach even the most sensitive of subjects."[19] *Dani* has been highly critical of corruption in high places in the Bosnian government, which is not surprising, given its leftist orientation. It is distributed in both Entities, as well as abroad. It has an online version which culls some of the printed articles in Bosnian. Contact information: Editor, Senad Pečanin. Fax: (387) (71) 651 789. E-mail: bhdani@bih.net.ba, or dani@soros.org.ba. Web access at http://www.freespeech.org/ex-yupress/musbos.html, and also at: http://www.soros.org.ba/~dani/.

Ekstra magazin (Biweekly). Published in Bjelina; its editor was head of the Bosnian Serb Army Press Center during the war. Contact information: Editor, Jovica I. Petković. Fax: (381) (076) 45 797. Web access at http://www.ekstramagazin. com/.

Magazin "M": muzičko kulturni časopis (Biweekly). A music periodical published by "3 M Company."

Nasa Riječ (Biweekly). This liberal paper is published in Zenica and serves that city and region, with only local distribution. Contact information: Editor, Jasminka Ahmetspahić. Fax: (387) (72) 38 053.

Novi prelom (Bi-Weekly). A liberal and intellectual newspaper, it is a proponent of the future reintegration of Bosnia's two political Entities, and is distributed in cities throughout both the Federation and Republika Srpska. Contact information: Editor, Miodrag Živanović. Fax: (387) (58) 60 676.

Polikita: satirični list (Biweekly). A satirical literary periodical published in Lukavac. Its title is a lewd play on the word "politika."

Prosvjetni list: list prosvjetnih, kulturnih i naučnih radnika BiH (Biweekly). A professional magazine for educators.

Sezam: zabavno-enigmatska revija Sarajevo (Biweekly). Devoted to light entertainment containing games, humor, etc.

TIM [Tržište i marketing] (Biweekly). Devoted to business, marketing and economics, published in Zenica.

Zmaj od Bosne (Biweekly). Published in Tuzla, this title is moderate-conservative, at times reflecting SDA (Muslim ruling party) positions. Contact information: Editor, Vedad Spahić. Phone and Fax: (387) (075) 234 808.

Serial Publications and Series

It is often very difficult to ascertain if a title is still being published. If an issue was published after 1994, its title is included here. If an issue of a serial was not published after the war, but evidence of its currency exists, then its title has been included. Any titles not having frequencies in their descriptions have either unknown frequencies, or irregular frequencies.

General

Djela (Akademija nauka i umjetnosti Bosne i Hercegovine). The flagship publication of the Bosnian Academy of Sciences and Arts, it contains scholarly articles concerning numerous topics.

Gradja (Akademija nauka i umjetnosti Bosne i Hercegovine). Contains summaries of scholarship in various areas.

Radovi Filozofskog fakulteta u Sarajevu. Published about once a year by the Faculty of Arts and Sciences of Sarajevo University.

Agriculture

Za [Zadrugar]: magazin za poljoprivredu, ekologiju i domačinstvo. Published quarterly, it also covers ecological issues pertaining to Bosnia.

Archaeology

Glasnik (Zemaljski muzej u Sarajevu). A scholarly journal, covering ethnology, archaeology, and the natural sciences.

Naše starine. Published by the Bureau for the Preservation of Cultural Monuments of Bosnia and Hercegovina.

Balkan Studies

Djela (Akademija nauka i umjetnosti Bosne i Hercegovina. Balkanološki institut). A scholarly journal treating all aspects of the Balkans.

Culture

Alem: list za kulturu i društvena pitanja KDM "Preporod." A newspaper devoted to Islamic cultural and social life, published in Novi Travnik.

Bosanska vila: list za nauku, kulturu i društvena pitanja. Published by the Serbian cultural society, Prosvjeta, this publication focuses on social and cultural life. It continues the earlier title *Bosanska vila,* published in the late nineteenth century by the same society.

Članci i gradja za kulturnu istoriju istočne Bosne. A scholarly journal published by the Museum of Eastern Bosnia in Tuzla.

Kolo: kulturno humanitarna revija. A monthly humanitarian and cultural review published by the Circle of Serbian Sisters.

Krijesnica: glasilo Matice Hrvatske Ogranak Zenica. Publication of the Zenica (Hercegovina) branch of Matica Hrvatska.

Moria: magazin za subkulturu. Monthly magazine published by UMCOR, United Methodist Committee on Relief. It covers social and cultural life.

Odjek: revija za umjetnost, nauku i društvena pitanja. Biweekly published by the Cultural and Educational Assembly of Bosnia and Hercegovina, devoted to art, critical thinking and social enquiry.

Stećak: list za kulturu i društvena pitanja. Monthly published by Napredak, devoted to social and cultural issues.

Vjesnik. Monthly published by "Preporod," the Bošnjak cultural society.

Znak Bosne: list za kulturni preporod Bosne. Monthly devoted to the cultural revival of Bosnia.

Ecology

Eko-oko: ekološka revija. As the title indicates, this monthly is devoted to a review of ecological issues.

Fondeko: znanstveni časopis. Annual devoted to ecological and quality of life issues.

Economics

Djela (Akademija nauka i umjetnosti Bosne i Hercegovine. Odjeljenje privredno-tehničkih nauka). Scholarly journal devoted to applied economics.

Education

Naša škola: teorijsko obrazovni časopis. Periodical devoted to educational theory.

Émigré Publishing

For the Bosnian Institute and its publications, see the text following "Newspapers."

Bosna Press. Émigré current political affairs publication published by Rijaset of the Islamic Union in Bosnia and Hercegovina.

Bošnjak: časopis za nauku, književnost, kulturu i informisanje. Published in Munich, it covers all cultural interests of Bosnian émigrés.

Bošnjak: list autohtonih sinova i kćeri BiH i Sandžaka. Focuses on émigrés and refugees from the Sandžak (the Muslim region of Serbia and Montenegro) and Bosnia and Hercegovina.

Informator: glasnik Kulturnog društva Bošnjaka "Preporod." Official publication of "Preporod," the Cultural Society of Bošnjaks.

Magazin Bosna: the only Australian Bosnian newspaper. Monthly. Published in Australia specifically for émigrés and refugees from Bosnia and Hercegovina.

Mjesečnik. A monthly publication for Bosnian refugees and émigrés in Ljubljana.

Zambak-BH odjek: list Bošnjaka Sjeverne Amerike. Periodical for the Bosnian Community in the United States, published in Chicago.

Ethnology

See *Glasnik. Zemaljski muzej* under "Archaeology."

Finance

Privredna banka Sarajevo. Report on finance issued by the Bank on demand.

Računovodstvo poslovne financije: časopis Udruženja računovoda i revizora BiH i preduzeća FEB Sarajevo. Monthly journal devoted to business and finance.

History

Djela (Akademija nauka i umjetnosti Bosne i Hercegovine. Odjeljenje istorijsko-filoloških nauka). A scholarly publication that covers history and philology. It has separate numbering for the series and the subseries.

Godišnjak Društva Istoričara BiH. Yearbook published by the Society of Historians of Bosnia and Hercegovina.

Prilozi (Institut za istoriju u Sarajevu). This is a scholarly history journal. Its past and present publication has been funded by private individuals, Soros, UNESCO, and SFOR.

Prilozi za orijentalnu filologiju [i istoriju jugoslovenskih naroda pod turskom vladavinom]. Scholarly publication devoted to historical and philological study of the Ottoman period in Southeastern Europe. Now uses the unbracketed form of its title.

Prilozi za proučavanje istorije Sarajeva. Published by the Museum of the City of Sarajevo, it focuses on the city's history.

Zbornik krajiških muzeja. Research published by the Museum of Bosnian Krajina, in Banja Luka.

Journalism

B-H journalist: revija za novinarstvo. This is a professional publication on journalism and journalists. It is published by the Union of Journalists of Bosnia and Hercegovina.

Maglajske novine. Published monthly by "Preporod," this publication covers journalism and journalists.

Juvenile

Aladin: poučno-zabavni dječji list. Monthly educational children's periodical.

Bubamara: dječji sportski list. Sports monthly publication for children.

Bulbulistan: list za mlade. A monthly publication for students, published in Travnik.

Dar: dječje novine. News magazine for children, published in Tuzla.

Evlad za pouku i zabavu: prvi islamski dječji časopis na bosanskom jeziku. Published by the Islamic Center in Mostar, this is an Islamic monthly for a juvenile readership.

Fan magazin: prvi BH magazin za kulturu mladih. Trimonthly magazine for young people.

Kevser: islamski list za djecu. An Islamic monthly for children.

Mirko. Published by IFOR in Sarajevo and Naples; for children.

Pupoljci islama: islamski list za djecu. Monthly Islamic newspaper for children.

Sarajevo calling: list učenika Prve gimnazije. Secondary school student newspaper.

Šubi-dubi: dječje novine. Monthly Tuzla publication containing news for children. The publisher is Radio Kameleon.

Law

Humanost: list Crvenog križa-krsta Tuzlansko-podrinjskog kantona. Published monthly in the Tuzla region by the Red Cross, this title focuses on martial law.

Library Science, Libraries and Archives

Anali (Gazi Husrev-begova biblioteka). Published by the Supreme Authority of the Islamic Community and the Gazi Husrev-beg Library. It contains scholarly articles on Bosnian Islam in all its aspects, from librarianship, to manuscript descriptions, to discussion of the relationship of Islam to other religions practiced in Bosnia.

Bibliotekarstvo: časopis Društva bibliotekara BiH. Scholarly journal devoted to library and information science, published by the Society of Librarians in Bosnia and Hercegovina.

Bosniaca: časopis Nacionalne i univerzitetske biblioteke Bosne i Hercegovine. This is a semiannual journal that contains scholarly articles on libraries and librarianship. It is published by the National and University Library of Bosnia and Hercegovina.

Fontes et Note Archaeologicae. This scholarly journal contains bibliographic analyses of archaeological publications, for example, indexing of citations from *Glasnik Zemaljskog Muzeja.* Published by the National and University Library for the Philosophical Faculty.

Glasnik arhiva i Društva arhivskih radnika Bosne i Hercegovine. Official publication of the Society of Archival Workers of Bosnia and Hercegovina.

Izdanje Arhiva Hercegovine Mostar. This publication contains descriptions of manuscripts and other archival materials in its collection. The Archive was severely damaged during the war in Bosnia and Hercegovina, and the future of this publication is not known.

Posebna izdanja (Orijentaljni institut u Sarajevu). In the past this publication focused on manuscripts held by the Oriental Institute, which was destroyed during the shelling of Sarajevo. Although many of its holdings were also destroyed, the Institute has continued to publish volumes devoted to scholarship on various aspects of Bosnian archival holdings. The Ministry of Education, Science, Culture and Sports is now the publisher of *Posebna izdanja.*

For other information on the National and University Library, see "National Bibliographic Compilations."

Linguistics, see Philology

Literature and the Arts

Baština: književno pozorišni časopis. Annual publication of the Museum of Literature and Theater Art.

Lettre internationale: tromjesečna europska revija. Published by ZID, this quarterly covers literature and literary trends.

Lica: časopis za kulturu. This monthly is published by the Society of Writers of Bosnia and Hercegovina.

Most: časopis za kulturu i društvena pitanja. Monthly published in Mostar, devoted to culture, particularly literature.

Novi izraz: časopis za književnu i umjetničku kritiku. Formerly titled *Izraz,* and published by Svjetlost, this literary quarterly is now published by Omnibus in Sarajevo.

Posebna izdanja (Akademija nauka i umjetnosti Bosne i Hercegovine. Odjeljenje za književnost i umjetnost). Scholarly publication that contains history and criticism of literature and the arts, which includes coverage of folk genres. It has separate numbering for the series and the subseries.

Putevi: časopis za književnost i kulturu. Literary journal published every two months in Banja Luka.

Život: časopis za književnost i kulturu, nova serija. Literary monthly published by the Society of Writers of Bosnia and Hercegovina, and the PEN Center of Bosnia and Hercegovina.

Mathematics

See *Djela (Akademija nauka i umjetnosti Bosne i Hercegovine. Odjeljenje prirodnih i matematičkih nauka)* under "Natural Sciences."

Medicine

Alergološko imunološki časopis: stručno medicinski časopis. Published twice yearly by the Society of Immunologists and Allergists.

Bilten (Državna bolnica Sarajevo). Bulletin for the State Hospital.

Bilten (Republički Zavod za zdravstvenu zaštitu, Sarajevo). Bulletin issued by the Bureau of Public Health in the Republic of Bosnia and Hercegovina.

Djela (Akademija nauka i umjetnosti Bosne i Hercegovine. Odjeljenje medicinskih nauka). Journal devoted to the medical sciences.

Folia anatomica Bosniaca: naučni časopis. Scholarly journal published twice a year by the Anatomical Society of Bosnia and Hercegovina.

Medicinski arhiv: časopis Sabora ljekara Bosne i Hercegovine. Medical journal published twice a year for the Congress of Physicians of Bosnia and Hercegovina.

Medicinski žurnal: informativni bilten Traumatološke klinike u Sarajevu. Official publication of the Trauma Clinic in Sarajevo.

Veterinaria: naučo stručni časopis. Quarterly published by the Veterinary Faculty in Sarajevo.

Music

Akordi: avazova muzička revija. Monthly musical review published in Sarajevo by Avaz.

Mega hit: ilustrovana revija. A music review published monthly.

National Bibliographic Compilations

Although these are not part of one series, they reflect a continuing effort to document publishing in Bosnia and Hercegovina.

Bibliografija monografskih publikacija 1992-1994: popis ratnih izdanja. This was the first national bibliography published by autonomous Bosnia and Hercegovina. Published by Nacionalna i univerzitetska biblioteka Bosne i Hercegovine in Sarajevo. The National Library regularly documents its current holdings, as well as retrospective holdings.

Bibliografija bosanskohercegovačkih serijskih publikacija 1945-1949. Published by the National Library in 1997 in Sarajevo, this monograph was intended for publication by the Bosnian bibliographer Đordje Pejanović, but was not completed in his lifetime.

Bibliografija serijskih publikacija 1992-1996. Published by the National Library in 1997.

Books and Publishers from Bosnia and Hercegovina. Published by the National Library for the Frankfurt Book Fair in Sarajevo, 1998.

Natural Sciences

See *Glasnik (Zemaljski muzej)* under "Archaeology."

Djela (Akademija nauka i umjetnosti Bosne i Hercegovine. Odjeljenje prirodnih i matematičkih nauka). Scholarly publication that covers both mathematics and the natural sciences.

Official Publications

Legislative Gazettes

Službene novine Federacije Bosne i Hercegovine. Biweekly. Official gazette of the Muslim-Croat Federation, which has legal instruments that have the force of law and other notices that are required by law to be published. It is published by Službeni list.

Službene novine grada Sarajeva: službeni informativni glasnik Skupštine grada Sarajeva i skupština opština: Centar Sarajevo, Hadžići, Ilidža, Ilijaš, Novo Sarajevo, Novi Grad, Pale, Stari Grad

Sarajevo, Trnovo i Vogošća. Monthly. Same as the above for the Assemblies of Sarajevo and the municipal districts listed above. It is published by the City Assembly.

Službene novine Kantona Sarajevo. Weekly. Same as the above for the Canton of Sarajevo, published by Službeni list.

Službene novine Srednjebosanskog kantona županije: službeno glasilo kantona-županije. Same as the above for the Central Bosnian Canton-District, published in Travnik by the local Assembly.

Službeni list Bosne i Hercegovine continues: *Službeni list Republike Bosne i Hercegovine.* Weekly. Same as *Službene novine Federacije,* but for the Republic of Bosnia and Hercegovina.

Constitution

Ustav Federacije Bosne i Hercegovine: Ustavni amandmani. Sarajevo: Službeni list, 1994. (Republička pravna biblioteka). The Constitution of Bosnia and Hercegovina first appeared in Annex 4 of the *Handbook on the Dayton Peace Agreement.* It was issued later in the *U.S. Department of State, Dispatch Supplement,* Vol. 7, No. 1, and can be found at the following Web site: http://www.state.gov/www/publications/dispatch/index.html, as well as in *Zbirka Ustava Bosne i Hercegovine.* Sarajevo: Službeni list, 1997. Sadiković, Ćazim. *Human Rights Without Protection.* Sarajevo: Bosanska knjiga; Pravni centar, Fond Otvoreno društvo BiH, 1999 also contains a reprint of Annex 4 of the Dayton Accords. *Zbirka Ustava,* mentioned above, also contains:

- *Dejtonski mirovni sporazum*
- *Ustav Republike Srpske*
- *Ustav Federacije Bosne i Hercegovine*
- *Annex 4 (Dayton Peace Agreement)*
- *Zbirka Ustava Kantona-zupanija Federacije Bosne i Hercegovine.*

Census

For statistical information concerning Bosnia and Hercegovina, the only publication that provides fairly recent coverage was published in Croatia: *Stanovništvo Bosne i Hercegovine: narodonosni sastav po naseljima,* edited by Jakov Gelo et al. Zagreb: Državni zavod za statistiku, 1995. Coverage relies on census data up through 1991.

Other

See "Medicine" for *Bilten (Republički Zavod za zdravstvenu zaštitu)*. *Statistički godišnjak Republike Bosne i Hercegovine*. Annually published by the Republic Bureau of Statistics.

Philology

Bosanski jezik. Published quarterly in Tuzla by "Prava riječ."

Djela (Akademija nauka i umjetnosti Bosne i Hercegovine. Odjeljenje istorijsko-filoloških nauka). A scholarly publication that covers history and philology. It has separate numbering for the series and the subseries.

See *Prilozi za orijentalnu filologiju [i istoriju jugoslovenskih naroda pod turskom vladavinom]* under "History."

Philosophy

Dialogue: a philosophical journal. Monthly sister publication of the Bosnian trimonthly below. This philosophical journal is also published by the International Peace Center in Sarajevo.

Dijalog: časopis za filozofska pitanja. Trimonthly sister publication of the English monthly, devoted to philosophical inquiry, published by the International Peace Center in Sarajevo.

Photography

Fotografija: stručni časopis. Professional quarterly, devoted to photography.

Politics

Bobovac: informativno glasilo Hrvata Vareša. Published by Napredak and the Vareš town council, this is an official publication for the Croats of Vareš (Bobovac).

Bilten (Stranka demokratske akcije). Bulletin for the SDA, the Muslim-Croat Federation's ruling party.

99 [Devedeset devet]: časopis slobodne misli. Published by Studio 99 in English.

Fenix: informativno političke novine. Monthly news magazine published in Zenica.

Narodne novine: informativno politička revija. A monthly political review published by the National Party of Bosnia and Hercegovina (Narodna stranka BiH).

Republika: nezavisni mjesečnik. Monthly devoted to politics.

Time-out: Sarajevo cultural guide. Monthly published jointly by Oslobodjenje and Slobodna Bosna.

Travnički ljiljani Zambak: list Okruga Travnik. Monthly political newspaper with a Muslim focus.

Zidne novine: posebno izdanje preduzeća "Zid." Bimonthly published by "Zid."

For "Literature," see "Literature and the Arts."

Publishing Abroad

Mirna Bosna. A political journal published by Solidarité Bosnie in Geneva.

Religion and/or Ethnic Identities

Advent News: religijski informativni vijesnik. This bimonthly gazette is published by the Seventh Day Adventists.

Bilten Franjevačke teologije. Semiannual covering Franciscan theology and Catholicism in general.

Bilten: glasnik Jevrejske zajednice Bosne i Hercegovine. Quarterly bulletin devoted to Judaism and Jewish theology.

Bosna Franciscana: časopis Franjevačke teologije Sarajevo. This publication covers Franciscan theology. It succeeds the publication *Nova et vetera.*

Bosna Srebrena: službeno-informativno glasilo Franjevačkog provincijalata u Sarajevu. The official publication of the Franciscan archdiocese in Sarajevo.

Djela (Akademija nauka i umjetnosti Bosne i Hercegovine. Odjeljenje društvenih nauka) Scholarly journal featuring articles about the social sciences.

Domovina: bošnjačko-hrvatski list. Monthly, published by Naša riječ, a publisher with a Croatian orientation.

Glasnik Rijaseta Islamske zajednice u BiH. Official publication

("Herald") of the Supreme Authority of the Islamic Community, published monthly.

Hikmet: list za vjersko-teološka pitanja. This Islamic publication has a theological focus.

Informator: glasnik Kulturnog društva Bošnjaka "Preporod." Official publication of "Preporod," the Cultural Society of Bošnjaks.

Kabes: popularni mjesečni časopis za duhovnu i nacionalnu afirmaciju. Monthly published in Mostar, devoted to "spiritual and national affirmation," that is, being both Muslim and Bosnian.

Napredak: hrvatski narodni kalendar za . . . god. After a period of almost fifty years, this yearly calendar is being published once again.

Naša ognjišta: informativni vjerski list. Monthly newspaper devoted to Roman Catholic issues. It is published by the Tomislavgrad Parish Church.

Preporod: islamske informativne novine. Monthly, covering Islamic news.

Prosvjeta: narodni almanah. Literary yearly almanac published by "Prosvjeta" in Sarajevo.

Svijetlo riječi: vjerski list. Monthly periodical published by the Head of the Franciscan Order in Sarajevo.

Takvim za . . . godinu. Yearly calendar published by the Supreme Authority of the Islamic Community.

Vjesnik bošnjačke dijaspore: vjerski časopis. Quarterly official publication of the Supreme Authority of the Islamic Community.

Vrhbosna: službeno glasilo biskupija Metropolije Vrhbosanske: Sarajevo, Banja Luka, Mostar, Trebinje. Monthly official record of the Metropolitanate of Vrhbosna (Bosnia today).

Zbornik radova Fakulteta islamskih nauka. Works published by the Faculty of Islamic Study at the University of Sarajevo.

Science

BH Elektrotehnika: znanstveno stručni časopis. Published twice yearly, contains research findings in engineering and technology.

Social Sciences

Hijatus: časopis za društvena pitanja i kulturu demokratije. Published in Zenica, this monthly deals with society and culture in a democracy.

Pregled: časopis za društvena pitanja. Monthly journal devoted to social issues, published by Oslobodjenje.

Pregled: časopis za društvena pitanja: izbor. Annual providing summaries of articles from the preceding year.

Sports

Bosna sport: prvi privatni list slobodne BiH. Contains sports coverage.

Champion: avazova sportska revija. A monthly review of sports, published by Avaz.

Dobojske novine: informativno sportske. Monthly, published in Doboj, covering the news in sports.

Tennis: prvi bosanskohercegovački magazin. Magazine devoted to tennis. This was being published during the shelling of Sarajevo.

Statistics. See *Official Publications, Statistički godišnjak.*

Veterans

Apel: bosanskohercegovačko glasilo Saveza ratnih vojnih invalida BiH. Official publication of the Union of Disabled War Veterans of Bosnia and Hercegovina, published in Sarajevo.

Glas antifašista: list Saveza udruženja boraca narodnooslobodilačkog antifašističkog rata Bosne i Hercegovine. Official publication of the Coalition of Associations of World War II Veterans.

Visually Impaired

Svjetlo misli: kulturno naučni časopis. Monthly magazine published by the Library for the Blind.

Zvučne novine: informativno revijalni časopis. Informational monthly published by the Society of Blind Citizens.

War and War Crimes

Bilten (Državna komisija za prikupljanje činjenica o ratnim zločinima u BiH). A bulletin covering wartime law and justice.

Bosanska vojna riječ: časopis za vojnu teoriju i praksu. Published by the Ministry of Defense of Bosnia and Hercegovina, this publication covers issues dealing with military theory and practice.

Zločin: glasilo Državne komisije za prikupljanje činjenica o ratnim zločincima na području Republike BiH. Quarterly dealing with collection of information on war crimes committed in Bosnia.

Women

Šumeja: revija za zene. Monthly review devoted to interests of Muslim women.

Žena 21 [dvadeset jedan]. A monthly magazine that delivers news, popular culture, personal interest stories and some in-depth coverage from a woman's point of view, published in Sarajevo.

Some Other Notable Publications

Within the past five years the publishing surge that Bosnia has experienced has provided libraries around the world with new, diverse and interesting material. Several items are worth noting, for their literary, historical, and sociohistorical significance.

Mehmedalija Huremović. *Moj vodić za otkup stana.* Sarajevo: Službeni list, 1997. During the shelling of Sarajevo countless numbers of citizens found themselves homeless, either due to shell damage, or because specific ethnic groups were forced to evacuate given neighborhoods. After the war the survivors had to deal with reclaiming their apartments. This book establishes the legalities for reclamation. At a time when scores of publications appeared dealing with personal wartime experiences, this title is an example of how a government publication can contribute to the reestablishment of civil infrastructure.

Bošnjačka književnost u književnoj kritici. Sarajevo: Alef, 1998. This is a multivolume set that contains literary scholarship on periods in and genres of Bosnian literary history. Separate volumes cover the following topics: (1) Old (premodern) literature; (2) Oral literature; (3) New literature–Poetry; (4) New literature–Prose; (5) New literature–Drama; (6) New literature–Literary criticism. Each volume contains documented articles by prominent scholars. The articles are grouped in subtopics according to areas of specialization. Included in each volume are a list of each author's works, a bibliography for each genre, and an index of proper names.

Suada Kapić. *Sarajevo Survival Map, 1992/3-1994/5.* Sarajevo: FAMA, 1996. A map of Sarajevo and its environs, including its landmarks and all military installations, as they existed during the siege of the city, 1992-1995. Text, describing life in the city from the point of view of daily cultural, social, and economic life, is printed on the back. This map emphasizes how determined the city was to not only survive, but thrive, despite death, destruction, and predictions of a bleak future.

Sarajevo Haggadah (Sarajevska hagada). The 200,000-volume library of Bosnia's National Museum (Zemaljski muzej, established in 1888) was successfully evacuated under shelling in the summer of 1992. The Sarajevo Haggadah, a fourteenth century illuminated prayerbook for the Passover Seder, was rescued as well. It had been brought to the city by Sephardic Jews, who fled the Spanish Inquisition four hundred years ago. During World War II it had been successfully hidden by its curator. During the siege the Haggadah became an issue when Bosnia was criticized for not giving it up to the world Jewish community. Bosnia refused on the grounds that it was part of the Bosnian multicultural heritage and rightfully belonged in Sarajevo. It remained safely hidden during the war. The Serbo-Croatian translation by Eugen Verber (accompanying a facsimile of the original manuscript) was originally published in 1983 by Svjetlost in Sarajevo. It was reissued in 1988, and is again available as a reprint.

Koran (Kur'an). Originally published in parallel Serbo-Croatian and Arabic texts by Besim Korkut in the Oriental Institute series Posebna izdanja (1977), this text has now been reprinted.

Alija Isaković. *Rječnik bosanskoga jezika: karakteristična leksika.* Sarajevo: Bosanska knjiga, 1995. When the term "ethnic cleansing" (Serbo-Croatian *etničko čišćenje*, literally translatable as either cleansing or purging) gained currency as a euphemism for genocide in 1992, Bosnians cast a critical eye on past cultural and historic interpretations. Among other things, at issue was the definition of the language spoken in Bosnia as being either Serbian or Croatian (but not Bosnian). Since then some have proposed "normalizing" the language back to the time when Bosnian was a language with traits that distinguished it from Serbian or Croatian. During this period *Rječnik bosanskoga jezika* was also published: a dictionary of common Bosnian vocabulary and its origins and references to published documentation.

Noel Malcolm and Quintin Hoare, editors. *Books on Bosnia: A Critical Bibliography of Works Relating to Bosnia-Herzegovina Pub-*

lished Since 1990 in West European Languages. London: Bosnian Institute, 1999. This bibliography lists and describes recent works pertaining to Bosnia. The categories include readings considered to be essential, other important readings, readings that illustrate a particular point of view, and in-depth reviews of specific publications. This should be considered an important work, not only for its descriptions, but as a collation of most titles pertinent to West European language study of Bosnia. Notable titles that might have appeared in the present essay were not included, because they are described in Malcolm and Hoare's book.

Bosnian Manuscript Ingathering Project. In 1992 virtually all manuscripts and documents housed in the Oriental Institute, as well as the structure itself, were destroyed in incendiary explosions. The purpose of this project is to establish a virtual collection of microforms and photocopies of manuscripts and documents once held by the Institute, which will be accessible worldwide. Information about the project is available at http://www.applicom.com/manu/ingath.htm.

BOSNIACA Bibliographies. Several projects were initiated during the war to establish "wish lists" for the National and University Library, whose collections had been destroyed. One of them has been completed, at the University of Michigan, and supplements are added regularly to update holdings. The holdings reflect those owned by the University of Michigan Library in Ann Arbor. It is available at http://www.soros.org.ba/~cuprija/bibi/bibi_lib.htm. Another project, initiated at OCLC in Dublin, Ohio, is still underway. When completed, it will have extracted Bosnian holdings from the OCLC database of catalog records. The resulting database will include BOSNIACA titles in collections held by most major American libraries. Information is available at http://www.oclc.org/oclc/new/n225/fs.htm.

PUBLISHERS AND COLLECTIONS

Unless otherwise noted, the publishers are located in Sarajevo.

Avaz–publishes titles that in most cases support positions taken by the SDA.

Avicena–publishes titles dealing with medicine, for example *Orijentalni medicinski rukopisi u Gazi Husrev-begovoj biblioteci u Sarajevu.* It also collaborates with other publishers on new authors' works, or works of import.

Bosanska knjiga–formed by a coalition of professionals, and including Gavrilo Grahovac, former Director of Svjetlost before Bosnia's independence. Its interest is in literature of lasting value, which includes reference materials. For example, it recently issued a two-volume set of *Kur'an* and *Tefsir*, translated by Enes Karić. During the war and in 1995, it issued several editions of *Riječnik bosanskoga jezika*. Although this company's editorial policy is not always politically correct, that is because it sees its role as that of a quality publisher and not of an idealogue.

Bosanska riječ/Bosnisches Wort–publishes in Tuzla and Wuppertal. It focuses on titles of literary merit, particularly those dealing with literary history or criticism. In 1998 it published *Antologiju savremene književnosti bošnjaka iz Sandžaka*. In 1993 it published *Bosna, bošnjastvo, i bosanski jezik: zbornik referata sa Osnivačke skupštine Matice Bošnjaka*.

Bosnian Institute–it provides education and information on all aspects of the history of Bosnia, with the intention of fostering the growth of institutions that would support a civil society. It also publishes its own titles, which includes two by Noel Malcolm. The Institute is located in London and is privately funded.

El Kalem–Arabic for "the pen," this publisher got its start before the war, but since then has become a major producer of literature (i.e., belles lettres) by Muslim writers. It is affiliated with the Supreme Authority of Islamic Communities.

Media Centar Prelom–publisher in Banja Luka that espouses tolerance and open dialogue. It is sponsored by the periodical *Novi prelom* and in the past collaborated with Radio Free Europe/Radio Liberty.

Mediapress–Publisher and advertiser of titles in multiple formats. It produces videos, audios, and printed materials.

Medunarodni Centar za Mir–during the war it published the works of those who couldn't publish elsewhere. It also advertised and arranged cultural events. Although it is listed in *Books and Publishers from Bosnia and Hercegovina*, it does not appear to have any recent publications.

Nacionalna i univerzitetska biblioteka Bosne i Hercegovine–has been publishing its own, and other, scholarly materials. For example, it published the last number of the Oriental Institute's *Posebna izdanja*. Please see more on the Library above.

Nezavisno udruženje novinara Republika Srpske–an independent publisher in Banja Luka. It obtains funding from the Soros Media Centar, which funds many independent publishing projects throughout the two entities. Nezavisno udruženje publishes a series, *Mala biblioteka*, which shares the name of its series with that of Srpska književna zadruga in Belgrade.

Nezavisna unija profesionalnih novinara Bosne i Hercegovine–appears to be the Sarajevo counterpart of the preceding publisher. It also issues the series *Mala biblioteka*. It recently published several titles dealing with publishing and journalism, including Fadil Ademović's *Bosanskohercegovačka štampa* (1998).

Oslobodjenje–very actively published books during the war. Its focus was and is on nonfiction, although its publishing profile is not as high as it was during the war.

Šahinpašić–is mainly known as a distributor of Bosnian materials in the United States, but he also distributes English-language materials in Bosnia. He has an extensive inventory, a small portion of which is published by him. He has an interest in supporting the publication of works having literary merit, and currently markets the two-volume Bosanska knjiga publication *Kur'an* and *Tefsir*.

Sarajevo-Publishing–in 1993 it became the successor to "Veselin Masleša," and continues to publish the series *Biblioteka kulturno nasljede*. The latter contains belles lettres, as well as literary history and criticism.

Službeni list–the official publisher for the two Entities, as well as for the Republic. In addition to producing the papers of record, it also issues works dealing with legal issues.

Svjetlost–a publisher before the war, it shared publishing with houses in Belgrade and Zagreb. Despite this former interreliance, it seems to have survived on its own. It publishes works of scholarly merit, as well as belles letters. A recent publication was *Usmena književnost Bošnjaka*, edited by Enes Kujundzić. It also published and reissued the *Sarajevo Haggadah*.

Vijeće Kongresa bošnjačkih intelektualaca–in addition to publishing its own almanac, this publisher issues critical works on political, social, and economic topics of current interest, for example, the role of the National Bank, the position of Croats in contemporary Bosnian society, etc.

Most university, Academy of Sciences and Arts, and other learned society publishers have resumed their publishing activities, but current activity cannot compensate for collection losses incurred during the war. It is quite possible that the strongest Bosnian collections in the world are located elsewhere: at the British Library in London, in Istanbul for the Ottoman Period holdings, in Vienna and Budapest for Austro-Hungarian Period holdings, and in the United States for later materials. It is also possible that a larger portion of contemporary materials is available in U.S. markets than is deposited with the National Library in Bosnia. The strongest American collections can be found at the following libraries: University of California, Berkeley; University of Chicago; Columbia University; Indiana University; University of Kansas; Library of Congress; University of Michigan; New York Public Library; Ohio State University; University of Washington; University of Wisconsin and Yale University. Very strong collections are held by both Harvard and University of California, Los Angeles, which also boast special collections containing a large number of Bosnian materials. UCLA owns the Halpern Pamphlet Collection, containing materials collected by Professor Joel Halpern in the Yugoslav republics in the 1960s. These items have a date range that covers the first half of the twentieth century, as well as a very broad subject range. Harvard's Milman Parry Collection is comprised of works gathered by Milman Parry in the 1930s. It supplemented other works acquired by the library, and in turn has been supplemented substantially. In 1976 the Parry Collection was twice as large as the original collection had been. This Collection also owns microfilm copies of archival holdings from most major repositories in the Yugoslav republics.

NOTES

1. Đordje Pejanović, *Štamparije u Bosni i Hercegovini*, 1529-1951 (Sarajevo: Svjetlost, 1952): 21.

2. That is, the language referred to by some as Bosnian, and by others as Serbo-Croatian, Croato-Serbian, Croatian or Serbian. For more information about the language spoken in Bosnia and what it is called, see Alija Isaković. *Rječnik bosanskoga jezika* in the section "Some Other Notable Publications."

3. It should be understood that these presses frequently changed hands and/or names. Pejanović cites as an example: In 1878 Austria occupied Bosnia, and Vilajetska pečatnja was handed over to the Austrian authorities. It was renamed Cezarsko-kraljevska tiskara. Under the new management *Bosansko-hercegovačka novina* was published. The press was refurbished in 1879, and its name changed to Zemaljska tiskara, and then changed again in 1895 to Zemaljska štamparija. After World War I it

took the name Državna štamparija, and then under Ustaša (Croatian) control in 1941 it became Hrvatska državna tiskara Zagreb–Podruznica Sarajevo. It reverted to its former name in 1945. Until 1951 Državna štamparija remained the single largest publisher in Bosnia. It then merged with Oslobodjenje under its name.

4. Pejanović, *Štamparije*, 21.

5. This occurred despite the fact that each item for publication had to be granted permission by the authorities.

6. Pejanović, *Štamparije*, 53.

7. Pejanović, *Štamparije*, 64.

8. Živorad K. Stoković, *Štampa naroda i narodnosti u SFRJ, 1945-1973* (Beograd: Jugoslovenski institut za novinarstvo, 1975): 20-24.

9. Robert J. Donia and John V. A. Fine Jr., *Bosnia and Hercegovina: A Tradition Betrayed* (New York: Columbia University Press, 1994): 165-66.

10. Robert J. Donia, *Bosnia and Hercegovina*, 173-4.

11. Kemal Kurspahić, *As Long as Sarajevo Exists* (Stony Creek, CT: Pamphleteer's Press, 1997): 33.

12. Kurspahić, *As Long as Sarajevo Exists*, 47.

13. Bosnia and Hercegovina. Republički zavod za statistiku, *Statistički godišnjak Bosne i Hercegovine*, vol. 19-24, 1985-1990 (Sarajevo: 1986-1991).

14. World Bank Group, *Countries: Bosnia and Herzegovina*, http://www.worldbank.org/html/extrdr/offrep/eca/ba2.htm. 18 February 2000.

15. *Bosnia and Hercegovina: 1996-1998 Lessons and Accomplishments*, http://www.seerecon.org/Bosnia/Bosnia.htm. 18 February 2000.

16. Nacionalna i Univerzitetska biblioteka Bosne i Hercegovine, *Bibliografija monografskih publikacija, 1992-1994: popis ratnih izdanja* (Sarajevo: Biblioteka, 1995): 4.

17. "Zakon o bibliotečkoj djelatnosti," *Službeni list Republike Bosne i Hercegovine*, 37, October 2, 1995.

18. *Bibliografija monografskih publikacija, 1992-1994*, 4.

19. Kurspahić, Kemal. *As Long as Sarajevo Exists*, 31.

BIBLIOGRAPHY

Bosnia and Hercegovina, 1996-1998: Lessons and Accomplishments. http://www.seerecon.org/Bosnia/Bosnia.htm.

Bosnia and Hercegovina. Nacionalna i univerzitetska biblioteka Bosne i Hercegovine. *Bibliografija monografskih publikacija, 1992-1994: popis ratnih izdanja*. Sarajevo: NiUbBiH, 1995.

Donia, Robert J. and John V.A. Fine, Jr. *Bosnia and Hercegovina: A Tradition Betrayed*. N.Y.: Columbia University Press, 1994.

Freespeech: Ex-YUpress. http://www.freespeech.org/ex-yupress/.

"Izdate knjige, brošure, listovi i časopisi." *Statistički godišnjak Bosne i Hercegovine*, 19-24 (1986-91): 331, 320, 314, 314, 292, 263. Sarajevo: Republički zavod za statistiku.

Kurspahić, Kemal. *As Long as Sarajevo Exists*. Stony Creek, CT: Pamphleteer's Press, 1997.

Pejanović, Đordje. *Štamparija u Bosni i Hercegovini: 1529-1951*. Sarajevo: Svjetlost, 1952.

Press now. *Free Press in South-Eastern Europe*. Amsterdam: Press Now, 1998.

Stoković, Živorad K. *Štampa naroda i narodnosti u SFRJ, 1945-1973*. Beograd: Jugoslovenski institut za novinarstvo, 1975.

World Bank Group. *Countries: Bosnia and Herzegovina*. http://www.worldbank.org/html/extdr/offrep/eca/ba2.htm. 18 February 2000.

"Zakon o bibliotečkoj djelatnosti." *Službeni list Bosne i Hercegovine* 4/37 (1995): čl. 30-48. Sarajevo: Službeni list.

SERBIA

MAP 4. Serbia

Source: *Serbia and Montenegro*. Scale 1:1,375,000. Washington DC: Central
Intelligence Agency, 1997

Publishing in Serbia

Ivana Nikolić

SUMMARY. The history of Serbian publishing is inextricably tied to Serbian and Yugoslav history in general. The author discusses publishing in the territory from the beginning, concentrating on the period 1990-1999. She deals with statistics, and basic themes and problems from this period. She then compares censorship in communist Yugoslavia to that in 1990-1999. Finally, the article lists leading Serbian publishers from this recent period and their profiles. *[Article copies available for a fee from The Haworth Document Delivery Service: 1-800-342-9678. E-mail address: <getinfo@haworthpressinc.com> Website: <http://www.HaworthPress.com> © 2000 by The Haworth Press, Inc. All rights reserved.]*

KEYWORDS. Serbia, Yugoslavia, publishers and publishing, censorship

HISTORICAL OVERVIEW OF SERBIAN PUBLISHING

The origins of printing in Serbia are linked to the press established in Cetinje in 1493 by Đuradj Crnojević, the eldest son of Ivan Crnojević, the ruler of Zeta (the early designation of Montenegro). At that time Zeta was the last free territory of the formerly powerful Serbian state that fell under Turkish rule in 1389 after the Battle of

Ivana Nikolić is Acquisitions and Exchange Librarian, National Library of Serbia, Skerlićeva 1, 11000 Beograd, Serbia.

[Haworth co-indexing entry note]: "Publishing in Serbia." Nikolić, Ivana. Co-published simultaneously in *Slavic & East European Information Resources* (The Haworth Information Press, an imprint of The Haworth Press, Inc.) Vol. 1, No. 2/3, 2000, pp. 85-126; and: *Publishing in Yugoslavia's Successor States* (ed: Michael Biggins, and Janet Crayne) The Haworth Information Press, an imprint of The Haworth Press, Inc., 2000, pp. 85-126. Single or multiple copies of this article are available for a fee from The Haworth Document Delivery Service [1-800-342-9678, 9:00 a.m. - 5:00 p.m. (EST). E-mail address: getinfo@haworthpressinc.com].

Kosovo Polje. In an attempt to defend Zeta from Turkish aspirations to the land, Ðuradj Crnojević sought an ally in Venice. He dispatched a monk named Makarije to Venice to purchase a printing press and learn the trade of printing. In this way Serbia, in straitened circumstances, acquired a press just thirty-seven years after the invention of movable type. The most outstanding specimens of Serbian incunabula were printed on this press–the Oktoechos, a psalter, prayer books, and the Gospels. This press ceased to function when Zeta fell under Turkish control and Ðuradj Crnojević himself fled for his life to Venice.

It was owing to these circumstances that the second Serbian press was established outside the country's borders, in Venice, by Božidar Vuković in 1520. The press produced mostly religious books, all of them finely printed. Vuković's son, Vicenzo, inherited the press from his father and reprinted his books. In 1597 the press passed into the hands of an Italian named Giorgio Rampazetto, who printed two very important books–the Collection for Travelers and the earliest Serbian language primer. In Venice in the 1670s Jerolim Zagurović, a native of Kotor (Montenegro), was active as a printer.

Throughout the sixteenth century in the Serbian lands, presses were generally established within monasteries, with monks serving as printers. Sheltered within these remote, inaccessible monasteries, far removed from trade routes and the control of the Turkish usurpers, these presses produced religious books and in so doing rendered a great service by preserving the religious, spiritual and cultural identity of the Serbian people under oppressive, violent conditions. The best known presses were established in 1519 in Goražde, at the monastery of Rujno near Užićka Požega, at the monastery of Gračanica in Kosovo, and at the monastery of Mileševa near Prijepolje. In 1552 the press of Trojan Dimitrijević in Belgrade was opened. Ten years later, in 1562, a monk named Mardarije established a press in the church at Mrkša. The last Serbian press operating in the sixteenth century was in Skadar (today Shkoder, in Albania, near the border with Montenegro).

Escaping the intolerable conditions of life under Turkish rule, a large number of Serbs fled to Vojvodina in the great migration of 1690. In Vojvodina the Serbs tried repeatedly to get permission to establish a press, but the Habsburg authorities, fearful of the potential loss of control, refused this permission until the end of the eighteenth century. Under the considerable political, economic and religious pressures of Austrian rule, lacking schools, books and an educated class, the Serbs turned to Russia and began importing books from there. However, the Habsburg authorities quickly grasped the potential threat inherent in that relation, and forbade the import of books from Russia. In these circumstances the Serbs were forced to print their books in Rîmnicu Vîlcea (Romania), Venice and Leipzig. In 1770 the Austrian authorities gave their permission to the well-known Viennese printer, Josef Kurzbeck, to print books for Serbs, albeit under the censor's eye. In his lifetime Kurzbeck printed 151 Serbian books, and it was in his shop that the first Serbian newspaper was printed–*Serbskija povsednevnija novini* (Serbian Daily News, 1791-1792).

The first Serbian press in the nineteenth century, the Royal Serbian Press ("Knjaževsko-srpska knjigopečatnja") was purchased in St. Petersburg and began operating in Belgrade in 1832. It issued the works of Dositej Obradović, Vuk Karadžić, the *Novine srpske* (Serbian News), and eventually the publications of the Serbian Royal Academy (Srpska kraljevska akademija), all official publications, and university and school textbooks. It continued to operate to the end of World War II. The most prominent individual associated with this press was Gligorije Vozarović, the first Serbian publisher, who in the decade from 1835 to 1845 published about 20 books. Vozarović gathered around himself the most important cultural figures of his day, and it was in his house that the National Library of Serbia was founded in 1832.

The social and cultural life of the Serbs in Vojvodina is closely linked to the activities of the "Serbian Home" Society (Matica srpska). A publishing crisis experienced by the periodical *Serbska letopis* (Serbian Chronicle), which began publication in Budapest in 1824, served as the occasion for the Matica's founding. In order to keep the periodical alive, a group of Serbian citizens resolved in 1826 to establish a society that would assume responsibility for continuing to publish not just the Chronicle, but also Serbian books. Today the *Letopis Matice srpske* is the oldest continuously published periodical in the world, with an unbroken record dating to the 1820s. In 1864 the Matica srpska relocated from Budapest to Novi Sad, where it continues to function as the oldest existing Serbian literary, cultural and scholarly institution. Also in Novi Sad, beginning in 1893 the city was home to a press that produced religious and school textbooks, the official publications of the Serbian church authority, and reproductions of icons and other pictures with religious or national significance. Later this press was relocated to Sremski Karlovci.

In 1842 the Society of Serbian Letters (Društvo srpske slovesnosti) was founded, setting for itself large goals–the establishment of a new orthography, the publication of school textbooks, the establishment of scientific terminology, and publication of the Society's periodical, the Herald (*Glasnik Društva srpske slovesnosti*). In 1864 the Society was renamed as the Serbian Learned Society (Srpsko učeno društvo), and in 1886 as the Serbian Royal Academy (Srpska kraljevska akademija), the forerunner of the present-day Serbian Academy of Sciences and Arts (Srpska akademija nauka i umetnosti, or SANU) in Belgrade.

The Matica srpska and Serbian Academy of Sciences and Arts are two world-class national institutions which, from their founding to the present day, have worked to strengthen the social and cultural consciousness of Serbia's citizenry and have exerted decisive influence on important historical and social movements in the country.

Alongside these two institutions one should also mention several publishing and book selling enterprises which were active from the beginning of the twentieth century until World War II. The Serbian Literary Cooperative (Srpska književna zadruga) was founded in 1892 and continues in existence today as one of the country's oldest and most respected publishers, specializing in Serbian and foreign literature and major historiographic works, literary studies, criticism, essays, and dictionaries. Svetislav Cvijanović, a book seller and publisher in Belgrade from 1902 to 1948, was responsible for producing around three hundred books of mostly popular literature. The publishing house "Dositej Obradović" existed from 1927 to 1948 and produced several excellent catalogs of antiquarian books under the direction of its owner, Dragoslav Petković, a rare and new book seller in Belgrade. In affiliation with the French publishing firm ASET, the Franco-Serbian Bookstore (Francusko-srpska knjižara) also operated from 1927 to 1948, and was owned by Aleksandar Popović, a bookseller and publisher in Belgrade; it became best known for its children's series "Radost." Luka Jočić, a publisher and bookseller in Novi Sad, was active from around 1870 to 1906, publishing school textbooks and, for a time, the periodicals *Stražilovo* and *Javor*. The Brothers Jovanović (Braća Jovanović) was owned by the brothers Kamenko and Pavle Jovanović in Pančevo, and from 1872 to 1910 published a famous series titled the "National Library of the Brothers Jovanović" (Narodna biblioteka braće Jovanovića) and about 350 other books. The publishing house and bookstore of Toma Jovanović and Lazar

Vujić in Belgrade, founded in 1898 and continuing to 1948, published more than one thousand books, mostly geared toward a broad readership–songbooks, collections of tales, calendars, icon reproductions, school textbooks, and children's books. Geca Kon, whose bookstore in Belgrade was home to the largest combined bookselling and publishing operation in Serbia, remained in existence from 1901 to 1941, publishing more than 3,500 books on all subjects, including belles lettres. Jugoistok ("Southeast") was the name of the German publishing concern that took over Geca Kon's operation during the occupation (1941-1944); and out of Jugoistok emerged, after the liberation, a new publishing concern named Prosveta (Enlightenment), which remains in existence today. Kosmos, a private publishing house in Belgrade, was active from 1932 to 1941 and again from 1945 to 1947. Napredak ("Progress"), owned by Armin Švarc, a bookseller and publisher from Belgrade, existed from 1920 to 1938, issuing around 200 books, most of them translations of foreign belles lettres. Narodna prosveta (National Enlightenment), owned by Antonije Ivanović in Belgrade, published anthologies and editions of authors' collected works. Narodno delo (National Works), owned by Petar Petrović in Belgrade, was founded in 1922 and survived until 1948, also specializing in collected works editions. Nolit (1928-1948), established by Pavle Bihali in Belgrade, specialized in leftist literature. Svetozar Ognjanović was active from 1894 to 1925 as a publisher and bookseller in Novi Sad, responsible for the publication of about three hundred books. The brothers Popović, booksellers, publishers and printers in Novi Sad, maintained their business from 1870 to 1907, producing books with broad popular appeal, and were the first Serbian publishing concern to publicize and distribute its stock using mail-order catalogs. Rajković and Ćurković were active as partners in a bookselling and publishing concern in Belgrade from 1898 to 1932, specializing in pedagogical and children's literature, and textbooks. Slavija, a bookstore in Novi Sad, owned by publisher Vladimir Lezimirac, was an active publisher from 1923 to 1948. The socialist bookstore Tucović, which maintained a bookstore in Belgrade, was a publisher of leftist literature from 1906 to 1935. Some of the many other publishers active before 1945 include: Slovenska knjižara (Belgrade, from 1910 to 1948), Svetlost (Belgrade, from 1930 to 1941), Velimir Vazović's bookstore (Belgrade, 1853-1935), Vreme (Belgrade, 1921-1930), and Zadruga Jugoslovenskog profesorskog društva (1933-1941).

During the war year of 1914 (August-December), and for part of 1915, there was very little publishing activity in the country. What few titles were produced were mainly periodicals and newspapers sponsored by the Serbian military: *Ratni dnevnik* (Military Daily), published first in Valjevo, then in Kragujevac, and later in Thessaloniki, charting by its successive imprints the steady retreat of Serbian forces; *Ratni vesnik* (War Reporter) and *Ratni zapisi* (War Notes), both published in Belgrade; *Velika Srbija* (Greater Serbia), published in Niš; a different publication by the same title, *Velika Srbija*, published in Valjevo. Due to the occupation of Serbia in 1915, independent publishing ceased almost totally, and any existing publications were controlled by the forces of occupation, such as the occupation newspaper *Beogradske novine* (Belgrade News) and the *Zbornik zakona i uredaba Cesarske i Kraljevske vojne uprave u Srbiji* (Collection of Laws and Decrees of the Imperial and Royal Military Administration in Serbia). Any significant publication of Serbian books, and particularly periodicals, took place abroad. Among the most important periodical titles published in exile were *Gusle: list srpskih djaka u izbeglištvu* (Gusle: publication of Serbian students abroad) was published twice per month in Lyons; *Velika Srbija* also appeared as a daily newspaper from 1916 to 1918 in Thessaloniki; *Napred = En avant* (Forward) was another daily, published in Bizerte, Tunisia, from 1916 to 1918; *Naša nada: organ srpskih daka u Francuskoj* (Our Hope: publication of Serbian students in France) appeared weekly in Lyons in 1916; *Ratni dnevnik: organ Vrhovne komande* (War Daily: Publication of the High Command) appeared daily, in 1914 out of Valjevo, in 1915 out of Kragujevac, and from 1916 to 1918 in Thessaloniki; *La Serbie* was published weekly in Geneva from 1916 to 1919; *Skerlić: organ djačke družine u Užes* (Skerlić: publication of the student organization in Gard) was a handwritten publication reproduced by mimeograph, issued every two weeks; *Slobodna Srbija = Libre Serbie* appeared twice per week from 1916 to 1919 in Geneva; *Srpske novine* (Serbian News), the official newspaper of the Kingdom of Serbia, appeared three times per week on Corfu, from 1916 to 1918; *Srpski glasnik = L'echo serbe* was published daily from 1916 to 1919 in Thessaloniki; *[La] Patrie Serbe* was a monthly journal for young Serbs living in exile, appearing in Paris from 1916 to 1918; *Srpski orlić* (The Serbian Eaglet) was the weekly publication of the Serbian students in the lycée in Bastille, Corsica; and *Srpski glas* (The Serbian Voice) was a handwritten publication of Serbian prisoners of war detained in camps in Hungary, produced in 1917.

Serbia's publishing landscape during World War II was very similar. Within the country itself, only publications approved by the German forces of occupation could be legally issued, such as the official records of proclamations (e.g., *Obznane i objave nemačkih vlasti u Srbiji = Bekanntmachungen und Veröffentlichungen der deutschen Behörden in Serbien*, issued in Belgrade), but also some magazines featuring light, entertaining and neutral contents. The Partisans' illegal printing presses, concealed in remote, inaccessible locations or on liberated territory, produced mostly brochures, flyers, posters, propaganda materials and newspapers. Individual Partisan brigades or newly formed governmental authorities in the liberated territories served as the publishers, with most of the material being produced on typewriters and reproduced using mimeograph machines. The following newspapers were published abroad: *Službene novine Kraljevine Jugoslavije* (Official News of the Kingdom of Yugoslavia) published in London and Cairo from 1941 to 1944; *Naši dani* (Our Days), from 1942 to 1944 the newsletter of the prisoners of war in Stalag XVIIB, composed by hand; *Srpski glasnik = Serbische Lagerzeitung* was issued monthly from 1942 to 1943 in Stalag IIB, and was also reproduced by mimeograph; *Srpski vesnik = Serbische Lagerzeitung Stalag VIIIA* was published by rotopress in 1943; the *Vojno-sanitetski pregled* (Medical Corps Review) was a monthly publication of medics involved in the Yugoslav forces of national liberation from 1944 to 1945 in Bari, Italy, and in Belgrade. *Logorski jež* (The Camp Hedgehog) was a hand-produced publication of Serbian prisoners of war in campus C and D at Osnabrück, and *Vesti* (News) was the title of a newsletter produced by the Yugoslav inmates at Dachau, appearing occasionally during 1945.

During the first postwar years in Yugoslavia, most frequently published were books dealing with the Partisans' struggle against fascism, or those that encouraged a spirit of collectivism and national renewal. Also significant during this period, of course, was the large role played by the government in shaping the new publishing landscape by creating and financing the major new publishing houses. This decisive role played by the government–extending to the government's right to shape the ideology emanating from published materials–remained in force in Serbia until the collapse of the federal Yugoslav government in 1991.

Two main, parallel tendencies dominate Yugoslav and Serbian post-war publishing throughout the Tito era (1945-1980). The first was the vast corpus of officially sanctioned and encouraged publications–material published pertaining to World War II as it took place in Yugoslavia–including diaries and memoirs of participants, literary works by writers who had been participants in the fighting (Branko Ćopić, Antonije Isaković, Dobrica Ćosić, Jovan Popović and many others), monographic histories of individual Partisan brigades, regiments and divisions, historical and political studies of the war in Yugoslavia and elsewhere; but also the Marxist classics, books pertaining to current Yugoslav political theory (e.g., self-management, non-alignment, socialist economics), the full texts of government resolutions, stenograms of government meetings and party congresses, and collections of other official documents. The most frequently published authors were Josip Broz Tito and Edvard Kardelj (Tito's number two in command for ideology), as well as many Yugoslav politicans of the time. It is clear that the intention of these publications was the glorification of the existing political ideology and system. At the same time, it would occasionally happen that certain books, journal and newspaper issues, theatrical productions and films were banned after publication as inappropriate.

The second main tendency in the post-1945 period was provoked by the desire and need to educate broad segments of the society, and books provided popularized education among both industrial and agricultural workers. Cheap paperback editions of books were published in large print runs, most often featuring Serbian or foreign literary works, presentations of popular medicine, agriculture, and other subjects. In order to make books readily accessible to everyone, a vast network of libraries was established in schools, factories, farming cooperatives, workers' universities, and palaces of culture. This trend, growing from an intention to educate the people in the earliest postwar decades, in later years and as Yugoslavia became more open toward the outside world, became part of a concerted effort to link the country to the world's scientific and cultural currents, and to make the world's scientific and cultural achievements accessible to the Yugoslav populace. Numerous translations of famous foreign authors active in all disciplines of the sciences, arts and culture were commissioned and published, and foreign books and periodicals were imported and made available not just in libraries, but also for sale in bookstores. There was now also greater variety in the Serbian and Yugoslav belles lettres–both contemporary and older classics–that were published. New newspapers and periodicals were founded, including literary journals and specialist technical ones. The publishing industry opened up, and in addition to the major established firms, museums, institutes, and university departments also became active as publishers. Private publishing at this time existed only to an insignificant extent, in the form of occasional books published independently at their authors' expense.

Publishing and Printing in Serbia From 1990 to 1999: A Statistical Overview

The collapse of Yugoslavia in 1991, with its subsequent wars, economic crises, and the emergence of new nation states, was clearly reflected in the field of publishing. Within the unitary Yugoslav state, cooperation among publishers had been a given and included informal agreements among publishing houses in different republics, joint publications (most frequently involving publishers in Belgrade, Zagreb, and Sarajevo), and arrangements whereby many Yugoslav publishers had their works produced by Slovene printers in accordance with the highest graphic and technical standards. Further givens were the shared Yugoslav book market (books and periodicals of all Yugoslav publishers could be acquired in bookstores throughout the country, directly from the publisher, or at the bookfairs that brought together all of the most significant publishers in the country) and an extensive, if diverse, reading public (Slovenes and Macedonians, as well as representatives of all national minorities in Yugoslavia, had publications in their own native languages, but at the same time were readers of materials published in Serbo-Croatian, the country's official language, and that of its linguistic majority). The formation of new nation states led to the diminution of the book market and to new demands on the part of the reading public.

Data on the number of book titles published in Serbia (Table 1) may serve as a point of departure for further publishing statistics for the decade from 1990 to 1999.

Table 2 provides an overview of the number of titles published each

TABLE 1. Number of Book Titles Published in Serbia, by Year

Republic of Serbia, including the Autonomous Regions of Vojvodina and Kosovo

Year	Total	Serbia only	Vojvodina only	Kosovo only
1990	3,888	2,989	625	274
1991	3,779	2,853	688	238
1992	2,380	1,833	522	25
1993	1,442	1,111	310	21
1994	2,705	2,382	303	20
1995	3,424	2,937	470	17
1996	4,943	4,444	407	92
1997	7,358	5,967	1,245	146
1998	6,910	6,190	613	107
1999	4,018	3,802	211	5

Note: Figures for 1990-1996 are taken from the Statistical Yearbook of Serbia *(Belgrade: Statistical Institute). Figures for 1997, 1998 and 1999 (through November 2, 1999) are derived from searches of the National Library of Serbia's bibliographic database, which is subject to continual updating, and should be viewed as provisional.*

TABLE 2. Number of Titles and Print Runs of Books and Brochures Published in the Serbian Republic, by Language of Publication

Year	Total Titles	Total Copies	Titles in Serbian	Total Copies in Serbian	Titles in Other Languages	Total Copies in Other Languages
1990	3,888	14,857,000	3,084	11,622,000	804	3,235,000
1991	3,779	15,270,000	3,072	12,115,000	707	3,155,000
1992	2,380	10,376,000	2,035	8,816,000	345	1,560,000
1993	1,442	8,307,000	1,214	6,610,000	228	1,697,000
1994	2,705	11,833,000	2,356	10,003,000	349	1,830,000
1995	3,424	9,292,000	2,953	7,587,000	471	1,705,000
1996	4,943	15,851,000	4,305	12,900,000	638	2,951,000
1997	7,358	---	6,964	---	394	---
1998	6,910	---	6,691	---	219	---
1999	4,018	---	3,939	---	79	---

Note: These figures are taken from the Statistical Yearbook of Serbia *(Belgrade: Statistical Institute) and are valid for the entire territory of the Serbian Republic, including the autonomous regions of Vojvodina and Kosovo. Official figures have not yet been published for 1997, 1998 and 1999; the figures cited here are derived from searches of the National Library of Serbia's bibliographical database through November 2, 1999. In the category of books published "in other languages," the languages of minority groups living in Serbia occur most frequently, but world languages such as English, French, German and Russian also occur.*

year in Serbian and other languages, as well as the total number of copies printed.

A glance at Table 1 shows the number of titles published and copies printed declining from 1990 to 1993. The year 1991 witnessed the outbreak of a war that brought enormous losses in human life, destruction of property and economic hardship throughout the greater part of the formerly unitary state. Those circumstances also brought about a crisis in publishing–a decline in the number of titles published, in print runs, and in the esthetic appeal and production standards of published materials, but also in the proportion of materials of high scholarly or literary value as against those of questionable value. At war's end (1996) new political formations arose which reduced both the territory and the potential reading public in each of the newly created states. The reduced readership is one of the causes for the decline in numbers of titles published and copies printed. Similarly, within each of the new countries the needs and demands of the reading public with respect to language, alphabet, subject matter, and pricing structure were now different.

By mid-1992 Yugoslavia (Serbia and Montenegro) was subjected to economic sanctions by the international community. The following year was one of never-ending economic crises, enormous inflation, tremendous disorder in the market, shortages of goods and a dramatic fall in the average standard of living. In such circumstances it was a tremendous feat for publishers to issue new books and for readers and libraries to buy them. The result was a dramatic fall in the number of published titles and of copies printed. In early 1994 Dragoslav Avramović introduced economic reforms and a fixed rate of exchange of one to one between the Serbian dinar and the German mark, leading to improvement in the economic situation and conditions more conducive to publishing. The number of published titles rose from year to year. In October 1996 the economic sanctions against Yugoslavia were removed, which led to an improved economy and the country's gradual reintegration into the international scientific and cultural community, a fact which is reflected in publishing–in 1997 the number of published titles reached 7,358.

The relationship between titles published in Serbian as opposed to those published in other languages is also noteworthy. From 1990 to 1996 the number of titles published in other languages fell in relation to the number of titles published in Serbian. The representation in the publishing industry of individual languages has changed sharply. In 1990 there were 84 books printed in Slovene in the Republic of Serbia, with a total print run of 105,000 copies. In 1992 only one Slovene-language book was printed, in 20,000 copies; and from 1993 on, not a single Slovene-language book has been printed in Serbia. In 1990 there were ten Macedonian-language books printed in Serbia, with a total print run of 14,000 copies. In 1991 the number rose to 15 titles and 25,000 copies, but since 1993 no Macedonian-language books have been printed in Serbia. These figures clearly reflect the disintegration of the country and the formation of the new states of Slovenia and Macedonia (and consequently, the absence of any need to print materials in those languages). In the course of 1990 there were 202 Albanian-language titles published in Serbia, with a total print run of 1,230,000 copies. In 1991, 195 titles were published with a total print run of 912,000 copies; but by 1992 only three books, with a combined print run of 9,000 copies, were published. These figures reflect the exclusion of the Albanian population in Kosovo from the Serbian Republic's system of education, and the formation of parallel schools and universities using instructional materials and textbooks imported from Albania. The number of titles and print runs of books in the languages of the remaining minority populations in Serbia did not change significantly during these years.

The figures representing publications in world languages also marked a decline from 1990 through 1993, followed by a steady increase until 1996, when the 1990 figure was reached again. For example, the number of English-language titles published in Serbia went from 67 in 1990, to 45 in 1991, then 36 in 1992, bottoming out at 32 in 1993. By 1996 the number had risen again to 69, with 103 English-language titles published in 1997.

The statistics also show a decrease in the number of titles translated from foreign languages into Serbian: in 1990 a total of 607 foreign titles were published in Serbian translation. By 1993 the number had dropped to just 168; but by 1996 it rose again to 653. In 1990 there were 55 published translations from English into Serbian; in 1991 just 39; in 1992 zero; in 1993 twenty-five; in 1994 twenty-four; in 1995 forty-nine; but in 1996 again none at all. The reduced number of titles published in world languages, as well as the drop in titles translated from foreign languages into Serbian were clear indicators of Yugoslavia's isolation during the years when the international community's sanctions were at their harshest. Besides their devastating economic effect, the sanctions brought about the nearly complete cultural and scientific isolation of Yugoslavia, resulting in the reduced number of translations of foreign authors, a fact demonstrated in Table 3.

It is clear that in 1993 the proportion of foreign authors to domestic ones was at the lowest level of the decade (every seventh published

TABLE 3. Books and Brochures Published in Serbia by Origin of Author

Year	Total	Serbian Authors	Foreign Authors
1990	3,888	3,205	683
1991	3,779	3,098	681
1992	2,380	1,969	411
1993	1,442	1,242	200
1994	2,705	2,297	408
1995	3,424	2,871	553
1996	4,943	4,164	779

author was a foreigner), and though the ratio subsequently began to increase again, even by 1996 it hadn't reached the 1990 ratio of 1 to 5.7.

Similarly, as a result of the collapse of Yugoslavia and the emergence of new states, there has been a noticeable change in the representation of authors from what had formerly been neighboring republics. Within the framework of Yugoslavia authors of all republics and regions had been published in all parts of the country, a fact that was most readily observed in school curricula, which included classics of all Yugoslav literatures. As a matter of course, Prešeren, Prežihov Voranc, Miško Kranjec, Miroslav Krleža, Kočo Racin and many other Slovene, Croatian and Macedonian authors were published in Serbia, just as Serbian authors were published in Slovenia, Croatia, Macedonia, and Bosnia and Hercegovina. With the emergence of the new states these authors were treated as foreign and their inclusion in publishing programs drastically diminished. For instance, over the past nine years only two works by Krleža have been published in Serbia, and one by Blaže Koneski. One can assume that an analogous situation now holds in other countries of the former Yugoslavia.

It is interesting to track the proportion of books, brochures, periodicals and other printed material published in the Cyrillic, as opposed to the Roman alphabet. While in 1990 Cyrillic-alphabet books numbered 1,809 and Roman-alphabet books 3,134, as early as 1992 the number of Cyrillic-alphabet titles already surpassed those published in Roman characters (1,747 in Cyrillic to 1,405 in Roman). The share of Cyrillic-alphabet titles grew through the decade, until they numbered 4,672 titles in 1996 as against 2,646 in Roman characters. Thus the proportion was reversed from 1990, when Roman-alphabet titles still outnumbered Cyrillic ones by a factor of two to one. This change in the status of the two alphabets is understandable as a result of political events. In 1990, when Serbia was still a part of the unified Yugoslav state, publishing in the Roman alphabet of the northern republics Slovenia and Croatia dominated, even though Serbia's traditional alphabet is Cyrillic–a fact which illustrates the central government's attempt to reenforce unity and downplay Serbia's national alphabet in favor of the Roman alphabet which was in use throughout the country. By contrast, in 1990 there were 2,474 Roman-alphabet titles published in Croatia, but just 56 in Cyrillic (according to the National Library of Serbia's database). With the collapse of Yugoslavia in 1991 and the creation of new states, Serbia's national alphabet enjoyed ever more widespread use. (See Tables 4, 5, and 6.)

Since data for 1997 through 1999 have not yet been published in the *Statistical Yearbook of Serbia*, we have supplied figures from *Bibliografija Jugoslavije. Serijske publikacije* (Beograd: Jugoslovenski bibliografsko-informacijski institut). In 1997 a total of 1,014 newspapers and periodicals were published in Serbia, twenty of them daily newspapers. In the same year thirteen official papers of political parties and movements were published. In 1998 1,188 newspapers and periodicals were published, including twenty daily newspapers and thirteen papers of political parties and movements. Figures for 1999 have not yet been published.

In 1990 there were in Serbia eighty-four newspapers and thirty-two periodicals published in the languages of the national minorities; of these, seventeen newspapers and three periodicals were published on the territory of Serbia proper, forty-six newspapers and eighteen periodicals were published in Vojvodina, and twenty-one newspapers and twelve periodicals in Kosovo. Six years later, in 1996, there was a total of thirty-eight newspapers and nine periodicals published in the languages of the national minorities.

BASIC CHARACTERISTICS OF PUBLISHING AND INFORMATION IN SERBIA, 1990-1999

Themes and Problems

To provide a better overview of the changes taking place in Serbian publishing from 1990 to 1999, we will give a brief summary of publishing in Yugoslavia during the preceding period, from 1945 to 1990.

TABLE 4. Number of Books (Titles) Published by Subject

	1990	1991	1992	1993	1994	1995	1996	1997	1998	1999
All Subjects	3,888	3,779	2,380	1,442	2,705	3,424	4,943	7,358	6,910	4,018
Philosophy	97	118	′42	24	61	51	97	173	203	98
Politics/Economics	314	202	178	110	188	245	278	328	324	222
Religion	43	73	65	34	48	73	134	121	124	82
Sociology	51	50	26	15	24	22	46	130	118	80
Law	241	260	188	148	238	313	521	271	323	199
Education	374	400	256	189	429	422	553	601	575	268
Medicine	186	207	110	87	108	204	246	316	336	216
Technology	158	153	83	41	63	111	105	96	134	98
Business	112	135	83	57	111	158	226	210	207	118
Art	19	14	13	11	10	20	24	39	54	4
Film, TV, Theater	138	123	171	42	84	114	137	56	144	17
Sports	45	39	19	12	10	27	49	74	86	37
Literature	1,110	1,174	682	384	787	927	1,365	2,051	2,461	1,528
Geography	111	100	42	43	92	102	170	74	95	53
Biography	6	10	3	23	35	115	203	264	307	135
History	20	31	33	14	32	18	40	135	151	83
General	248	170	42	29	107	112	193	207	236	190

This table is provided for the overview it gives of the proportion of titles published in broad subject areas.

TABLE 5. Newspapers Published in Serbia, by Periodicity

Year	Total	Daily	Weekly	Biweekly	Monthly	Irregular
1990	898	14	108	136	299	341
1991	745	10	106	134	249	246
1992	555	10	89	107	184	165
1993	418	10	78	83	124	123
1994	514	14	81	85	166	168
1995	539	16	84	83	154	202
1996	575	18	69	90	160	238

TABLE 6. Periodicals Published in Serbia, by Periodicity

Year	Total	Weekly	Biweekly	Monthly	Bimonthly	Quarterly	Irregular
1990	549	2	19	132	67	110	219
1991	489	2	18	114	55	104	196
1992	378	2	10	81	40	82	163
1993	315	2	6	64	25	75	143
1994	379	2	6	71	34	88	178
1995	423	2	6	71	35	104	205
1996	496	2	6	85	46	119	238

According to Lj. Lakičević, the postwar period of publishing in Yugoslavia can be divided into five phases. The first, from 1945 to 1949, saw the nationalization of all printing enterprises, bringing an end to all private publishing. The publishing industry was treated as a tool of the revolution, a means for building the new society and new consciousness. Most books published were in small formats, but large print runs, with political literature accounting for as much as one-third of all published titles and one-half of the total number of copies printed. There was a proliferation of pamphlets of an informational and propaganda nature, aimed at "enlightening and bettering the masses." About thirty percent of all published titles were translations of Soviet works on similar topics.

In the second phase, from 1949 to 1955, the number of publications increased, while print runs diminished overall. The variety and quality of the material published improved, and Western authors began to be translated. (Tito's break with the Soviet-controlled Informbureau was reflected in the smaller number of Russian and other Soviet authors translated, as Yugoslavia began to open to the West.) With the introduction of worker self-management the incidence of direct government intervention was reduced and publishing firms achieved a measure of independence as they slowly adapted to the market. As some major publishing houses lost their overriding federal (nationwide) orientation, conditions were created that were conducive to publishing within the narrower linguistic and national framework of a given republic.

The third phase (1956-1960) was characterized by slow but steady growth in the number of titles and print runs. The interests (and control) of society were protected by publishing councils and the requirement that each company issue a publishing plan in advance. The basic law governing publishing enterprises and institutions regulated their status, and their economic independence was fostered by legislation that permitted publishing houses to maintain their own presses and bookstores.

In the fourth phase (1961-1967) extraordinary progress was made, both in the variety of themes covered and the size of print runs, and in publishers' financial status (due to easier credits, government subsidies, and tax breaks). From 1956 to 1968 each republic had its Fund for the Advancement of the Publishing Industry, which supported the publication of works of educational, scholarly or cultural significance.

In 1968 this role was assumed by each republic's Fund for the Development of Cultural Activity.

In the fifth phase (1968-1972) the number of titles increased, while the figures for print runs fell. Publishing was not spared economic and social crises–the student revolt of 1968 and the events in Croatia in 1971 led to more intensive "ideological vigilance," criticism and "guidance" from the Party, and to new pressures placed on publishers; many publishing houses became insolvent.

In the 1970s and 1980s there was a tendency for publishing to withdraw behind the borders of its local republic or region (the Constitution of 1974 contributed to the slow dismantling of the federation). Efforts were made to correct the financial situation of publishing houses and to overcome the problems of their inadequate professional network, their lack of liquidity, the underdeveloped nature of the market, high production costs, insufficient demand for books, and the dual status of books (as both cultural artifacts and commercial products). In an attempt to help publishers distribute their publications and assist libraries in acquiring them, the Ministry of Culture of the Serbian Republic sponsored a program of coordinated acquisitions. From 1985 to 1993 this program served about 170 libraries throughout Serbia. The Ministry of Culture financed the purchase of books according to the libraries' selection, with the National Library of Serbia serving as coordinator of both acquisition and distribution.

Since some of the changes that have taken place in Serbian publishing since the collapse of Yugoslavia are covered in a previous section, what follows is an attempt to characterize the publications themselves, at least by broad categories.

The war taking place in the former Yugoslavia was reflected in Serbian publishing by numerous titles delving into the historical, political, religious, economic and other causes, aspects, and outcomes of the Yugoslav crisis. Many significant scholarly and analytical titles were published by major authors (Svetozar Stojanović, Zagorka Golubović, Slavoljub Đukić, Kosta Čavoški, Milovan Đilas, Aleksa Đilas, Branko Petranović, Milan Bulajić, Vladimir Goati, Borisav Jović, Veljko Kadijević, Ivan Čolović, Smilja Avramov, Slobodanka Kovačević, Nebojša Popov, and others). In pre-1991 Yugoslavia many of these authors had been blacklisted and their works banned, either in part or in whole. Throughout this period many books, pamphlets and propaganda materials were published that discussed the suffering of the Serbian people in the course of the war, and in this respect much published material is consistent with a longstanding tradition of documenting the dramatic vicissitudes of the nation's history. Most books of this nature are based on solid scholarship and are thoroughly documented, written by authorities in their fields and issued by respected publishers. However, it is important to stress that the war in former Yugoslavia had as both cause and effect an ever more strident nationalism in all parts of the former federation. This became obvious in publishing, in books whose contents lacked any scholarly foundation and which were colored by authors' partiality toward their own country and intolerance of any others. Distortions and arbitrary interpretations of Serbian history, traditions, and religiosity were typical of this kind of publication in Serbia–all in an attempt to demonstrate that the Serbs are the "oldest," the "elect," or the most venerable nation, in order to appeal to readers' baser instincts and bring in a quick and easy profit. In the rush to turn a profit, these books were financed and published by the authors themselves, or by small, private publishers lacking any scholarly credentials. During this period many undocumented and biased or nationalistically colored periodical articles were published, and occasionally even whole newspapers and journals. The end of open armed conflict in 1995 led to a gradual reduction in the number of this kind of publication.

After the introduction of a multi-party system and the first open elections in Serbia in 1990, publications relating to the ideologies and activities of various political parties (works of authors who were active members of political parties, newspapers and magazines, platforms, programs, and the parties' propaganda materials) began appearing in Serbia for the first time. There was a profusion of titles published by two authors in particular–Professor Mira Marković, the wife of Slobodan Milošević and president of the Yugoslav United Left (acronym JUL in Serbian), whose memoirs and diaries were published in multiple editions and large print runs, and in translations into numerous foreign languages; and Vojislav Šešelj, president of the Serbian Radical Party (Srpska radikalna stranka) and author of over two dozen books from the mid-1980s through the early 1990s. This volume of published material suggests the extent of these two parties' influence on the Serbian political scene, as well as the extent of their financial resources.

Aside from uncritical works in history and politics, during this period numerous cheaply produced books of unprepossessing contents were published–calendars, horoscopes, picture books, cook books, hastily compiled anthologies of poetry or quotations, advice books for living a healthy and happy or professionally successful life. These undemanding books were geared to the tastes of the least educated part of the reading public and brought their publishers a quick profit, with a minimum of effort or investment. The same interest in material gain was the driving force behind publishers of the tabloid press–newspapers and magazines that reported the "confirmed" version of the news, spread rumors, carried news of the smart set and revealed sensational details of the lives of public figures. Also characteristic of this period was the publication of a large number of collections of poetry by both unknown and lesser known authors; for the most part lacking literary value, they were generally published by the authors themselves or by their sponsors, including local authors' organizations.

A tendency of publishing in pre-1991 Yugoslavia continued into this period in Serbian publishing. B. Juričević estimates that school and university textbooks accounted for about forty percent of Yugoslavia's overall book production. Among the titles published in Serbia in the immediate post-1991 period, textbooks, collections of exercises, handbooks and similar materials designed for school and university consumption still amount to a large share of the total output: of 7,358 titles published in 1977, 1,055 of them were textbooks (i.e., almost every seventh book).

The positive aspect of the transition to a market economy–in the form of the many worthwhile titles published by government-sponsored publishers, but especially by newly established private publishers–is presented in the last section of this article. It must be stressed that it was extraordinarily difficult in the immediate post-1991 period for serious publishers–either government-sponsored or private–to produce worthwhile and well-crafted books. The country's economic crisis was reflected in the high printing costs which publishers were forced to absorb, and in book prices that were too high for the average Serbian reader to pay. Still, thanks to carefully developed publishing plans and contractual commitments to some outstanding authors, many publishers managed to produce books of lasting and real value.

Throughout the 1990s the enforcement of Serbia's legal depository copy law proved a serious problem. Some government-sponsored presses, as well as most new private presses, defaulted on their legal obligation to supply a mandatory copy of each published book to the National Library of Serbia. In some years the number of titles for which depository copies were not delivered reached alarming proportions. Given the circumstances, the National Library was forced to purchase books that were not delivered by mandatory deposit, even after repeated requests and warnings were made to printers. The reasons for this behavior on the part of printers are complex–negligence and forgetfulness, the lack of any sense that the materials they produce are a national cultural good, treatment of books merely as a commercial product (many printers complained of the losses they would incur delivering copies of their more expensive titles), and various obstacles to delivery (including gasoline shortages and postage costs).

During this period one more serious problem surfaced and became very widespread: many private publishers did not respect the legal requirement to produce cataloging in publication (CIP) and did not deliver their galley proofs to the National Library of Serbia in Belgrade (which creates the CIP for publications printed on the territory of Serbia proper, exclusive of outlying regions), to Matica srpska in Novi Sad (which creates CIP for publications printed within the Vojvodina Region), or to the National Library in Priština (which is responsible for CIP for publications printed in Kosovo and Metohija). The reasons for the disregard of this requirement are also negligence, an irresponsible concept of the publishing profession, and a view of books that sees them exclusively as commercial and consumer items designed to bring a profit. It often happens that the publishers themselves take the CIP information created for one of their earlier publications and arbitrarily–and quite wrongly–print it in a new book. This results in frequent, obvious mistakes and leads to enormous problems in tracking newly published books and acquiring legal depository copies for a given library's collection. Another consequence of the failure to supply legal depository copies and CIP information is the radical difference in the number of published titles recorded each year in the *Statistical Yearbook of Serbia* (which is based on the depository copies submitted in a given year) as against the number of Serbian imprints in a given year that appear in the National Library of Serbia's online catalog (the National Library's collections and catalog are, of course, continually being supplemented with late-arriving depository copies and newly purchased publications from earlier years that were not acquired on legal deposit). The disparity in the two kinds of statistics is obvious in Table 7.

CENSORSHIP IN YUGOSLAVIA (1945-1990) AND SERBIA (1990-1999)

Following World War II the Communist Party was the primary arbiter in all spheres of social life. It subordinated publishing–and culture in general–to its own immediate political interests and used it to develop a definite ideological consciousness among the citizenry. A strict, narrow range of permissible topics, an orthodox writing style, black-and-white presentations of events during the War, a positive tone in anything having to do with current Yugoslav reality, and an absence of critical thought were all characteristic of published work during this period. From that time to the present day, the ruling political forces have regulated the freedom of the publishing industry to varying degrees and in different ways, and have justified this as a necessary measure to prevent abuses by possible "enemies" of the people and the state, or as a defense of the ruling order against those same "enemies" who presumably were already at work. These "enemies" changed over time; after the War they were called the "remnants of fascist forces," "collaborators," traitors, or "remnants of defeated forces." Later they became adherents of the Communist Information Bureau (Cominform)–a catch-all designation for any politically deviant Yugoslav citizen after Tito's break with Stalin in 1948.

TABLE 7. Total Numbers of Book Titles Published per Year, by Statistical Source

Year	Statistical Yearbook of Serbia	National Library of Serbia	Percent Difference
1990	3,888	5,267	26%
1991	3,779	4,332	13%
1992	2,380	3,129	24%
1993	1,442	2,631	45%
1994	2,705	4,663	42%
1995	3,424	6,024	43%
1996	4,943	6,884	28%

Note: Statistics for 1997, 1998 and 1999 are given in an earlier section of this article, based on the online catalog of the National Library of Serbia. Official statistics have not yet been published for those years. In previous citations of statistics of books published per year we have used the government's official figures, since all other statistics cited here have been based on these sources.

Ultimately they were called unitarists, (anarcho-) liberals, or national-ists, in accordance with the various socio-political crises that periodi-cally threatened the ruling party. At the beginning of the 1960s the new orthodoxy formulated by the chief ideologue of the Communist Party of Yugoslavia, Edvard Kardelj, spoke of "freedom of form with limitations on content" in creative works. This brought about some changes and, at first blush, granted greater freedom of expression and more latitude to publish a variety of works. Kardelj proposed that "communists shouldn't decide, as Stalinists do, which schools of art are good and which are bad, nor should they prescribe limits and directions for scholarship and science," but rather that they should "fight for the political and social content of cultural products" and "fight against efforts made under the cover of art to produce antiso-cialist contraband, or to organize actions that undermine the efforts of our working people to build socialism." Clearly, there was still no real freedom, no opportunity for ideas to face off openly, because the limits to critical thought were strictly demarcated: it dare not threaten or negate the existing order and the ruling class.

In the 1960s the struggle against Stalinism, bureaucratism, and anarcholiberalism, along with the development of workers' self-man-agement, contributed to the development of a concept of real creative freedom. The official program of the Yugoslav League of Communists rejected the view that creativity had to serve immediate political inter-ests and that the Party had to serve as cultural arbiter. However, stu-dent demonstrations, economic crisis, and the rise of nationalism on the domestic political scene–hand in hand with events on the interna-tional level–all served to short-circuit the new anti-ideology. At the Congress of the Central Committee of the Serbian League of Commu-nists in July 1968, first mention was made of the "oppositionist activi-ties of the humanist intelligentsia," and limitations were set on criti-cism, because when it "manifests itself as the negation of any aspect of the political leadership . . . , or by assaulting the integrity of its previous and current work . . . , or in barely concealed attacks on Comrade Tito . . . , then this is no longer a struggle of ideas, but an outright political struggle which demands the engagement of all the means that our society has at its disposal to protect the socialist order."

With the development of self-managing socialism, the complete, direct and open control that the leadership had developed through its hierarchy and control of finances began to come apart. Under self-management, creative expression and the system of public information were technically free and legally instituted censorship did not exist, but the ideological control of the contents of information was maintained in many other, more subtle ways. One can identify three kinds of censorship: self-managing, Party-controlled, and police/juridically imposed. Censorship could be applied as a preemptive measure (through self-management, or by the Party) or as a repressive one (by the police or the courts). The League of Communists and its affiliated organizations performed preemptive censorship by placing the leadership of publishing houses, newspapers and other information media under an obligation of "political and moral appropriateness," by establishing publishing councils, by requiring publishers to issue their publishing plans in advance, and by creating party cells in each of the main publishing houses. The political elite decided the finances of each house, and thus decided on the employees' well-being. This system of control naturally led to self-managing censorship (Sveta Lukić refers to it as "house censorship"). "In defense of the interests of the working class," the workers themselves–the directors, editors, line workers, and Party comrades "spontaneously" gave their reactions within each institution itself, criticizing or punishing any colleague who overstepped the limits of what was permissible. In practice, this meant that incompetent or disaffected workers were able to advance themselves, and prevent their capable colleagues from advancing, through denunciations or avowals of loyalty. This kind of censorship was often much more effective than any applied from above by the leadership of the authoritarian state, because it derived from vigilance and action taken at the very bottom. What is characteristic of this kind of censorship is the total absence of any official document or prohibition to publish. The person who initiated the prohibition remained unknown, and it was put into effect by some of the author's most immediate colleagues. The original command for the prohibition could come from some unnamed high government official, or from someone within the leadership of the publishing house itself.

Party censorship was exercised by the political and party organizations within the publishing houses, generally by means of written directives, oral admonishments, plots conducted using the media (e.g., by arranging for bad reviews to be published about a writer or a specific work, or for "spontaneous" letters to the editor, which served as the "voice of the people"), by censure, or by expulsion from the Party.

Police/juridical censorship was repressive by nature and punished "violations" that had already been committed. The police would confiscate the printed copies, summon the author or other individuals responsible to an "informational meeting," threaten, and blackmail. Court trials could end in prohibitions against future public appearances, prison sentences, or loss of employment. All of these repressive measures reinforced self-censorship and the writers' fear. The "ideologically correct personnel" that the Party recruited was assigned to voice "appropriate" theoretical views and oppose critical thought. The ultimate and devastating result was the dominance of loyal, conformist, mediocre thinking over creative and critical thought in most spheres of social and creative life.

Because of the subtlety with which this form of censorship was applied in a variety of invisible ways, it is impossible to determine exactly the number of works that fell under its gun. The author of the book *Cenzura u Srbiji* (Censorship in Serbia. Belgrade: Andrejević Foundation, 1998), Želimir Kešetović, whose statistics we use in this article, estimates that in Yugoslavia from 1945 to 1990 approximately 1,300 works–including 570 books, 380 newspapers and periodicals, seventy-six films, seventy live theater productions, and five art exhibitions–were partly or completely censored. During that period there were secret blacklists of themes. These included international conflicts, the role of the Serbian Četnik movement, Croatian Ustaša crimes in World War II, the Cominform and Goli Otok (Naked Island– Yugoslavia's notorious penal colony for political offenders in the late 1940s and 1950s), the Brioni summit, the student demonstrations in 1968, the nationalist and liberal movements of 1971, scholarly research in contemporary history, critical portrayals of Josip Broz Tito or other Yugoslav leaders, the unmasking of abuses of power and privilege by government functionaries, biographies of political nonpersons, and any genuine criticism of social and political reality. There were also secret blacklists of authors who had overstepped allowable bounds. Some of these writers were barred from appearing in public or publishing their work, while others could not be mentioned in print in any way. These prohibitions and blacklists had a direct effect on many writers. The repression of the "black wave" in Yugoslav film, literature and painting fettered the creative efforts of such internationally renowned directors as Aleksandar Popović, Živojin Pavlović, and Želimir Zilnik. At the same time, a ban was placed on a group of independent sociologists and philosophers from Belgrade University who were the equals of European philosophers of that time.

In the 1980s the orientation of the official ideology began to undergo a gradual shift from social class to nation. The country underwent increasing decentralization, with many of the central government's functions shifting to the republics and regions, including the responsibility for censorship, which was now in the domain of the republic, regional, or local authorities. This led to considerable differences in the criteria for what constituted "appropriate," since there was no longer a central arbiter to decide. It would happen that local authorities would ban some work because they recognized some criticism of themselves in it. The degree of freedom of expression was different in different parts of the country. Even aside from these differences, and until the republics began assuming openly confrontational stances toward each other (around 1988), there continued to be a high degree of self-interested solidarity among the bureaucracies throughout the federation, and hence there was significant agreement regarding the extent to which freedoms should be restricted. The forces driving toward Yugoslavia's disintegration led to conflicts of interest among the centers of power within the republics, and those authors and works that were forbidden in one republic were frequently feted in another.

From 1945 to 1990, 148 publications were banned in Serbia. Presumably, the real figure is much higher, due to the hidden nature of the process of censorship. The most-censored works included histories and collections of political essays, theoretical work in the humanities and social sciences, literary works, and occasionally calendars, maps, and picture postcards. Banned were the literary works of Jovan Dučić (branded as a monarchist), Dragiša Vašić (a "collaborator"), Šima Pandurović (also a collaborator), Miloš Crnjanski (a "member of the defeated forces," which is to say, the so-called civic right), Meša Selimović, Dobrica Ćosić, Antonije Isaković, Slobodan Selenić, Vojislav Lubarda, Miodrag Bulatović, Dobrilo Nenadić, Mirko Kovač, Živojin Pavlović, and many others. For his collection of poetry titled "Woolen Times" (*Vunena vremena*), Gojko Đogo was sentenced to prison for "maliciously and falsely portraying social and political events in Yugoslavia, and for claiming allusively that there is no freedom or democracy here and that our system is based on the rule of terror of a single person." The works of historian, lawyer and politician Slobodan Jovanović (1869-1958), professor at the University of Belgrade, president of the Serbian Royal Academy and president of the Yugoslav government in exile (London) were also banned, as was any mention of him or his works in print–even though Jovanović is one of the key figures in recent Serbian history. Works by other authors who were part of the Yugoslav emigration suffered a similar fate–these books, along with other "inappropriate" works by native authors, were removed from the general collections of the National Library of Serbia and the Library of the Serbian Academy of Sciences and Arts (SANU) and put in a special collection which users could access only with special permission. The SANU Library opened this collection to general use by the public in the late 1980s, and in 1995-1996 the National Library transferred these books into its general collection for greater public access. Since then, the National Library has also begun to pay much closer attention to intensifying efforts at acquiring works published by the Yugoslav and Serbian emigration. Before 1990 these materials had been treated as "undesirable," and are largely lacking in library collections.

A particularly drastic instance of repression and censorship occurred when the Assembly of the Serbian Socialist Republic moved against a number of Belgrade University liberal arts professors in January 1975. By this decision, Zagorka Golubović, Dragoljub Mićunović, Mihailo Marković, Ljubomir Tadić, Trivo Indjić, Nebojša Popov, Svetozar Stojanović and Miladin Životić were dismissed from their posts and forbidden to publish in all but the most specialized and obscure periodicals.

Judgments about the degree of freedom and the influence of censorship on creativity and information in the former Yugoslavia and Serbia range from the belief that there was virtually no difference between Yugoslavia and the "East Bloc" countries in this respect (and that Yugoslavia even contributed the new category of self-censorship) to the opinion that Yugoslavia was significantly more liberal than the other socialist states (Leonard, Scammel).

The open, multiparty elections in Serbia in 1990 and the transition to party pluralism did not bring with them the automatic abolition of censorship. The social and political scene in Serbia was still marked by a low level of political culture, the remains of a totalitarian way of thinking, and the absence of democratic traditions. On the legal plane, the new constitution abolished the category of "verbal crimes," the information industry became freer and was no longer subject to censorship, and adherents of different political philosophies gained the right to organize into parties and participate in public life. The law on public information allowed for bans on distribution of the press and on media broadcasting in instances where these called for the violent overthrow of the government, damaged the territorial integrity or independence of the Serbian Republic, infringed on constitutionally guaranteed freedoms and human rights, or provoked national, racial or religious hatred. These restrictions were incorporated into virtually all regulations and legislation governing information in the former Yugoslavia. The law on publishing of 1991 abolished the industry's status as having "extraordinary national importance," as well as the participation of "representatives of the social community" in the management of publishing enterprises; it similarly did away with the requirement that editors demonstrate their "moral and political suitability" and that publishing houses issue in advance their plans for the coming year. The law also gave private individuals the opportunity to become involved in publishing and simplified the registration process. This regulation, along with the transition to a market economy, paved the way for the establishment of a large number of private publishing houses, which by the end of the 1990s had managed both to outnumber state-owned houses and to surpass them in terms of the number and quality of titles published.

In addition to private publishing houses and the new private radio and television stations that came into being, private newspapers and periodicals were also established, publishing a wide range of opinions which included sharp criticism of the country's ruling parties, social and political organizations, and leaders. Among the various media, the oppositionist press, with its mission to analyze and criticize the existing social order, was particularly noteworthy and included the newspapers and news magazines *Demokratija, Blic, Glas javnosti, Danas, Naša borba, Republika, Vreme, NIN, Srpska reč, Dnevni telegraf, Nedeljni telegraf, Evropljanin, Parlament, Novi Pančevac* (Pančevo), *Nova svetlost* (Kragujevac), *Nezavisni* (Novi Sad) and *Promene*, which later tracked the protests of the opposition in Belgrade. Among the nongovernmental, oppositionist radio and television stations, those that gained the greatest trust on the part of citizens of Belgrade were Studio B, Radio B92, and Radio-Index. Numerous private radio and

TV stations were founded in Serbia during this period, in nearly all of the country's larger cities.

In a period of nine years, and particularly during the war, Serbia, like other former Yugoslav republics, had its share of media which published uncritical, sensational news items, and presented the war option as the only possible solution to the country's crisis. They appealed to national and religious intolerance and hatred, and clearly suggest that no sense of responsibility for the publicly spoken word remains. Speeches filled with provocations and hatred were delivered in the media under the direct or indirect oversight of government authorities and radical parties, provoking as a result ever more strident nationalism and a flood of kitsch. The effect on the consciousness and personal development of individual listeners and readers has been devastating. This phenomenon had its parallel in the media war conducted against the Serbian people by international news media: CNN, Sky News, the BBC and other networks broadcast unconfirmed information, rumors and fabrications about Serbia, yet remained silent about crimes committed against Serbian citizens, and helped foster hatred against the Serbian nation. The media war in the former Yugoslavia and the conspiracy of the foreign media against Serbia almost certainly produced as much hatred as did the armed conflict, demonstrating that unprofessional, unobjective reporting is capable of aggravating the military conflict.

By all indications, one might conclude that practically no effective censorship remains. From 1990 to 1997 there is only one documented instance of a temporary ban of a printed publication in Serbia. In 1990, on the initiative of officials from the Army, the Yugoslav League of Communists and the Union of World War II Veterans, Filip Radulović's book *Ljubavi Josipa Broza* (The Loves of Josip Broz. Belgrade: Grafos, 1990) was banned for "damaging the memory of the late president." This was the last year in which the image and work of Josip Broz Tito remained "untouchable." The following years would bring a spate of critical studies, incisive criticism, and even accusations that the former president was responsible for Yugoslavia's crisis and wars in the 1990s. Although formal censorship through repression and bans has not existed in this period, the aggressive propagandizing that dominates the media, accompanied by disregard and discrimination against others can be viewed as a kind of de facto censorship which leaves little room for those who think differently. Instead of the "defense of the revolution, brotherhood, unity and the power of the working class" which prevailed in pre-1991 Yugoslavia, the focus is now on the defense of the "endangered nation and national interests." Pacifists and real peacemakers are subject to attack as traitors and foreign mercenaries. In general there are no absolute values being defended; instead, immediate political needs determine what is permitted and what isn't. The attacks on dissidents intensify during periods of social crisis and just before important political events (elections, protests, demonstrations), as shown by the following instance.

At the end of 1996 Serbia found itself in an extreme social and political crisis resulting from both long-term and more immediate causes–the Yugoslav war which had inflicted human losses and the economic exhaustion of the Serbian people, the presence of hundreds of thousands of refugees in Serbia, international sanctions, a grave economic crisis, soaring unemployment, a standard of living that verged on poverty, disastrous political leadership, grave abuses of power and self-aggrandizement on the part of leading politicians, and an election that the ruling party had just stolen. In many large Serbian cities, the growing discontent of the populace was organized by the oppositionist political parties into a months-long mass protest that lasted throughout the winter of 1996/1997. Seeing the threat to its power, the ruling elite used both repressive police tactics and the government-sponsored media to settle accounts with the opposition and the participants in the protests. The state-controlled media glossed over the causes and the enormous scale of the protests with silence. The ferocious attack by the country's highest politicians against their own people will be long remembered: they did not hesitate to call the protesters and their leaders "fascists, traitors, foreign mercenaries, hooligans, and riff-raff." It was an all-out media war which provoked hysteria and hatred among the political dissidents and deep, passionate political divisions among Serbia's citizens.

Since then, fearing for its power, the ruling elite has used a whole repertory of repressive measures: dismissing officials and replacing them with its own loyal people, who are given a free hand to enrich themselves at public expense; cutting public budgets and rationing gasoline and other commodities in cities and towns that are governed by the opposition, and supplementing municipal budgets where the leadership is loyal; provoking crises and complicating civic issues in cities where the opposition is in power. Discerning the threat which the media pose to it, the leadership has turned the blade of repression and censorship toward them. The methods vary–confiscation of radio frequencies, or arbitrary delays in the granting of frequencies, jamming broadcasts, police raids on studios and printing presses, theft of equipment, economic pressures, dismissals of editors and producers, forced paid leave for "unsuitable" journalists, and the withdrawal of accreditation from foreign journalists. The independent radio stations Radio Index and B92 fell victim to these tactics, and were forced several times to stop broadcasting, abandon their studios and find new ones. In the case of Radio B92, the regime appointed a new head producer, retained the station's old name, and totally changed the station's programming, causing most of its reporters to resign and found a new radio station, B292. Now both Radio Index and B292 share their studios with Independent Television Studio B and broadcast from there.

With the promulgation of the law on public information in October 1998 a drastic reckoning with opposition newspapers, periodicals and broadcast media was set in motion. Some complaints are lodged by the Ministry of Information, but the repressions are usually carried out by concealed means: a political leader lodges a private complaint when he discovers some injurious mention of himself or a malevolent interpretation of his words in a newspaper article. Then follow court proceedings which inevitably lead quickly to such enormous monetary fines imposed on the publishers, editors and printers of the newspaper that it is impossible to pay them. The final step is the confiscation of the newspaper's property–its offices and printing press–and the end of its existence. In this way the publishers of the newspapers and magazines *Blic, Glas javnosti, Naša borba, Čačanski glas, Kikindske novosti, Niške novosti, Dnevni telegraf, Pančevac, Evropljanin* and some others have all been convicted. All together, these newspapers have had to pay fines totaling one million German marks. As one of the most drastic examples one can cite the case of the printing press ABC Glas, which in November 1999 was fined a total of 533,000 German marks for failing to register the newspaper *Promene* with the authorities, and for printing thirty-seven issues of that bulletin, which reported on the opposition protests in Belgrade. The newspaper *Naša borba* went out of business after it was unable to pay a similar fine and had its property confiscated. Faced with unpayable fines, the newspaper *Dnevni telegraf* and the magazine *Evropljanin* moved from Belgrade to Podgorica, capital of Montenegro. When the Serbian police began to confiscate the press runs of this newspaper and magazine as they were being transported across the administrative border from Montenegro into Serbia, both ceased publishing. In April of this year the editor of both *Dnevni telegraf* and *Evropljanin*, Slavko Ćuruvija, was murdered in mysterious circumstances.

As these repressions take place, the aggressive propaganda of the state-sponsored media continues its war against the opposition on both television and radio. In a country which has been immersed in crisis for nearly ten years and which recently suffered severe human losses and destruction inflicted by NATO, the state-sponsored media show the "victory of politics," the "successes" of a devastated economy, and portray the "renewal of the country" and the "record-breaking reconstruction" of targets destroyed by NATO, ascribing all these successes to the country's leadership. The state media and newspapers are once again printing fabricated "letters to the editor" and "telegrams of support," while at the same time continuing to organize the "mass meetings of support" that over the past nine years have been a proven means of propping up the ruling elite and discrediting the opposition in times of social crisis. The activities of the opposition are passed over in silence, or distorted, and its leaders are called traitors or NATO mercenaries.

For the duration of the NATO attack on Yugoslavia the publication of books was drastically reduced, and the media found themselves in an unfamiliar position. Many newspapers reduced the number of pages printed and focused exclusively on the destruction and human losses, the vital problems of citizens under conditions of war. Instructions were published for surviving in conditions of chemical pollution, or without electricity or water. The domestic, and especially government, media presented a unified picture of reality in a country fighting a defensive war, and wartime censorship was introduced. Reports by the opposition media about conditions in areas especially affected by the war were limited, but not totally prohibited. Aside from the fact that they were exposed to bombardment and at risk of losing their lives, the citizens of Serbia were once again faced with a media war between their own and the foreign media, which were constantly accusing each other and, each in its own way, glossing over the truth when it didn't suit the official policies of their respective countries. Regardless of whether Serbian state television reported objectively or not, and whether that reportage suited the officials of NATO or not, the bombardment of the building of Radio-Television Serbia and the death of RTS's technical staff members placed a crucial question before world opinion: did the freedom of information which is such an important part of the Western democracies also include the right to kill someone who thinks differently? Even the most embittered oppositionist critics of Serbia's state-sponsored media had to condemn that act of violence and feel sympathy with its innocent human victims.

OVERVIEW OF LEADING SERBIAN PUBLISHERS, 1990-1999

The law on publishing of 1991 made it possible for private individuals to become involved in publishing for the first time. This new government regulation, along with the country's general movement toward a market economy, provided favorable conditions for the emergence of a large number of privately owned publishing houses. The large, government-sponsored houses were deprived of their previous subsidies and fell upon a time of considerable crisis, a fact which was reflected in their shrinking, ever more monotonous title lists. Some government publishers transformed themselves into private ones, but a large number of the private companies were founded now for the first time. From year to year the number of private publishers increased until, by the late 1990s, they constituted the majority. During this period more than nine hundred state-sponsored and private publishers were registered with the government.

State-Sponsored Publishers

- Bagdala (Kruševac). From 1990 to 1998 this publisher produced 348 titles. Its series Istočnik (The Source) specializes in Serbian medieval literature–original texts, as well as history and criticism–and pre-1945 literature. It publishes contemporary Serbian poetry and prose, contemporary short stories from around the world, literary works by Serbs living in diaspora, and books for children and young people. Its series Biblioteka Tragovi (Footprints) focuses on the literature and mythology of the peoples of Asia, Africa and South America.
- Beogradski izdavačko-grafički zavod (BIGZ), Belgrade, published 754 titles from 1990 to 1999. Sadly, even this publisher,

once the flagship of the industry, has reached a point of crisis which is clearly visible in the steadily contracting number of titles it has produced each year–while in 1990 it published 158 titles, in 1995 it published only 102, and in 1998 just 37. BIGZ publishes contemporary Serbian literature as part of its series titled Nove knjige domaćih pisaca: Poezija and Nove knjige do- maćih pisaca: Proza (New Books by Native Writers: Poetry and New Books by Native Writers: Prose). As part of its series Džepna knjiga (Pocket Book) it sponsors the subseries Beletristi- ka (Belles Lettres), Ljubavni roman (Romance), Klasika (Clas- sics), Lektira (Reading), Kriminalistički roman (Mystery Nov- els), Džepna knjiga za decu i omladinu (Pocket Books for Children and Young People), Filozofija (Philosophy), Sociologi- ja (Sociology), Rečnici (Dictionaries), and Praktična knjiga (How to . . .). It also publishes memoirs, translations of works by major philosophers (Filozofska biblioteka), books for childen and young people (Biblioteka Zlatna jabuka), dictionaries, and encyclopedias. Independently or jointly with other publishers, BIGZ has issued the selected or complete works of Borislav Stanković, Slobodan Jovanović, Meša Selimović, Vladan Desni- ca, Dobrica Ćosić, Danilo Kiš and Mihailo Marković.

- Dečje novine (Gornji Milanovac). Between 1990 and 1999 this publisher produced 662 titles, 149 of them in 1990 and only 15 in 1998. It publishes Serbian and foreign literature in translation, literary studies and collections of essays, children's literature and picture books. It also specializes in works on Serbian national history and, as co-publisher with Matica srpska and Vukova zadužbina, the series Biblioteka Studije o Srbima (Studies About Serbs).
- Filip Višnjić (Belgrade) has published 157 titles from 1990 to 1999, including books about the social and political crises in Yu- goslavia and Serbia, political studies about Europe and Eastern Europe in the twentieth century, literature and literary essays, dictionaries, and books for children.
- Gradina (Niš) has published 338 titles over the past ten years. It specializes in work about the history of Niš and Southern Serbia, and publishes the Encyclopedia of Niš (*Enciklopedija Niša*). It also publishes contemporary foreign prose and poetry, philoso- phy, sociology, mythology, law and politics.

- Kairos (Sremski Karlovci) publishes poetry by Serbian classic authors (Aleksa Šantić, Jovan Dučić, Vojislav Ilić, Jovan Jovanović Zmaj, Milan Rakić, Momčilo Nastasijević and others) in its series Stražilovo.
- Književna opština Vršac (Vršac) published 147 titles during the 1990s, mostly Serbian and world literature. Most notable are its publications of works by winners of the European Poetry Prize awarded by the Literary Community of Vršac.
- Matica srpska (Novi Sad), one of Serbia's oldest and most respected publishers, published 419 titles from 1990 through 1999. In its series Biblioteka srpski pesnici it publishes works of classic Serbian poets; and in its Bibliotcka Poezija it publishes contemporary Serbian poetry. Its Biblioteka Romani includes works by both native and foreign novelists. Matica srpska has published the collected works of writers whose life and work is connected to the region of Vojvodina, including Laze Kostić, Jakov Ignjatović, Jovan Sterija Popović and Boško Petrović. It publishes literary criticism and essays, works on Serbian national history and especially the history of Vojvodina. It also publishes works on psychology, philosophy, art (cultural and historical monuments, monasteries, and painting in Vojvodina), Serbian orthography, dictionaries, encyclopedias, and children's books.
- Medunarodna politika (Foreign Affairs), Belgrade, publishes documents and studies concerning contemporary European politics, law and economics.
- Naučna knjiga (Belgrade) published 964 books from 1990 to 1999–330 in 1990, 27 in 1995 and just 16 in 1998. It publishes technical manuals and textbooks in the social and natural sciences, collections of study exercises, and dictionaries.
- Nolit (Belgrade) published 466 titles from 1990 to 1999, including 105 in 1990, 55 in 1994, and 26 in 1998. As part of its Biblioteka Izbor it publishes contemporary Serbian poets, and Serbian prose writers in its Biblioteka Kratki roman. Its Biblioteka Nolit: Proza has seen the publication of works by Mikhail Bulgakov, Marguerite Duras, James Joyce, Botho Strauss, Marguerite Yourcenar and others. Its Filozofska biblioteka and Psihološka biblioteka publish works of foreign experts in these two areas. In its Ljubičasta biblioteka it publishes contemporary Serbian children's literature.

- Prosveta (Belgrade), another of Serbia's most respected publishers, produced 1,071 titles during the ten-year period–104 titles in 1990, 104 in 1995, and 100 in 1998. It publishes works of twentieth-century Serbian and world literature (Meša Selimović, Branko Ćopić, Milorad Pavić, Erih Koš, Pavle Ugrinov, Matija Bećković, Slobodan Selenić, Dobrica Ćosić, Svetlana Velmar-Janković, Momo Kapor, Laurence Durrell, Berthold Brecht, Milan Kundera, and others), literary criticism and essays (in its Biblioteka Savremeni esej). Its Biblioteka Savremena poezija and Biblioteka Savremena proza present the work of younger Serbian authors. Prosveta has also published the complete works of early and contemporary classics such as Vuk Stefanović Karadžić, Borislav Stanković, Ivo Andrić, Danilo Kiš, Borislav Pekić, and Aleksandar Tišma. It publishes works in Serbian history and dictionaries of Serbian and other languages.
- Prosveta (Niš) published 146 titles during the ten-year period. It publishes textbooks in all subjects, especially medicine, economics and mathematics. As part of its series Ogledi, studije, rasprave it publishes titles in philosophy, sociology, mythology, philology, and literary criticism. Its Biblioteka Beleg features works on the history of the Niš region, and on Serbian history and literary history. In the series Slovenski svet (The Slavic World) it publishes Serbian and other Slavic work in ethnology, mythology, and the cultural identity of the Serbs and other South Slavs. The series Biblioteka Balkanski krug features literary works from different Balkan countries. The Biblioteka Svet kulture brings together works in philosophy, sociology, linguistics and ethnology by Serbian and foreign authors. Its two series, Savremena domaća poezija and Savremena domaća proza, feature Serbian authors.
- Rad (Belgrade) published 660 titles from 1990 to 1999. In its series, Biblioteka Znakovi pored puta, it features works of contemporary Serbian literature. In its major series, Reč i misao, it has published over 500 titles to date, representing the very best of Serbian and foreign literature. The series Dom i škola includes works by native and foreign authors which are part of the standard school curriculum. Its Biblioteka Satirikon features contemporary Serbian political and social humor.

- Srpska književna zadruga (SKZ), Belgrade, was founded in 1892 and is one of the country's oldest and most respected cultural institutions. From 1990 to 1999 it published 702 titles–99 in 1990, 74 in 1995, and 32 in 1998. It publishes anthologies of Serbian and world poetry and prose, classics of Serbian and world literature, works pertaining to Serbian history, and children's books. Its Kolo Srpske književne zadruge is a major series which has published over 600 works of Serbian and world literature and history to date. Independently, or jointly with other publishers, it has issued the selected or complete works of Shakespeare, Dušan Baranin, Momčilo Nastasijević, Matija Bećković, Slobodan Rakitić, Ljubomir Simović, and Veselin Čajkanović. Its series, Atlas and Savremenik, features contemporary Serbian poetry and prose. Its Mala biblioteka Srpske književne zadruge specializes in mostly recent literary works, history and collections of essays in small-format hardbound editions. The series Srpski memoari publishes source materials for the study of the Serbian historical and political scene in the late nineteenth and twentieth centuries. The series Do granice čuda (Verging on a Miracle) is intended for children. This publisher's major project is the ten-volume *Istorija srpskog naroda*, which covers the history of the Serbian nation from the earliest times to 1918 and was published from 1981 to 1993.
- Službeni list SRJ (Belgrade) published 245 titles during this period, consisting of the text of legislation or pertaining to law, economics and politics. It also publishes books on Serbian history, the history and politics of various Balkan nations, including the Kingdom of Yugoslavia and Socialist Yugoslavia, as well as works on the Yugoslav crisis, disintegration and wars. Its series, Klasici jugoslovenskog prava, brings together the most eminent South Slavic authors in the field of law.
- Zavod za udžbenike i nastavna sredstva (ZUNS), Belgrade, published 3,740 titles from 1990 to 1999–261 in 1990, 515 in 1995, and 408 in 1998. With support from the government, this firm has primary responsibility for publishing Serbia's elementary and secondary school textbooks, both in Serbian and in the languages of the national minorities. It also publishes university textbooks, psychological and pedagogical literature for educators and university faculty. This publisher's major projects include selected works or complete editions of many of the most outstand-

ing Serbian scientists, scholars and writers, including Milutin Milanković, Jovan Cvijić, Branislav Petronijević, Stevan Stojanović Mokranjac, Josif Pančić, Svetozar Marković, Nikola Tesla, Mihalo Pupin, Mihailo Đurić, Ivan Lalić, Boško Petrović, Petar Džadžić, Milovan Vitezović, Živojin Pavlović, Stevan Raičković, and Tanasije Mladenović. Its series, Izbor, includes classics of Serbian and world literature that figure as part of the secondary school curriculum. The series Portret knjizevnog dela (Portrait of a Literary Work) and Tumačenje književnosti (Literary Interpretation) are potentially of interest for literary studies at any level. This publisher also issues works in philology and linguistics, history and geography, as well as dictionaries and encyclopedias. Biblioteka Societas is comprised of titles in sociology, and the series Saznanja (Insights), Psihološke paralele, Andragoška biblioteka, and Pedagoška biblioteka are also significant. Its series Medijske imperije (Media Empires) offers interviews with about fifty major media figures in the USA, Great Britain, Germany and France.

Aside from these publishers and others omitted from this listing, numerous cultural and scientific institutions also engage in publishing as a major activity, including archives (Arhiv Jugoslavije, Arhiv Srbije, Arhiv Vojvodine). Libraries (Narodna biblioteka Srbije, Biblioteka grada Beograda, Biblioteka Matice srpske, Narodna i univerzitetska biblioteka in Priština, and the national and city libraries in Serbia's major cities, including Despotavac, Čačak, Kruševac, Kragujevac, Pirot, Sombor, Subotica, Zrenjanin, and Užice) publish professional literature for the library profession, bibliographies, photoreprint editions, catalogs of their collections, and literary works. University departments and colleges (such as the universities of art in both Belgrade and Novi Sad, nearly all major departments of the Universities of Belgrade, Novi Sad, Kragujevac and Niš) publish scholarly studies and textbooks in their respective fields. Research institutes (the Institute of Economics, Institute for Agricultural Economics, Economics Institute, Institute of International Management, Institute of Finance and Development, Institute of Social Science, Institute of International Politics and Economics, Institute of Recent Serbian History, Institute of Contemporary Serbian History, Institute of Political Science, Institute of Comparative Law, Institute of Literature and Art, Film Institute, Institute of Philosophy and Social Theory, Institute of Architecture and Urban Studies in Serbia, Institute of Nuclear Science, the Kirilo Savić Institute, the Mihailo Pupin Institute, as well as the institutes that operate as part of the Serbian Academy of Sciences and Arts–the Balkanological Institute, Ethnographic Institute, Historical Institute, Mathematical Institute, Section for Rural Studies, the Institute of Byzantine Studies, and others–publish monographic scholarly studies in their respective fields, and some professional journals. Museums and galleries (such as the National Museum in Belgrade, the Museum of the City of Belgrade, the Museum of Modern Art, the Museum of Applied Art, the Museum of the Serbian Orthodox Church, the Museum of Theatrical Arts, the Museum of Science and Technology, the Historical Museum of Serbia, Museum of Vojvodina, Historical Museum of Vojvodina, and the national museums in Serbia's larger cities) publish catalogs of exhibitions and holdings, as well as monographs on the works of individual artists and art works. The Ministries (Ministry of Information of the Republic of Serbia, Ministry of Science and Technology of the Republic of Serbia, and others), foundations (Vuk Karadžić Foundation, Ilija M. Kolarac Foundation, Ivo Andrić Foundation, Miloš Crnjanski Foundation, Desanka Maksimović Foundation, Andrejević Foundation–which publishes the major series Dissertatio, a collection of doctoral dissertations, and new studies in all fields–the Nikola Pašić Foundation, and others) publish critical editions of the authors' collected works, as well as studies of the life and works of their respective authors, and books by winners of the foundations' prizes. Government-sponsored foundations are also active as publishers, including the Republic Foundation for the Preservation of Cultural Relics, the Republic Foundation for International Scientific, Educational, Cultural and Technological Cooperation, the Federal Foundation for Statistics, and the Republic Foundation for Statistics.

Private Publishers

- Clio (Belgrade) published 107 titles from 1990 to 1999, pertaining to marketing, the media, cultural theory and criticism, and art (music, theater, film, painting).
- Čigoja štampa (Belgrade) published 185 titles during this period, mainly economics, management, marketing and law. It also published the complete works of the linguist Ranko Bugarski and the

selected works of Đura Šušnjić. Its Biblioteka XX vek includes works of native and world authors in the fields of ethnology, anthropology, mythology, linguistics, and sociology.

- Dereta (Belgrade) published 202 titles between 1990 and 1999–seven in 1990, eight in 1995, and 54 in 1998. Its series include Biblioteka Savremena srpska književnost, Biblioteka Džepna knjiga (Serbian and foreign literature), and Biblioteka Roman decenije (selections of the best Serbian novels of the second half of the twentieth century). Dereta publishes the selected works of leading contemporary authors Svetislav Basara and Milovan Vitezović. It also publishes dictionaries and children's literature.
- Draganić (Belgrade) has published 318 titles in the 1990s–sixteen in 1990, seventy-two in 1995, and forty-two in 1998. Its series, Nasledje (Heritage), features monographs about Belgrade, Serbian Orthodox monasteries, and medieval Serbian art. The series Nasledstva includes classics of Serbian literature. It has published individual works by classic authors such as Petar Petrović Njegoš, Lazar Kostić, Borisav Stanković, Petar Kočić, Simon Matavulj, Stevan Sremac, Miloš Crnjanski and others. It has also issued the collected works of such leading contemporary authors as Desanka Maksimović, Dobrica Erić, Momo Kapor, Miroslav Josić Višnjić, Vuk Drašković and Milorad Pavić. Its series, Studije, publishes works on law and the legal history of the South Slavic nations, as well as medical works.
- Izdavačka knjižarnica Zorana Stojanovića (Sremski Karlovci) published 110 titles from 1990 to 1999. This house is known for its publications of literary translations, particularly of German and French works in philosophy, mythology, religion, sociology, history, psychology, politics, philology, linguistics, and literary history. It also publishes the work of Serbian linguists (such as the complete works of Pavle Ivić, and various descriptive grammars).
- Narodna knjiga–Alfa (Belgrade) has been marking steady growth since 1994 and has become one of the leading private publishing houses. In its series Sto klasika Narodne knjige (100 Classics of Narodna Knjiga) it has published the classics of world literature, from Homer, Dante, and Boccaccio to Tolstoy, Proust, and Samuel Beckett, alongside Serbian classics of Ivo Andrić, Vasko Popa, and others. The series Kraj veka (End of the Century) includes works by Dobrica Ćosić, Dragoslav Mihailović,

Borislav Pekić, Ivan V. Lalić and Miodrag Pavlović. Serbian literature is further represented in the series Savremeni srpski pisci and Antologija jugoslovenske pripovetke. The collected works of leading poet David Albahari were also published by Narodna knjiga–Alfa. The series Megahit features bestselling foreign authors, both past and present.

- Paideia (Belgrade) has published 120 titles since its founding in 1994. It publishes translations of works by the most outstanding writers in 20th-century world literature (Fernand Pessoa, Kazimierz Brandys, Eugene Ionesco, Otto Weininger, José Samarago, Joseph Brodsky, Isaac Bashevis Singer, and others).
- Prometej (Novi Sad) has published 318 titles in the 1990s. As part of its series, Antologija, it publishes Serbian literary classics. It also publishes contemporary Serbian poetry, works on Serbian history, albums about monasteries in Vojvodina and Serbia, and the works of Serbian and foreign writers on film, theater, and Serbian language.
- Radio B92 (Belgrade) has published 115 titles from 1993 to present. It publishes books by Serbian and foreign authors having to do with current events in the former Yugoslavia, and particularly works concerned with the role of the media in the Yugoslav crisis. Its publications have also dealt with relations between the Serbian government and the political opposition, and protest movements in Serbia in the 1990s. Its series, Apatridi, features literary works by both Serbian and foreign authors.
- Svetovi (Novi Sad) has published 143 titles during the 1990s, mostly translations of foreign literary authors, anthologies of Serbian and foreign prose and poetry, and literary criticism, as well as philosophy and psychology.
- Stubovi kulture–Vreme knjige (Belgrade) has published 217 titles in a total of 257 editions since its founding in 1993, and has assumed the role of foremost publisher in Yugoslavia. Its books have won 48 awards, and 47 of its titles have been translated into world languages. Bringing together under one roof many of today's leading Serbian authors, economists, legal scholars and essayists, Stubovi kulture (formerly Vreme knjige) has become the primary publisher of 67 major writers, including Dušan Kovačević, David Albahari, Radoslav Petković, Dragan Velikić, Svetislav Basara, Aleksandar Jerkov, Sava Damjanov, Mileta

Prodanović, Vladimir Arsenijević, Vladimir Pištalo, Vojislav Despotov, Žarko Trebješanin, Svetlana Velmar-Janković, Aleksandar Tišma, Ljubomir Simić, Vida Ognjenović, Stojan Ćerović, Ljubodrag Dimić, Mladjan Dinkić and others. It publishes belles lettres, history, economics, essays, film theory and reviews, and numerous translations of foreign authors (György Konrad, Peter Esterhazy, Bohumil Hrabal, Arthur C. Clarke and others).

Under its owner, Predrag Marković, this house has been actively engaged in the social and political life of Yugoslavia. During the spring 1999 bombardment of Serbia and Kosovo by NATO forces, Stubovi kulture initiated a project to track the economic consequences of the bombing in detail; the project's report was published just ten days after the end of the war, collectively authored by the ad hoc Group G 17 under the title *Final Account: The Economic Consequences of the NATO Bombing: An Assessment of Damage and the Resources Required to Rebuild Yugoslavia's Economy* (*Završni račun: ekonomske posledice NATO bombardovanja: procena štete i sredstva potrebna za ekonomsku rekonstrukciju Jugoslavije*). Promotional events for the book attracted several thousand people throughout Serbia and Montenegro; as a consequence, Predrag Marković developed a political plan to bring the country out of its crisis. Together with Mladjan Dinkić he invited citizens to meet on August 19, 1999, in support of a plan of radical economic reforms and a transitional government consisting of economic and technological experts. Despite obstacles put in its way by some political parties, this meeting grew into one of the largest-scale mass meetings in Yugoslavia in the past ten years. In addition to the writers who were part of the original Group G 17, Marković enlisted still other authors to contribute, thus forming the Group G 17 Plus, an expert group whose mission is to assist Serbia's citizenry.

To fill out this picture we list a few of the smaller private publishing houses which, though less prolific, have made a positive contribution to Serbia's publishing scene through well-reasoned production plans leading to some worthy new titles: Ars Libri (Belgrade) publishes Serbian belles lettres and historical works, the collected works of Vladimir Ćorović and new works by Vladeta Jerotić; Bookland, Dečja knjiga and Zebra are all Belgrade publishers which specialize in children's picture books; Gutenbergova galaksija (Gutenberg Galaxy) in

Belgrade publishes work in philosophy, history, lexicography, poetry and prose; Idea (Belgrade) publishes work on Serbian culture; Itaka (Belgrade) publishes translations of foreign authors about Serbia, its history and culture; Esotheria (also in Belgrade) specializes in works on religion and the occult; Kreativni Centar (Belgrade) publishes educational picture books, handbooks for parents and teachers, and books on educational methods and psychology which promote creative relations in the family, in school, and in society in general; Pešić i sinovi (Belgrade) publishes work on Serbian history and culture; Plavi jahač (Blue Rider) in Belgrade publishes literary works of Serbian and foreign women writers; and Verzal Press publishes Serbian and foreign literature.

Among the nongovernmental organizations that published material in the 1990s, of particular note are Fond za humanitarno pravo (Foundation for Humanitarian Law), Fond za otvoreno društvo (Open Society Institute), the Helsinki Committee, Media Centar, Centar za ženske studije (Center for Women's Studies), Ženski centar (Women's Center), and Žene u crnom (Women in Mourning).

The following government-sponsored and private publishers specialize in audio-visual materials: PGP Radio-Televizija Srbije, Studio B, Beograd-ton, Beograd-disk, B92, Global musik, Good taste, Imago, Jugodisk, Komuna, Metropolis, Music Land, UFA Media, Multimedia, Multi soft, Central Group, Institute of Foreign Languages (Institut za strane jezike), Radionica duše (Workshop of the Soul), all in Belgrade; and Diskos in the city of Aleksandrovac.

MONTENEGRO

MAP 5: Montenegro

Source: *Serbia and Montenegro*. Scale 1:1,400,000. Washington DC: Central
Intelligence Agency, 1993

Publishing in Montenegro

Vesna Vučković

SUMMARY. Publishing and printing in Montenegro are very much connected to the history of Montenegro and its people. The author discusses publishing in the territory until 1990, and then from 1991 to the present. Approximately 40 new, private publishers have emerged in the past decade. She discusses current major publishers, old and new, along with their profiles and recent notable titles. She then lists important periodicals. The article concludes with the hope that Montenegro will soon break out of its isolation and become a more integral part of the East European market for the printed word. *[Article copies available for a fee from The Haworth Document Delivery Service: 1-800-342-9678. E-mail address: <getinfo@haworthpressinc.com> Website: <http://www.HaworthPress.com> © 2000 by The Haworth Press, Inc. All rights reserved.]*

KEYWORDS. Montenegro, Yugoslavia, publishers and publishing, printing

PUBLISHING IN MONTENEGRO UNTIL 1990

Publishing and printing in Montenegro have a long and rich tradition. Tracing the fate of books within the confines of this small nation, one also traces the history and evolution of the Montenegrin people. Any historical overview of publishing in Montenegro must begin with

Vesna Vučković is Acquisitions and Exchange Librarian, Central National Library of Montenegro, Bul. crnogorskih junaka 163, 81 250 Cetinje, Montenegro, Yugoslavia.

[Haworth co-indexing entry note]: "Publishing in Montenegro." Vučković, Vesna. Co-published simultaneously in *Slavic & East European Information Resources* (The Haworth Information Press, an imprint of The Haworth Press, Inc.) Vol. 1, No. 2/3, 2000, pp. 129-156; and: *Publishing in Yugoslavia's Successor States* (ed: Michael Biggins, and Janet Crayne) The Haworth Information Press, an imprint of The Haworth Press, Inc., 2000, pp. 129-156. Single or multiple copies of this article are available for a fee from The Haworth Document Delivery Service [1-800-342-9678, 9:00 a.m. - 5:00 p.m. (EST). E-mail address: getinfo@haworthpressinc.com].

an analysis of the work of Đurdje Crnojević in the fifteenth century. Considering its small land mass, low level of commerce, and sparse population, Montenegro figures remarkably in this earliest period of the history of printing, with an abundance of printing presses and book dealers. The first printed book in the Cyrillic alphabet among the South Slavs appeared in 1494 in the vicinity of Cetinje. It is, in fact, Đurdje Crnojević, the ruler of this small Balkan nation–officially called Montenegro since the end of the fifteenth century–who is generally considered its first publisher, responsible for the purchase of a printing press and for printing the earliest Cyrillic-alphabet religious books. Since the Middle Ages, the confluence of cultures in this small, but strategically important territory resulted in the creation of written documents of exceptional value. For a long time medieval churches and monasteries remained the only centers of spiritual and cultural life–places in which learned people, writers and scribes gathered and worked. Among them there were extraordinarily creative individuals, such as Makarije, who worked at Crnojević's press. These centers had their own libraries as early as the thirteenth century. Bookstores appeared only during the latter half of the nineteenth century, and in Cetinje. The eighteenth century was Montenegro's age of national awakening, accompanied by a new efflorescence of culture and writing in the vernacular. This was the age of rulers from the dynasty of Petrović-Njegoš, themselves writers and poets and, in fact, Montenegro's most widely translated authors, whose works can be found in all major libraries of the world. The nineteenth and early twentieth centuries–until Montenegro's loss of independence in 1916–are marked by periodic spates of energy and cultural accomplishments on a scale comparable to those of the great centers of Europe.[1] The most notable characteristic of this period is the discontinuity in publishing that runs parallel to the discontinuities in Montenegro's struggle for national independence. The successes of Montenegro's earliest printing presses proved to be atypical and unique. The oldest publishing house still functioning today is Obod, which was established in 1860 as the government printing press and today is one of Montenegro's largest publishing houses and printers. Toward the end of the nineteenth century and in the early twentieth century five or six new printing presses, which also functioned as publishers, were established in Cetinje, Nikšić and Kotor.

The period between the two world wars was one of considerable stagnation in Montenegrin publishing. Following World War II, publishing experienced a new upswing. From 1945 until 1990 and the collapse of Yugoslavia, there were extreme disparities in the degree to which publishing was developed among the Federation's various republics and regions; in Montenegro, unfortunately, publishing was developed to a lesser extent than in the other republics, and even within Montenegro it received less support than did other cultural industries. Some statistics may illustrate this reality: in the 1940s and 1950s between fifteen and twenty book titles were published in Montenegro each year; newspapers were published mainly by political organizations; and only a few periodicals were published (two dealing with literature, one with medicine, one with history, and one devoted to entertainment). The broadsides and newspapers that were published immediately after the war were intended to mobilize the masses to defend and rebuild their country. They served the one-party system exclusively and soon ceased publication, as the need for them diminished. Only one title dating to that period continues to be published today, the daily newspaper *Pobjeda*. Many periodicals in the former Yugoslavia were established for specific purposes and went out of existence immediately after their goals were accomplished. In terms of themes covered, over seventy percent of all books produced during those years were either textbooks or belles lettres, while all other subjects were largely neglected.[2] During the 1950s and 1960s the number of titles and size of press runs of scholarly and technical books declined, and art books (museum and exhibition catalogs, albums, and scholarly treatments) virtually did not exist as a category. One of the rare exceptions is the catalog of the Art Gallery of Cetinje, which was issued in 1958 as the first publication of this kind. The same holds true for cultural history, where one of the few instances of a work published was *Studies in the Cultural History of Kotor* (*Studije iz kulturne istorije Kotora*). At the end of World War II there was only one actual publishing firm in existence–Narodna knjiga, which was active from 1949 until 1958; however, various scholarly institutes also functioned as publishers, including the Historical Institute (Istorijski institut), the Institute for Geological Research (Zavod za geološka istraživanja), the Scientific Society (Naučno društvo), the Society of Physicians (Društvo ljekara), and Society of Folklorists (Društvo folklorista).[3] Companies such as Obod, Pobjeda, Grafički zavod, Kole, and A. Paltasić intensified their publishing programs and also began to contract for printing jobs with Yugoslav publishers outside of Montenegro. Throughout the 1960s the number of publishers in Montenegro increased as the republic's publishing industry finally entered a period of sustained growth. Besides Pobjeda, Obod and the Republički zavod za unapredivanje školstva (Republic Institute for the Support of Education), whose primary business was publishing, institutions and organizations such as the University, the Montenegrin Academy of Sciences and Arts, the Historical Institute (Istorijski institut), the Lexicographical Institute (Leksikografski zavod), the Crnojević Central National Library (Centralna Narodna Biblioteka "Đurdje Crnojević," political organizations, citizens' groups, cultural centers, and writers' associations all began to publish materials as part of their activities. However, based on the number of titles published each year, the size of the press runs and the subjects covered, the conclusion is inevitable that even this activity was not highly developed. In the 1970s and early 1980s Pobjeda published from forty to seventy titles per year, constituting one-half of the total annual output of books in the entire republic. Press runs went as high as one thousand copies, with belles lettres, history, political literature and, of course, textbooks dominating. Translations from foreign languages were only rarely published. There was a paucity of children's literature, essays, literary criticism and scholarly monographs. Aside from the fact that honoraria were very small, authors had little influence on the publishing programs of the various houses. The bigger publishers, such as Obod and Pobjeda, collaborated with publishing houses in the other republics to issue some very successful joint publications, such as collected works of major authors, multi-volume encyclopedias and the like. Yet there was insufficient cooperation between these trade publishers and Montenegro's research institutions, with the result that much valuable scholarly work had to wait for years to be published, or was not published at all. A major problem throughout Montenegrin publishing history is the persistently low capitalization of the major firms and their constant need for financial support. The high cost of printing and paper, compounded by the population's low standard of living and purchasing power, had an inevitably negative effect on the sale of books.

Responsibility for developing a network of bookstores was left in the hands of the publishers. In the 1970s and 1980s only Pobjeda had a well-developed network of sales outlets (twenty-seven of them throughout Yugoslavia). Viewed as a whole, the diffusion of books was sluggish, there was no organized system for promoting new books, and the network of libraries was also underdeveloped, with insufficient numbers of new books added to their collections.[4]

From 1945 until 1980 (the year of the death of Josip Broz Tito, Yugoslavia's head of state and head of the country's communist party), the publishing industry deferred entirely to the wishes of party organizations and the party's leaders. It tried to survive as an industry by performing a balancing act between satisfying the needs of its sponsors–the government, which at that time was the sole financier of all larger publishing enterprises–and the needs of the reading public, whose more sophisticated elements could not be satisfied with a market that neither evolved nor underwent significant modifications in the course of several decades.

PUBLISHING FROM 1991 TO THE PRESENT

The past decade–the period which began with the dissolution of Yugoslavia–has been characterized by severe economic and political crises, and international isolation. All of these powerful forces have affected the development of publishing in Montenegro; fortunately, one can say that the effects have not been wholly negative. Despite these difficulties, publishing is experiencing some remarkable changes. The number of publishers has risen to around seventy (though it is difficult to cite an exact number), and altogether they are producing more than five hundred monographs per year. A significant number of private publishers has come into being, and some previously government-owned houses have been privatized. The use of desktop computers to prepare typescripts has lowered printing and publishing costs and accelerated the entire process. The most prolific Montenegrin publisher in this decade has been Univerzitetska riječ, which has recently changed its name to Unireks, Nikšić. Similarly, the Republički zavod za unapredivanje školstva has undergone a change of name to Zavod za školstvo, Podgorica. Previously established publishers have expanded, producing a great number of new titles, supporting first publications by young authors, issuing works in history, ethnography and folklore focused on particular regions of Montenegro, or promoting the development and adoption of a native Montenegrin variety of written Serbo-Croatian.

During this period the works of Montenegrin authors have also

been published abroad. For instance, in Belgrade 272 different publishers have issued books by Montenegrin authors, with belles lettres
and textbooks dominating in this instance, as well.[5] Data about émigré
publishing over the past ten years–analogous to the works of Milovan
Đilas, the publicist and politician who was deposed from his government office in 1954 and who was published in the U.S. by Harcourt
Brace–are difficult to come by. Montenegrin publishers are going
through this period of transition and privatization without adequate
preparation. In unified Yugoslavia before 1991, barely more than one
percent of the country's entire annual book output came from Montenegro. Bearing in mind that publishing is by its very nature a low-turn-
over activity, that government subsidies of the publishing industry
have significantly decreased, and that the nation's standard of living
has been in constant decline, one can only conclude that the recent
flourishing of the industry in Montenegro, facilitating the appearance
of numerous works whose publication was unthinkable in the former
Yugoslavia, is due first and foremost to the capability of entrepreneurs
who have fully invested their business sense and feel for the diverse
needs of the reading public into their enterprises. These ventures are
financially risky, but play a decisive role in the transformation of the
country's cultural climate.

Several factors work against the development of a more efficient,
high-quality publishing industry. Foremost among them is the absence
of a consistent policy toward publishing on the part of the government
agencies that are supposed to oversee it. The government budget allocated in support of publishing varies from year to year and depends on
the severity of the government's (non-) liquidity in a given year (the
allocation is supposed to be around two percent, but this figure has
never been honored). With the establishment of an open competition
in just the past two years, the Ministry of Culture has provided all
publishers with the opportunity to compete for funds that will at least
partly cover the costs of producing titles of exceptional merit. A second factor is the absence of legislation that would systematically regu-
late this sphere of culture. Of the approximately seventy publishers
now active in Montenegro, only a small number are registered with the
Ministry of Culture, despite the fact that this is a legal requirement.
This suggests that a large proportion of the total number are businesses
and institutions whose primary activity is something other than publishing. The majority of publishers issue only several new titles per

year, and consequently devote scant attention to properly distributing them. The absence of a consistent government policy toward cultural activities in general is conducive to chaos in the publishing industry. At a time when the developed world has begun to contemplate the growing dominance of electronic media and the possibility that books as physical artifacts may become obsolete, the small nations of the Balkans, including Montenegro, have not even managed to support this fundamental medium of communication in an adequate way. Publishers have been left to their own devices, do improvised marketing, have their own distributors and buyers, and go looking for sponsors that will enable them to publish a book, advertise it in the press, and take it to book fairs. A new Association of Publishers and Printers of Montenegro has been *in statu nascendi* for several years and, even once it is officially established, is unlikely to be able to contribute toward progress in this area.

The absence of associations at the republic level is partly offset by the energetic presence of the Soros-sponsored Open Society Institute (OSI) in Montenegro. OSI has had an office in Podgorica since 1993, and since 1997 it has begun actively underwriting the publishing costs of selected titles in the social sciences and humanities. In allocating its support, the OSI gives preference to small publishers that issue titles on current topics of social import, such as the social transformation of East European countries. The OSI is also active in training library personnel, donating books and computer equipment to libraries and other cultural institutions, translating contemporary literature into various East European languages, and many other areas. Apart from its sporadic, idiosyncratically allocated financial assistance, the Ministry of Culture has no legal obligation to support the publishing industry in any particular way. Printed materials are generally exempt from the country's basic sales and service tax, but it is the obligation of each publisher to expressly request this exemption for each title published. At the end of each calendar year publishers are required to pay a tax on their profits, with no deductions allowed for that part of the year's profit which they plan to invest further.

Censorship no longer exists, nor does any authority which might be able to exercise censorship. Each publishing house makes its own decision as to what merits publication. Until several years ago there was a requirement that reviews had to be submitted alongside manuscripts being considered for publication, and the opinions of the reviewers were one of the main factors in making a decision to publish or not.

With the collapse of Yugoslavia, Montenegrin publishers, and especially printers, lost an enormous share of the Serbo-Croatian-speaking market. Political circumstances, closed borders and unconvertible currencies have made normal book trade and even the simple exchange of publications among the former members of the Yugoslav Federation all but impossible. There is tremendous interest on all sides in reestablishing normal trade relations, but nothing progresses beyond isolated attempts. This results in a huge loss to all cultural institutions in all the countries of the former Yugoslavia, but especially to the national libraries. The national libraries' decades-old practice of exchanging depository copies of all books published within their borders with their peer libraries in the other republics–Slovenia, Croatia, Bosnia and Macedonia–ceased, for all practical purposes, in 1991. The National Library of Montenegro now exchanges legal depository copies of materials published in Montenegro only with Serbia. Political events, the accelerated rate of democratization in Montenegro (in contrast with the deeply rooted regime of Slobodan Milošević in Serbia), and the occasional interruption of trade between Montenegro and Serbia even in such fundamentals as foodstuffs all point to the imminent demise of this federation resting on poor foundations. In the past ten years Montenegrin publishers regularly participated in the International Book Fair that takes place in Belgrade in October of each year. By 1998 only twenty Montenegrin publishers participated.

Judging from the interests of the reading public, the greatest demand at present is for historical monographs, religious literature, and translations of foreign popular literature and belles lettres, and Montenegrin publishers have attempted to respond to this demand. Only modest financial support is allocated toward the participation of Montenegrin publishers in the Belgrade book fair, and as a result they have attracted correspondingly little attention amid the fair's hubbub. There have been some occasional successes, such as the Makarije Prizes awarded to DOB Publishers from Podgorica for its recent book, *The Petrović Dynasty: Writers, Priests, Rulers* (*Petrovići: pisci, duhovnici, vladari*), and to CID Publishers for the exceptional physical design of its translation of *Don Quixote*. A major step forward in the presentation of Montenegro's book production to the world was its involvement in the 1998 Frankfurt Book Fair. This was the first time that

Montenegrin publishers, with support from the government of the republic, participated in a book fair outside the boundaries of the former Yugoslavia. "The Frankfurt Book Fair is the dream of every author, publisher, and librarian. Just to get there is a huge success. To see, from our quarantined perspective, how the rest of the world makes and displays its books, and what level of professionalism it has reached. A person makes many useful contacts there, and one of the great practical advantages of the fair is that participants get included in its printed catalogs and directories. You get the sense there that the greatness of a people is not in its history, but in the level of its culture. And you realize that we are just losing time and missing opportunities in the most brutal Balkan way–squandering time with our political mess . . . "[6] The effect could have been even greater, if only the vitiating factors mentioned above did not exist. Unfortunately, the interest in Montenegrin books brought about by their sudden presence at one of the world's largest book fairs dissipated just as suddenly due to the insurmountable difficulties posed by Montenegro's current geo-political reality–such as obstacles to paying authors, shipping books, etc.

Representatives of publishing houses in Slovenia and Croatia showed particular interest in Montenegrin books at the Frankfurt fair. The books displayed at Frankfurt covered a four-year period of publishing activity, from 1995 through 1998. For the occasion a catalog was published with the title *Izdavaštvo u Crnoj Gori = Books of Montenegro: From 500 to 504 Years After the Oktoekhos*. CID was the only publisher from Montenegro that participated in the book fair independently and at its own expense.

MAJOR PUBLISHERS, THEIR PUBLISHING PROGRAMS, AND A BRIEF OVERVIEW OF RECENT NOTABLE TITLES

CID (Centar za izdavačku djelatnost) is a private publishing house established in summer 1994. Over the past five years it has published some eighty monographic titles. While this record does not make it a large-volume enterprise, judging by quality of output it is exceptional. It is run by a young, four-member team, with Žarko Radonjić at the helm as director. For individual projects, CID frequently hires outside editors, compilers, translators and other contributors, as necessary. The basic concept of this new publishing house consists of three main elements: every new title must consist of high-quality content; all titles are issued in one of a variety of series, each devoted to a different topic; and every title must be realized according to the highest technical, esthetic and graphic standards. *Svjedočanstva* (*Testimonies*) is the title of the most notable of CID's topical series; it publishes important texts pertaining to the history of Montenegro, translations of travel diaries kept by foreign scholars who visited Montenegro to conduct field work, and memoirs of foreign visitors who lived in Montenegro in the eighteenth, nineteenth, or beginning of the twentieth centuries. Up to this point, twenty-seven titles, most of them unknown to most readers and translated into Serbo-Croatian for the first time, have been published in this series. Titles such as *Krvna osveta* (*Blood Revenge*) by Christopher Boehm, an American ethnographer who lived in Montenegro in the 1960s and later published his doctoral dissertation on this subject, appeal to the interests of Western readers, and particularly humanities scholars, historians, ethnographers and sociologists. One of the most popular titles in the series is *Montenegro: Travel Diaries by Kurt Hassert*, in two volumes, followed by *Crna Gora u izvještajima mletačkih providura 1683-1735* (*Montenegro in the Reports of Venetian Envoys, 1683-1735*), published in a bilingual edition in cooperation with the Italian Embassy. Also, for the first time a translated book has proven to be of extraordinary importance for understanding the history of Montenegro: L.C. Vialla de Sommieres' *Voyage historique et politique au Monténégro*. The author served as an officer of the French army in these lands from 1807 to 1813, and this work contains his extensive descriptions of Montenegro from that period. CID's series entitled Sofia is dedicated to Russian religious and philosophical thought from the end of the nineteenth and early twentieth centuries; to date eleven titles have been published in this series, mainly translations of Russian thinkers whose work is now appearing in Serbian translation for the first time. Alongside this series, another one titled Nomos offers translations of Western philosophers, sociologists and legal theorists. Of the ten titles published in this series to date, three deserve special attention: Herbert Hart's *The Concept of Law* (*Pojam prava*), John Rawls's *A Theory of Justice* (*Teorija prava*), and *Constitutional Government and Democracy* (*Konstitucionalizam*) by Carl Joachim Friedrich. CID has published about a dozen books pertaining to Montenegrin history, most of them translations from English (William Denton) or French (Paul Coquelle), but also from Czech (Josef

Holeček) and other languages. CID's publications of works by native Montenegrin authors have mostly been bibliophile editions, such as the collected works of the writers and rulers of the Petrović-Njegoš dynasty–Petar II and Nikola I–followed by the works of Marko Milja-nov and others. They have been awarded prizes for best designed book of the year for their editions of world classics, including Goethe's *Faust, Don Quixote*, and the *Divine Comedy*.

CID is one of the few publishers whose sole commercial activity is publishing. On occasion they receive support from the Open Society Institute and the Ministry of Education, which buys CID's publications to stock school and municipal libraries. Like the majority of publishers, CID does not have its own bookstore. In a 1998 competition sponsored by the Ministry of Culture, the company won a cash prize with which it was able to finance up to sixty percent of the costs of publishing the five books it had submitted for the competition. True for all publishers is the fact that the printing of a book is the most costly aspect of its production, amounting to anywhere between forty and sixty percent of the total cost, depending on the quality of the paper and printing. The staff of CID explain their financial success by pointing to the company's strategy of seeking maximum sales for each title (it typically takes four to five years to sell out a press run of 1,000 to 1,500 copies) in order to cover employee salaries and honoraria, and then investing the remaining profit in the production of future titles. Last year, thanks to its high-quality, attractive books, CID was invited as a special guest to the Frankfurt Book Fair.

A quite different mission in publishing–possibly, even, a diametri-cally opposed one–is espoused by the Kulturno-prosvjetna zajednica Podgorice (Cultural and Educational Association of Podgorica). This institution supports the development of amateur cultural and artistic creativity and has organized scholarly, cultural and artistic presenta-tions in and around the capital city of Montenegro. In accordance with this mission its publishing activity has promoted the same values–the cultural tradition of Podgorica and its surroundings, amateur perfor-mance and art, and folk ways in Montenegro throughout its history up to the present day. With nearly four hundred titles published over the past ten years, KPZ has grown into one of the most extensive and important publishers, with one prominent feature that sets it apart from other publishers seeking popular acclaim–namely, the equal attention it gives to beginners and amateurs, to potential artists in the making as well as established names. This institution has been in existence since 1984, but it has been active as a publisher only since 1991, thanks to the enthusiasm of one of its editors, Novak Vukčević, who has successfully woven the company's disparate commitments into a harmonious whole. By publishing the work of beginning poets, KPZ noticeably enriches the cultural spectrum of Montenegro. Great financial success is not one of the company's goals, but it does seek to influence the sensibilities of Montenegro's reading public with its new discoveries. Several of KZP's titles deserve particular mention. In 1994 it published a book by Dr. Radoslav Vešović, *Tolstoy and the Problems of Moral and Religious Education* (*Tolstoj i problemi moralnog i religioznog vaspitanja*). This 1936 doctoral dissertation from the Sorbonne waited sixty years to be translated. Similarly, a novel by Stevan Dučić, *Ili Kuč*, had to wait a century before it was finally published in 1997, causing a sensation. This biographical novel about a hajduk (a Balkan outlaw) is written in highly imaginative prose. The author was a close colleague of Marko Miljanov, a collector of ethnographic material about the Kuči tribe at the turn of the last century. Among the books that deal with Podgorica's past cultural milieu (these being the publisher's bestsellers) are works by such authors as Ilija Zlatičanin, Kosta Čakić, Vlatko Ivanović, and Dušan Ičević. Second only to the Montenegrin Academy of Sciences (CANU) and the Historical Institute, this institution publishes the most conference proceedings of any in the country. It has published papers from conferences devoted to Marko Miljanov and Danilo Kiš, and also university textbooks. Among titles devoted to the history of Montenegro, the most deserving of mention include: *Commander Mitar Martinović, 1870-1954* (*Divizijar Mitar Martinović*) by Dušan Martinović; *The Contribution of Bokelji to the Development of the Russian Naval and Merchant Fleets in the 18th and 19th Centuries* (*Doprinos Bokelja razvoju ruske ratne i trgovačke flote u 18. i 19. vijeku*) by Gojko Vukčević; and *Sales Contracts in Kotor in the 14th Century* (*Ugovori o kupoprodaji u Kotoru u 14. vijeku*) by N. Bogojević-Gluščević. Other monographic series are devoted to collections of poetry, children's literature, or collections of aphorisms. As an organizer of cultural events, this publisher uses those occasions to publish and distribute its books. Its financing derives mostly from private donations. It is a regular participant in the Belgrade and Herceg Novi book fairs, where its books on the cultural history of Podgorica are its fastest selling items. Most of its remaindered stock is donated to schools and libraries. KPZ collaborates with the Historical Institute and with the Central National Library in joint publications. It also works closely with Medunarodna knjiga, the Belgrade book exporter, and with publishers in Macedonia and Vojvodina.

DOB–Društvo za očuvanje baštine (Society for the Preservation of Heritage)–has been in existence for two years as a private publisher with offices in Podgorica. In this short time it has achieved remarkable success with its attractive reprint editions and publications of contemporary work, which–in the words of the company's director, Goran Sekulović–united past and present in both an intellectual and national sense. As part of its series, Library of Montenegrin Classics (Biblioteka Crnogorski klasici), it published *Petrovići: pisci, duhovnici, vladari* in three volumes, comprising 2,600 pages, bringing together the complete works of all seven writers of the famous ruling dynasty. At the 1997 Belgrade International Book Fair this collection was awarded the Makarije Prize for the best-designed book. Among many quality titles, of particular note are *Vladalačka kuća Petrović-Njegoš* (*The Ruling House of Petrović-Njegoš*), a reprint of the 1910 edition, which was originally published on the occasion of the proclamation of Montenegro as an independent kingdom; alongside texts authored by King Nikola I, it includes portraits of members of the dynasty and all European dynasties with whom they were related. In the series Baština (Heritage), it recently issued the memoirs of Heinrich von Hessen, *The Crystal Chandelier of Helen of Savoy* (*Kristalni luster Jelene od Savoje*, originally *Il Lampadario di cristallo*). The author of this book is the grandson of Helen of Savoy, King Nikola's daughter. To commemorate the centennial of motion pictures in Montenegro, DOB published film director Gojko Kastratović's outstanding book *Montenegrin Cinematography and Films About Montenegro* (*Crnogorska kinematografija i filmovi o Crnoj Gori*). Its most recent bestseller, published in the series Museums of Cetinje (Cetinjski muzeji), is Anda Kapičić's *The Art Collection of the State Museum in Cetinje* (*Umjetnička zbirka Državnog muzeja na Cetinju*), which has an introduction written by Prince Nikola, King Nikola's great-grandson, who lives and works in Paris. The catalog includes some 130 color illustrations. DOB is rapidly approaching West European standards for electronic publications; it has already formatted a great deal of textual material, accompanied by film footage and sound clips, into CD-ROMs. Some of these projects are being realized in cooperation with Multimedia (a Belgrade firm), considering that electronic publishing in Montenegro is still in its early stages. The complete corpus of material pertaining to the life and work of Petar II, the 19th-century Prince Bishop of Montenegro, has already been issued on CD-ROM. Similar projects are being planned for the collected works of King Nikola, and for DOB's other major editions of collected works. Aside from the Montenegrin classics, DOB also expects that its meticulously produced CD-ROM *Enigmatic Charisma: Milo Đukanović* (*Enigma jedne harizme: Milo Đukanović*) by Goran Sekulović will meet with considerable commercial success. This will be a novelty in the Montenegrin book market–alongside textual material, the CD-ROM will include film footage depicting the development of his political career. Additionally, with the sponsorship of the Open Society Institute, valuable documentary material about Montenegro in the form of a television series titled *Montenegro on Documentary Film* (*Crna Gora u filmskim dokumentima*) will soon be produced on CD-ROM.

Pobjeda is one of the oldest publishing houses in Montenegro, with origins dating to the first publication of the daily newspaper by the same name (October 24, 1944). Next to Obod, during the period preceding the collapse of Yugoslavia, Pobjeda was one of the largest houses, particularly after it merged with Grafički zavod (Printing Institute) in 1974. As a result of its organizational transformation, from 1985 to 1995 Pobjeda no longer functioned as a publisher, only as a printer and bookstore chain. In 1995 it resumed its publishing activities, and its current director, Goran Sekulović, has expressed hopes that since the firm has long since made its major capital investments and developed its professional expertise and marketing strategies, it will soon achieve its former success. Over the past four years it has published some fifteen titles, primarily on philosophical and religious subjects, including five works by Slobodan Tomović, Montenegro's former Minister of Religious Affairs.

Oktoih is a young publishing house named for the first Cyrillic book printed among the South Slavs, the Oktoechos. It was established in 1991 with Radomir Uljarević as editor-in-chief. It publishes about thirty titles per year. It has managed to achieve a balance of foreign literature (translations of contemporary world authors, philosophy, religion, anthropology) and domestic, predominantly contemporary authors, such as Milorad Pavić, Matija Bećković, Dušan Kovačević, Vida Ognjenović, and Svetislav Basara. Oktoih's publishing efforts center around several main series which deal with current trends in the Montenegrin and international literary scene. For students of classic Montenegrin literature, the most interesting one is the Njegoš series (Biblioteka Njegoš), which is in the process of publishing, in twenty volumes, the most important interpretations of Njegoš's literary work. Authors representing a variety of specializations–writers, philosophers, psychologists–offer their interpretations of this inexhaustible object of study.

Obod in Cetinje is Montenegro's oldest publisher, considered the successor to the Njegoš Press (Njegoševa štamparija). Between the two world wars it was known as Banovinska štamparija Obod. It was established in 1946 as a publishing and printing enterprise with its own chain of bookstores. In 1974 the publishing programs were separated from the larger business and intensified. Obod primarily publishes works of Montenegrin writers, both in smaller, individually titled editions and as editions of collected works, as well as historical studies, dictionaries, encyclopedias and handbooks–in short, the kinds of publications that are most in demand. In the 1990s it also underwent a transformation, becoming a joint stock company based mostly on private capital. It receives government subsidies particularly to support its large-scale projects. Obod has largely retained its former publishing plan and now issues about forty titles per year. The Obod monograph series that have had the greatest success over the past ten years include the Novel in Montenegro (Roman u Crnoj Gori), published in twenty volumes with a print run of a thousand copies, *Literature in Montenegro from the Twelfth to the Nineteenth Centuries* (*Književnost u Crnoj Gori od 12. do 19. vijeka*), published in twenty-three volumes and with a comparable print run. At present Obod is in the midst of publishing the complete works in ten volumes of čedo Vuković, Montenegro's greatest living writer, the first volume of which has already come out. In 1998 it issued a facsimile reprint of the *Law Code on Property of the Principality of Montenegro* (*Opšti imovinski zakonik za knjaževinu Crnu Goru*), in a handcrafted leather binding. *Montenegro's Mountains* (*Crnogorske planine*), a title for which Obod served as co-publisher in 1994, has been in high demand beyond Montenegro's borders. A large share of Obod's business is given over to bilingual dictionaries–both standard, desktop editions and smaller pocket-sized ones, particularly for Serbian and Russian, English, German, Italian, or Latin. Within unified Yugoslavia Obod printed 50,000 copies of each of its dictionaries each year. In the past few years those press runs have contracted to between 10,000 and 12,000 copies per year. Although the dictionaries' retail prices have risen as a result, they continue to sell well. Obod has an outlet in Belgrade and a network of outlets in Bosnia, and has its dictionaries distributed on the foreign market through Jugoslovenska knjiga in Belgrade.

The Montenegrin Academy of Sciences and Arts (Crnogorska akademija nauka i umjetnosti–CANU) was established in 1973 as the Society for Science and Art of Montenegro (Društvo za nauku i umjetnost Crne Gore), and renamed in 1976 as the Academy. It sponsors both regular and irregular periodical publications, monographic series, bibliographies, Festschriften and memorial editions for deceased members of the Academy. In its history it has published 220 books on a wide range of scholarly topics, with one copy of each presented to the public at a specially organized conference in the Academy. Of the more than eighty titles published in the past ten years, over twenty of them have been collections of papers from these conferences. The authors are members of the Academy or otherwise outstanding scholars. Aside from Conferences (Naučni skupovi), its most voluminous series, CANU has published a number of monographs on the social and legal structure of Yugoslavia in the series Special Editions of the Division of Social Sciences (Posebna izdanja Odjeljenja društvenih nauka). Some significant monographs on art history have been published as Special Editions (Posebna izdanja): Pavle Mijović's *Typology of Church Architecture in Montenegro (Tipologija crkvenih spomenika u Crnoj Gori)*, a catalog of Milo Milunović's paintings, and Slobodan Raičević's *Montenegrin Painting in the New Age (Slikarstvo u Crnoj Gori u novom vijeku)*. As co-publisher it has issued Tatjana Pejović's outstanding and much sought-after *Monasteries in Montenegro (Manastiri na tlu Crne Gore)*. Also as co-publisher, in 1994 it produced an extensive study of Montenegro's capital, *Cetinje 1482-1982*. The Njegoš Institute (Njegošev institut) operates as a unit within CANU's Division of Art, and to date it has published three linguistic studies.

Beginning in 1997 the Academy committed its resources to producing the new *Encyclopedia of Montenegro (Enciklopedija Crne Gore)*, which involves contributions from nearly five hundred authors. Among its periodical publications are the *CANU Annual (Godišnjak CANU)* and the *Reporters* (*Glasnici*) of its various divisions, which are published irregularly. The Academy donates copies of its publications to its members, employees, interested peer institutions, and all major Slavic studies research libraries around the world. Consistently, CANU's social science publications, together with those of the Historical Institute (Istorijski institut), are the most important and influential ones published in the country.

The Historical Institute was founded in Cetinje in 1948, and its mission has been to study material of historical importance for Montenegro. In 1957 its seat was relocated to Podgorica. The Institute publishes the results of its research in the journal *Historical Notes* (*Istorijski zapisi*). Besides historical work, in the past ten years the Institute has published titles dealing with foreign policy, diplomatic relations of Montenegro with other countries, law, ethnology, genealogy, medieval art in Montenegro, and a large number of titles devoted to various aspects of World War II. At the 1998 Belgrade Fair the Institute received an award for the publishing project of the year for its five-volume collection of documents *Montenegrin Law Codes: Legal Sources and Political Documents of Significance for the History of Montenegro* (*Crnogorski zakonici: pravni izvori i politički akti od značaja za istoriju državnosti Crne Gore*).

Of the numerous smaller publishers in Montenegro several deserve particular attention. Charlie and Son Company, based in the coastal city of Bar, has published *The Hidden Side of History: the Montenegrin Riot and Outlaw Movement, 1918-1929* (*Skrivana strana istorije*) by historian Šerbo Rastoder. This four-volume work published in 1997 contains 1,759 documents from a variety of personal archives, most of them published for the first time. They deal with some of the most important issues arising from the dramatic and protracted conflict between two disparate concepts of the federation of Serbia and Montenegro. The same publishing house recently changed its name to Conteco and published several exceptionally successful titles, among them the *Chronicle of Priest Docleas* (*Ljetopis popa Dukljanina*)–Montenegro's oldest systematic work of history, which has been an object of study for native and foreign scholars on account of its important source material for general European history, in addition to local, South Slavic history. Conteco maintains a Web site at http://www.conteco.cg.yu, which supplies a list of its publications and information for placing orders for them over the Internet.

Svetigora is the publishing and informational office of the Monte-negrin-Littoral Archbishopric, with its seat in Cetinje. It developed out of the Archbishopric's official periodical *Svetigora*, which began publication in 1992. It is named for an underground stream that emerges aboveground in the form of a waterfall from beneath a famous medieval monastery, symbolizing the publishing house's mission to propagate the Orthodox written word, both past and present, throughout the South Slavic lands. It began functioning as a book publisher with the St. Peter of Cetinje Series (Biblioteka Sveti Petar Cetinjski) in 1995. Since then it has published about twenty new titles per year; in 1999 the number jumped to fifty, with a total print run for all titles published of over 100,000 copies per year. Some of its monographic series are: *Holy Mysteries and Holy Virtues* (*Svete tajne i svete vrline*), *The Rule of Faith* (*Pravilo vjere*), *Comforts of the Lord* (*Utjehe gospodnje*), *Orthodoxy and the Present Day* (*Pravoslavlje i novo doba*), and *Documents* (*Dokumenta*). Through the many volumes published in its various series, readers can obtain authentic answers of the Orthodox Church to the questions facing the individual and this particular nation today. Many of them are works by Serbian, Russian, Greek, American and French authors, theologians and scholars. The series *Svetigora's Books About Sects* (*Svetigorine knjige o sektama*) comprises seven titles which are in high demand. Translations from the Russian of two books by Igor Shafarevich–*Socialism as a Phenomenon of World History* and *Russia and World Crisis* have also sold well. A work currently in progress is the *Missionary's Dictionary* (*Azbučni misionar*), an alphabetically arranged catechism of basic issues of faith. Svetigora had the distinction of opening the international book fair in Herceg-Novi in 1998. One of its translations of works by Russian publicist Igor Shafarevich was awarded the prize for best translation of the year. Svetigora has its own bookstore in Cetinje and an outlet in Belgrade.

Our Lady of the Rocks (Gospa od Škrpelja) is a new publishing house named for a famous holy place on a small island in the Bay of Kotor. Brother Don Srećko Majić is its founder and sole representative. It was founded in 1995 with the intention of reviving the spiritual values of Montenegro's Roman Catholic population, whose cultural level has always risen above its surroundings, but unfortunately for many years has been ignored in print. The few titles already published by this house range from theological literature to belles lettres to several titles dealing with the history of Perast, a small coastal town with a rich maritime tradition. The first of these books, *The Cultural History of the Town of Perast* (*Kulturna povijest grada Perasta*), had waited since 1951 to be published. Ten years ago the emergence of a publisher like Gospa od Škrpelja was all but unthinkable. Now that it exists, it is forced to struggle for its continued existence using only its own resources, since it receives no public support and no attention from the media, even though it richly deserves both for nurturing an important segment of Montenegrin Littoral life which has always enriched and diversified the unique cultural climate of that multinational region of the country.

The Kotor City Archive (Arhiv grada Kotora), the oldest archive in Montenegro, which celebrated its fiftieth anniversary in November 1999, is an institution with a small number of extremely productive specialists. As part of an ongoing project to digitize the Archive's collections, a CD-ROM is being planned, an early version of which was demonstrated at Expo '98 in Lisbon. Its contents comprise the two rarest and most frequently used medieval documents. The CD-ROM includes an overview of documents of cultural and historical importance from throughout the municipality of Kotor and presents in electronic form a reconstruction of daily life in the Bay of Kotor in the 14th century. Shorter excerpts can be viewed on the Web at http://www.matf.bg.ac.yu/iak, which also provides an overview of the Historical Archive of Kotor. Of the Archive's print publications, an important critical edition of the Statute of the City of Kotor (Statut grada Kotora) dating to 1616 will be published in late 2000; as well as a new, expanded edition of the guide to the archival collections of the City of Kotor, essential for any serious research, which is being updated for the first time in twenty years.

The Crnojević Central National Library (Centralna narodna biblioteka "Đurdje Crnojević"–CNB) in Cetinje is the national depository and the universal research library with the largest collection of books, periodicals and other printed materials in Montenegro. It is located in Cetinje, the historic capital of Montenegro, which for nearly five hundred years was the center of the country's social, political and cultural life. Since its founding in 1946 it has striven to fulfill its primary mission, to develop an exhaustive collection of Montenegrina with the unique status of a national treasure. In building this collection the Library offers scholars the opportunity to do the most thorough research possible on topics relating to Montenegro. The CNB is a full-service library and serves as the center of the country's library and information system. The previous system of exchanging legal depository copies of each book published in the Republic with the national libraries of the other federal republics–in Slovenia, Croatia, Bosnia and Macedonia–ceased to function in 1991. The Montenegrin national library exchanges legal depository copies only with the National Library of Serbia, and even that exchange is now burdened by worsening political relations. It does remain the depository library, offering the single best overview of all materials published on the territory of the Republic, since the Library acquires and catalogs all of them. However, its collections are not complete, due to the failure of some publishers to honor the Law on Publishing, and the absence of regulations that would provide for fines against publishers and printers that fail to submit their legal depository copies. The CNB conducts an exchange of books and journals with more than sixty libraries worldwide. This is the only way for it to add to its collections important work published abroad, and at the same time an important way for the world's major Slavic studies collections to acquire the current Montenegrin titles they need. Recent attempts to reestablish cooperative and exchange ties with the National and University Library in Sarajevo have been encouraging, giving hope that similar contacts with the national libraries in other former Yugoslav republics may also be restored.

The CNB devotes a great deal of effort to carrying out its publishing mission, despite the modest resources at its disposal for financing new books. The Library structures its publishing activities in accordance with its institutional goals, issuing books and journals in several well-established series, including: Special Editions (Posebna izdanja), Photoreprographic Editions (Fototipska izdanja), Bibliography and Biobibliography (Biografija i biobibliografija), Catalogs (Katalozi). The CNB began functioning as a publisher in the 1950s when it issued the *Overview of Publishing and Printing From the Fifteenth Century and Crnojević's Press Until Modern Times* (*Pregled izdavačko-štamparske djelatnosti od 15. vijeka i Crnojevića štamparije do novijih vremena*). In the 1970s, with Dr. Dušan Martinović's directorship of the Library, these activities intensified. To the present day somewhat more than one hundred monographic titles have been published, as a result of which it is now possible to say that Montenegro has been bibliographically fully researched.

The number of titles has not been large, but the repertory that exists has been carefully developed. In the Special Editions series (Posebna izdanja) E.L. Nemirovski's book *The Beginnings of Printing in Montenegro* (*Počeci štamparstva u Crnoj Gori*) stands out for the quality of its contents and design. P.A. Rovinskii's *Montenegro Past and Present* (*Crna Gora u prošlosti i sadašnjosti*), a translation from Russian, is of enormous importance to the nation's scholarship and culture. In four volumes Rovinskii describes Montenegro and his stay there at the turn of the last century. He organized the authentic source material that he collected and the results of his investigations into separate chapters on geography, history, ethnography, archaeology and current events–amounting to a compendium of crucially important background information for anyone studying the complexity of life in Montenegro. In the Photoreprographic Series several reprint editions of Slavic incunabula printed by Crnojević at the end of the 15th century have appeared. These are texts of the church liturgy printed in old, pre-Petrine Cyrillic, a Cyrillic type that remains unsurpassed for its aesthetic appeal. There have also been reprint editions of the first Montenegrin periodicals from the 19th century–*The Montenegrin* (*Crnogorac*), the first paper of politics and literature, and *Crnogorka*, the first literary journal. The most voluminous title in the Bibliography Series (Bibliografija) is Dušan Martinović's *Portraits of Authors (Portreti autora*). The six volumes of this title published to date include bibliographic sketches of more than a hundred leading Montenegrin writers, past and present.

   The Bibliography of Montenegro, 1494-1994 (*Crnogorska bibliografija 1494-1994*) occupies a special place among the CNB's publications, representing one of the most important cultural and scholarly undertakings in Montenegro. The very first important publication of a bibliographic nature was the *Overview of Printing and Publishing in Montenegro, 1494-1954: A Retrospective Bibliography of Books and Periodicals* (*Pregled izdavačke djelatnosti u Crnoj Gori 1494-1954*). A large number of biobibliographies have appeared in the journal *Bibliographic Herald* (*Bibliografski vjesnik*). *The Bibliography of Yugoslavia* (*Bibliografija Jugoslavije*), issued by the Yugoslav Bibliographic Institute in Belgrade, is replete with citations of Montenegrin publications. Many individual periodicals have had specialized bibliographies devoted to them. The CNB has engaged in bibliographic work since 1957, when it began to publish *Bibliographic Data on Montenegro and the Bay of Kotor* (*Bibliografski podaci o Crnoj Gori i*

Boki). Over time these first attempts grew into the need for a systematic register of material from and about Montenegro. In view of the fact that publishing in postwar Montenegro amounted to only one to two percent of Yugoslavia's total publishing output, it was believed sufficient to publish occasional issues of a current bibliography. Given the complications of working on national bibliographies in a multinational state such as Yugoslavia, a multilateral agreement had to be reached concerning the standards to be used, so that all bibliographies could eventually be merged in a single machine-readable database. For instance, the Slovenes' task in this regard (one nation, one language) was far simpler than that encountered in the other, multinational regions, such as Montenegro, with its considerable proportion of Moslem, Albanian and–to a lesser extent–Catholic population (on the Littoral). One of the inadequacies of the bibliographies produced before the collapse of Yugoslavia was that a whole category of writers and scholars–i.e., political emigrants writing against the socialist system–was simply left unregistered. Work on the retrospective bibliographies of the various republics was entrusted to the national libraries, where the respective national collections were most complete. Work began in 1980. Soon afterward, the Bibliographic Division of the CNB was formed, which from that time carried responsibility for both retrospective and current bibliography. The editorial board of the Montenegrin bibliography decided that it would include material published and printed in Montenegro, material of Montenegrin publishers printed elsewhere, works of Montenegrin authors published elsewhere, and works published anywhere pertaining to Montenegro. Recently the part of the Montenegrin Bibliography that describes monographs reached volume one, part nine. In a period of just five years (1990-1995) a total of 3,525 items have been registered. The most extensive category of materials are textbooks for elementary and high schools (more than 800 citations). Among belles lettres the most extensive subcategory is poetry, with 528 citations, followed by novels with 154. Since the beginning of the project in 1985, all Montenegrin monographic publications through 1995 have been described, as planned by the project.

Volume II carries the title *Serial Publications (Serijske publikacije)*. It covers the period from 1835 to 1984. Over the past 150 years more than 700 serial titles have been published in Montenegro, of which 231 titles existed for only one year or less. The CNB owns, if not a complete, then at least the most extensive collection of newspapers and periodicals, as well as one copy of most extant rare and antiquarian items. It was precisely because of scholars' and other library users' high demand for copies of Montenegrin periodicals that photographic reprints of some titles from the nineteenth century have been produced. The bibliography of serial publications presents both retrospective and current material at the same time, an innovation that the other Yugoslav national libraries did not introduce when developing their bibliographies.

Volume III carries the title *Essays, Articles and Literary Works in Serial Publications* (*Rasprave, članci i književni radovi u serijskim publikacijama*). At this point 1835 to 1955 has been covered, including articles by Montenegrin authors published outside the Republic's borders.

Volume IV publishes bibliographies of material about Montenegro in Russian (1722-1989), Italian (1532-1941) and English (1593-1993). The Library is seeing to it that the more than 160,000 bibliographic citations that have been recorded are digitized on CD-ROM as soon as possible.

The *Bibliographic Herald* (*Bibliografski vjesnik*) is a periodical that has been appearing for more than four decades as a joint publication of the CNB and the Association of Librarians of Montenegro (Društvo bibliotekara Crne Gore). It was begun in 1961 and experienced a ten-year hiatus in publication (1965-1975). In categories such as Bibliography, Biobibliography, From Our Cultural History, and others, it has offered a constant stream of information about Montenegro and works about the nation's cultural history. In comparison with other European countries, librarianship got its own periodical here relatively late. Libraries are underfunded and there are few professional librarians who could participate in publishing a periodical. The founder, Niko S. Martinović, began the journal when he grasped the importance of bibliography to scholarship. From its first issue the *Herald* has been publishing bibliographies of the earliest Montenegrin newspapers and literary papers, biobibliographies of leading scholars, current national bibliography, summaries of contents of scholarly journals, overviews of publishing activity by year, reviews of books on literary history, observances of authors' anniversaries, and the like. After the decade-long hiatus in publication, it revived with the beginning of Dušan Martinović's directorship of the National Library, growing in size, format and contents. It also introduced ISBD (International Standard Bibliographic Description) for catalog and bibliographic entries to Montenegro. A number of foreign experts, especially ones from St. Petersburg, have written for the journal. For the past several years its editor has been Čedomir Drašković, the CNB's director. This journal, which has served to secure the status of books in Montenegro, is issued three times per year and is sent to over a hundred libraries around the world.

HIGHLIGHTS OF CURRENT PERIODICALS

Newspapers and News Magazines

- *Pobjeda* (http://www.pobjeda.cg.yu) was begun in Nikšić in 1944 as the official newspaper of the National Liberation Front. Since 1954 it has been published in Podgorica, becoming a daily in 1977. A daily section on cultural events publishes news about the publishing industry, theater, film, and art. Its regular Features section publishes serial excerpts of longer studies, mostly historical. There is also a 5-page Sunday supplement titled The World of Culture (Svijet kulture).
- *Vijesti* (http://www.vijesti.cg.yu) is the other main daily newspaper, which recently marked its second anniversary. It is gaining in popularity and lately has become a serious competitor of *Pobjeda*. Its format is similar to *Pobjeda*'s, except that it presents a more critical picture of political events.
- *Monitor: crnogorski nezavisni nedjeljnik* (*Monitor: Montenegro's Independent Weekly*). Podgorica: Montenegropublic, 1990- . The most widely read independent news weekly, *Monitor* has staff and contributors who are Montenegro's most outstanding journalists. They provide cutting-edge coverage of political events in former and present-day Yugoslavia; as a result, *Monitor* has been banned in Serbia. Every issue includes articles about the current art and music scene, and reviews of newly published literary works. Its Internet site (http://www.monitor.cg.yu) also includes an overview of books published by *Monitor*.

Culture and Cultural History

- *Ovdje: list za umjetnost, kulturu, nauku i društvena pitanja.* Podgorica: Kulturno-prosvjetna zajednica Crne Gore, subsequently Centar savremene umjetnosti Crne Gore, 1969- . Quarterly.
- *Almanah: časopis za proučavanje, zaštitu i prezentaciju kulturno-istorijske baštine Muslimana-Bošnjaka.* Podgorica: Udruženje Almanah, 1997- .
- *Boka: zbornik radova iz nauke, kulture i umjetnosti.* Herceg-Novi: Zavičajni muzej, 1969- .

Research Institutions

- *Godišnjak CANU.* Podgorica: CANU, 1973- .
- *Glasnik Odjeljenja društvenih nauka.* Podgorica: CANU, 1975- . Published irregularly.
- *Glasnik Odjeljenja prirodnih nauka.* Podgorica: CANU, 1974- .
- *Glasnik Odjeljenja umjetnosti.* Podgorica: CANU, 1976- .
- *Godišnjak Pomorskog muzeja.* Kotor: Pomorski muzej, 1952- . (Maritime, economic and cultural history of the Bay of Kotor.)
- *Zbornik Fakulteta za pomorstvo.* Kotor: Fakultet, 1975- .
- *Zbornik Pravnog fakulteta.* Podgorica: Pravni fakultet Crne Gore, 1978- .

Social Sciences

- *Luča: časopis za filozofiju i sociologiju.* Nikšić: Društvo filozofa i sociologa Crne Gore i Odsjek za filozofiju i sociologiju Filozofskog fakulteta, 1986- .

Statistics

- *Mjesečni statistički pregled Republike Crne Gore.* Podgorica: Zavod za statistiku, 1959- .

Governmental Gazettes

- *Službeni list Crne Gore. Podgorica: Službeni list.* Also available at http://www.sllrcg.cg.yu.

History and Archives

- *Istorijski zapisi. Podgorica: Istorijski institut, 1948- .* Quarterly.
- *Arhivski zapisi: časopis za arhivsku teoriju i praksu.* Cetinje: Državni arhiv Crne Gore, 1994- . Two per year.

Economics and Business

- *Privreda: informativni bilten Privredne komore Crne Gore.* Podgorica: Privreda komora, 1967- .
- *Adriatico: A Review of the Centre for Mediterranean Studies.* Podgorica: Centre for Mediterranean Studies, 1994- . Topics include cooperation among Mediterranean countries, economic and environmental issues. In English.

Foreign Affairs

- *Montenegrin Journal of Foreign Policy.* Kotor: Institut za istraživanje spoljne politike, 1997- . In English.

Education

- *Vaspitanje i obrazovanje: časopis za pedagošku teoriju i praksu.* Podgorica: Republički zavod za unapredivanje školstva, 1975- .
- *Prosvjetni rad: list prosvetnih radnika Crne Gore.* Podgorica: Udruženje prosvjetnih radnika, 1954- .

Belles Lettres

- *Stvaranje: časopis za književnost i kulturu.* Podgorica, 1946- . 3 to 4 issues per year.
- *Ars: časopis za književnost, kulturu i društvena pitanja.* Podgorica: Crnogorsko društvo nezavisnih književnika. Alongside Montenegrin literature, it presents contemporary work from the other former Yugoslav republics; Slovenia was featured in a recent issue.
- *Zapis: list za književnost i kulturu.* Podgorica: Udruženje književnika Crne Gore. The first issue was published in spring 1999.
- *Znak: časopis učenika Filološke gimnazije.* Podgorica: Oktoih, 1993- .

Art, Music, Theater

- *Most: ljetopis Galerije Most.* Podgorica: Galerija, 1997- . Annual.
- *Muzički glasnik Crne Gore.* Podgorica: Udruženje kompozitora Crne Gore, 1997- .
- *Gest: časopis za pozorišnu umjetnost.* Podgorica: Udruženje dramskih umjetnika Crne Gore, 1999- . (Continues Svjetla pozornice.)

Youth Magazine

- *Trend: časopis mladih.* Podgorica: Univerzitet Crne Gore, 1997- . Also at http://www.trend.cg.yu.

CONCLUSION

The collapse of Yugoslavia and the post-totalitarian period have wrought significant changes in Montenegro's publishing landscape. Approximately forty new, mostly small, private publishing houses have emerged in a shrunken market, while most previously established houses continue to exist, though without making significant changes in their publishing programs. A review of overall book and periodical production over the past ten years yields nothing fundamentally new or revolutionary, with some areas remaining as neglected as they were before. West European trends have made deep inroads. At the moment, history is and will probably remain one of the most popular fields for publishing. Notable progress has been made only in the sense that greater attention is now being paid to the accuracy of historical documents, while interpretation has receded to the background. Although each publisher is different in the amount of weight it sets on any given topic, they all appear to share an equal obsession with history and a lack of interest in contemporary topics. A search for lost traditions distracts them from the many issues that should be of concern to society in an age of multiculturalism, electronic media and globalization. The presence of a large number of new publishers in a country which is going through a phase of decentralization and democratization should bring with it the transformation of institutions, innovations in all spheres of culture, and an independent and diversified publishing industry. As the format most suited to reacting quickly to trends and events, magazines and journals should logically have been revolutionized, but paradoxically not a single new periodical title targeting young, educated people and focused on the opening of Montenegrin society has appeared. Yet there has been some positive movement, thanks precisely to small, private publishers. Faced with financial problems in the struggle to survive, they have created an atmosphere of healthy competition. Interest in translations of foreign literature, electronic publishing, and marketing has increased, so that under the pressures of increased demand and market economics Montenegro has gradually begun to become a part of an ever more diverse East European market for the printed word. Meetings and agreements concluded with publishers from the erstwhile republics of the former Yugoslavia have revived the possibility of Montenegro's gaining back the market that was lost to it not so very long ago–and, more importantly, of breaking through its isolation by opening itself to new, more humane themes in social relations and interpersonal communications.

NOTES

1. Martinović, Dušan. *Crna Gora u Gutenbergovoj galaksiji: istorija crnogorskog štamparstva s kraja XV vijeka do 1916. godine.* (Podgorica: Crnogorska akademija nauka i umijetnosti, 1994): 215.

2. *Izdavačka delatnost i štampa u FNR Jugoslaviji u 1953. godini.* (Beograd: Savezni zavod za statistiku i evidenciju, 1954): 102.

3. *Izdavačka djelatnost u NR Crnoj Gori, 1945-1958.* (Cetinje: Centralna narodna biblioteka "Đurdje Crnojević," 1959), 2: 117.

4. *Aktuelna pitanja razvoja crnogorske kulture.* (Titograd: Republička samoupravna interesna zajednica kulture, 1984): 492.

5. Dušan Martinović, ed., *Crnogorska bibliografija.* (Cetinje: Centralna narodna biblioteka "Đurdje Crnojevića," 1998), vol. 10, *Monografske publikacije,* 1990-1994.

6. Čedomir Drašković, director of the Central National Library of Montenegro and a representative of Montenegrin publishers at the Frankfurt Book Fair, as quoted in *Vijesti,* 27 Nov. 1998.

KOSOVA/KOSOVO

MAP 6. Kosova/Kosovo

Based on: *Kosovo*, administrative divisions. Scale 1:1,050,000. Washington DC: Central Intelligence Agency, 1998

Publishing in Kosova/Kosovo

Frances Trix

SUMMARY. Albanian-language publishing in Kosova during the 1990-1999 period was very much affected first by Serbian censorship and persecution, then by the war. The situation has improved since the fighting stopped in the summer of 1999, with most of the seven main publishers having reopened. The author reviews major newspapers, news magazines and other periodicals from Kosova, then lists books by important authors brought out by various publishers. The Internet has proven an important means of communicating news and culture, especially during the recent disruptions; several sites are listed. A section follows showing some significant library collections of Kosovar Albanian material. The author suggests acquiring such publications directly from their publishers and gives contact information. Finally, there is an English-language bibliography of recommended reading about Kosova in general. *[Article copies available for a fee from The Haworth Document Delivery Service: 1-800-342-9678. E-mail address: <getinfo@ haworthpressinc.com> Website: <http://www.HaworthPress.com> © 2000 by The Haworth Press, Inc. All rights reserved.]*

KEYWORDS. Kosova, Kosovo, Serbia, Yugoslavia, Albanian, publishers and publishing, censorship

Frances Trix, PhD, is Associate Professor of Anthropology, 165 Manoogian, Wayne State University, Detroit, MI 48202 (E-mail: ad1993@wayne.edu or ftrix@umich.edu).

The author would like to thank Ella Hoxha and Kelmend Hapçiu for research assistance. Mr. Hapçiu, long a journalist for Rilindja, was especially helpful in finding publications of new presses and ways of contacting editors at a time when the communication system in Kosova was severely damaged. Dr. Siglind Bruhn also was instrumental in finding the appropriate contact in the Bavarian State Library. They discussed the lists of recommended works in Albanian with several Kosovars. From this group the author especially thanks Mr. Rexhep Goçi and Mejreme Goçi for sharing their knowledge.

[Haworth co-indexing entry note]: "Publishing in Kosova/Kosovo." Trix, Frances. Co-published simultaneously in *Slavic & East European Information Resources* (The Haworth Information Press, an imprint of The Haworth Press, Inc.) Vol. 1, No. 2/3, 2000, pp. 159-183; and: *Publishing in Yugoslavia's Successor States* (ed: Michael Biggins, and Janet Crayne) The Haworth Information Press, an imprint of The Haworth Press, Inc., 2000, pp. 159-183. Single or multiple copies of this article are available for a fee from The Haworth Document Delivery Service [1-800-342-9678, 9:00 a.m. - 5:00 p.m. (EST). E-mail address: getinfo@haworthpressinc.com].

RECENT HISTORY AS CONTEXT FOR PUBLISHING

Few Kosovar Albanians joined the Partisans during World War II. Kosovar Albanians were largely traditional Muslims and Roman Catholics and, as such, they were not drawn to Communism. Nor were Kosovar Albanians drawn to organizations locally led by Serbs who had oppressed them throughout the 1920s and 1930s. In the first decades after the war there were reprisals, harassment, and, as a last resort, many Albanians left Kosova for Turkey. However, Tito's government gradually became fairer to the Albanians. Schools in the Albanian language were allowed. Publishing, which had been forbidden Albanians throughout the 1920s and 1930s, was permitted for the first time. Gradually in the late 1960s the University of Prishtina was organized and, with it, institutes like the Institute for Albanology. In 1974 Kosova was granted the status of an autonomous region within Serbia, which allowed Albanians to take part in the running of the region. At this time the demographics of the province were seventy-five percent Albanian and twenty-five percent Serb or Montenegrin. An architecturally impressive library was built in the center of Prishtina and completed in 1982.

The last two decades of the twentieth century saw a decline in the situation of Kosovar Albanians. In 1981 a large demonstration in Prishtina, triggered by student discontent at the university, turned into a demonstration for more political rights for Albanians. Albanians wanted Kosova to gain the status of a seventh republic in Yugoslavia, which the Serbs refused. The demonstration was put down severely and martial law was imposed. Many professional Albanians were fired from their positions. Throughout the 1980s the economy worsened and many Serbs left Kosova for economic reasons. At the same time there were police pressures on Albanians. Many Albanian writers and community leaders were given long prison sentences. The Yugoslav secret police remained very much in control. However, the political cohesion in all Yugoslavia was deteriorating, and Serbian and Croatian nationalisms were growing. In 1987 Slobodan Milošević came to national prominence by building on Serbs' fear and resentment of the much larger numbers of Albanians in Kosovo, who by that time represented eighty-five percent of the population. In 1989 Milošević took away the autonomous province status of both Kosova in the south and Vojvodina in the north, thereby centralizing power in Belgrade.

Throughout the 1990s conditions progressively worsened for Kosovar Albanians. In 1990 Serb authorities established martial law in Kosova and took over the police, judiciary, and military. Most Albanian media, including all radio, television and the main publisher and newspaper, *Rilindja*, were closed. Albanians were fired from most jobs by 1991. Albanian students from elementary school through high school were forbidden to enter schools as of fall of 1991. All Albanian staff of the University of Prishtina were fired and all 27,000 Albanian university students expelled that year. Helsinki Rights Watch documented instances of harassment, brutality and property destruction, committed in the course of alleged weapons searches. The response of the Albanian populace, under the leadership of literary scholar and president of the Writers' Union, Ibrahim Rugova, was non-violence. A parallel educational system was set up by Albanians, funded by Albanians in the diaspora. Still, as in Bosnia, harassment, arrest and beatings of Albanians, particularly doctors, teachers and intellectuals, continued. In Bosnia at that time NATO finally intervened, the fighting was brought to a close, and in 1995 the Dayton Peace Accords were negotiated. Albanians had been led to believe that when Bosnia was settled there would be justice for them as well.

The Dayton Peace Accords, however, failed to mention the plight of the Kosovar Albanians. From this time on, the non-violent policy of Rugova was seen as ineffective, and armed resistance among Albanians slowly grew. Still the Kosovar Liberation Organization (KLO: later, KLA for Kosovo Liberation Army) did not gain popular support until the killing by Serb forces of fifty-one members of the Albanian Jashari family in Drenicë in the winter of 1998. Throughout 1998 Serbian paramilitary groups operated along with Serbian police and the Yugoslav military to counter the KLA. The result was terrorizing of the populace, largely Albanian but also Serbian, and the destruction of Albanian homes, villages, and food sources. By September of 1998 there were 300,000 internal refugees in Kosova. The October ceasefire and agreed-upon Serb troop withdrawals were not carried out. Rather, there was a massive build-up of Serbian police and military in Kosova, particularly during the time of the "peace" negotiations in Rambouillet in France in early 1999. In the spring, Milošević implemented "Operation Horseshoe" to expel large numbers of Albanians from Kosova. NATO bombing of Serbia began on March 24, 1999. It lasted for eleven weeks during which time the Serbian police, paramilitary, and military forcibly expelled over 850,000 Albanians from Kosova, burned five hundred Albanian villages, and killed an estimated 12,000 Albanians. During this time Milošević was indicted by the International Criminal Tribunal in the Hague.

On June 10, 1999, NATO bombing stopped and a Military-Technical Treaty was signed. The United Nations supported the peace plan and Serbian forces withdrew by June 20, with the simultaneous entry of NATO troops. At this time many Serbs left, while Kosovar Albanian refugees began returning. By the end of July over 700,000 Albanians had returned. Under UN auspices, the civic institutions are gradually being rebuilt. In the fall of 1999 schools and the University of Prishtina opened for Albanian students for the first time in eight years.

STATE OF PUBLISHING SINCE 1990

During the 1990s publishing in Albanian in Kosova was severely disrupted. In 1990 the Serbian police forcibly removed editors and directors of *Rilindja*, the main Albanian language newspaper in Kosova since 1945. This newspaper was just one of the publications of the major Albanian publishing house in Kosova, also known as Rilindja. The publishing house was closed by Serbian police in 1993, and its offices given over to the Serb publisher Panorama. Closure of the publishing house also entailed closure of numerous bookstores and over five hundred kiosks throughout Kosova. Staff of the publishing house, under editor Nazmi Rrahmani, rented a private house and continued to publish despite many hardships. Some of Rilindja's publications were subsequently brought out in Slovenia and Croatia, and for a while in Switzerland, too. After the closure of the newspaper *Rilindja*, members of its staff went to the agricultural periodical, *Bujku*, and turned it into a daily. Smaller Albanian presses in Prishtina also published sporadically until 1996. Outside Prishtina, a press in Pejë (Peć) published until 1997. In December 1998 the Serbian publisher Panorama refused to print *Bujku* and it closed. In March 1999 large fines were imposed on Kosovar editors and copies of their papers were confiscated. During the first week of fighting, the offices of independent newspaper *Koha Ditore* were destroyed and its watchman killed. However, its editor brought out several editions from Tetovo in Macedonia, and the paper resumed publication in Prishtina after the fighting stopped. The newspaper *Rilindja* resumed publishing in July 1999.

The press in Pejë, known as Dukagjini, also resumed publication in the summer of 1999. As for market conditions, with eighty-five percent unemployment among Albanians in much of the 1990s in Kosova, there was not much discretionary income. On top of this, book prices, which previously had been relatively low, skyrocketed. However, funds came in from the Albanian diaspora, and writers have continued to be productive. Writings by Kosovar Albanians are well respected throughout Albanian speaking regions (Albania, western Macedonia, southern Montenegro) and in the Albanian diaspora (Turkey, Germany, Switzerland, Canada, United States). Albanian books and newspapers are highly prized, particularly among refugees and in the diaspora. Many Albanian books were destroyed by Serbian police in 1998 and 1999, and text books are in short supply. Thus there is an urgent need for publishers to return to full production.

CENSORSHIP AND SELF-CENSORSHIP

Censorship in its baldest forms was practiced by Serb authorities. Publication of any news unfavorable to the Serbian regime was seen as criminal behavior. For example, journalists who covered the demonstrations in support of the Kosovar Albanian miners' strike in February 1998 were arrested. News stories in newspapers were the most strictly censored; however, commentaries were less closely scrutinized. Another gross form of censorship took place in the mid-1990s and involved the confiscation of books of the Albanian-language publisher Rilindja, and the pulping of these books and other Albanian books from the National Library at a paper mill in Lipjan south of Prishtina.

Throughout the 1990s newspaper reporters were routinely picked up by police and beaten. Presses were closed down. At first the equipment was transferred to Serbian presses; later, equipment was simply destroyed. The Public Information Law, passed in Belgrade in November 1998, gave a legal basis for more censorship, and even Serbian-language media were strictly controlled. In response, some Albanians refused to criticize their own people, including Rugova or the KLA. However, the independence of most Albanian media allowed for such criticisms. That independence is well documented by the Prishtina newspaper, *Koha Ditore*, which was one of the first to question the efficacy of Rugova's policy of nonviolence and later the wisdom of some KLA actions and decisions. Its editor has continued to take positions of conscience challenging those who supported revenge against the Serbs.

In August of 1999 the Organization for Security and Cooperation in Europe proposed a limited regulatory commission to ensure that Kosovar media, principally radio and television, did not become tools of partisan propaganda, thus avoiding the potential incitement to ethnic violence that was characteristic of Milošević's regime throughout most of the 1990s.

OVERVIEW OF MAJOR PUBLISHERS IN KOSOVA

Rilindja. The primary publisher for Albanian books, newspapers, and periodicals in Kosova has long been Rilindja. It was created by an act of the Kosovo Parliament. Its offices have long been located in a sixteen story building in Prishtina, and in the late 1980s it had over 500 employees and produced over 40 newspapers and periodicals. Its main newspaper, *Rilindja*, began publishing in 1945, and published continuously, largely on a daily basis, until its forced closure in 1990. It also published the weekly *Zëri*, as well as many books. In 1993 it was taken over by the Serb publisher Panorama. After the fighting, some Albanian staff returned and brought out the newspaper *Rilindja* in the summer of 1999.

Dukagjini. Despite its relative newness, Dukagjini has become one of the most serious and respected publishing houses of the Albanian language in Kosova. Formally known as Ndërmarrjes Botuese Grafike Librare "Dukagjini" nga Peja (Publishing Graphic House "Dukagjini" from Peć), Dukagjini was founded in 1987 in Pejë, a city in western Kosovo, by University of Prishtina Professor of Philosophy and Sociology, Gani Bobi. The vision of its founder and the expertise of its current staff, including publisher Agim Lluka, the editor-in-chief Eqrem Basha, and its other editors, are credited with its ongoing quality. It has two main sections. One is known as *Fryma* ("spirit") for philosophical, sociological, and cultural works that portray and reflect the spirit of this transitional period. This section includes as well translations of late-twentieth-century seminal books (Eco, Kuhn, Lyotard, Lefort, Morin) into Albanian. The other section is known as *Rozafet* for contemporary fiction, poetry and drama by Albanian authors, as well as translations of world literature. Dukagjini has also brought out Botime të Veçanta ("Special publications"), including monographs on authors, educational texts and children's books. It closed in late 1998 as the political situation became untenable. By May of 1999 most of the Albanians of Pejë and its surroundings were expelled or killed. In 1999, however, Dukagjini resumed publishing under Agim Lluka.

Gjon Buzuku. Along with Rilindja and Dukagjini, Gjon Buzuku is the third-best-known publisher in Kosova. It was founded in 1990 as one of the first private publishing houses. It has focused largely on works of literature by Albanian authors as well as writings of Albanian dissidents.

Instituti Albanologjik (The Institute for Albanology). The Institute for Albanology published two series of *Gjurmime Albanologjike* (Albanian Research), one for historical research, another for folklore and ethnology. It began publishing in 1971, but by 1989, due to Serbian pressure, it had stopped its regular journals. The Institute also published scholarly books. Despite the political hardships of the 1990s for Albanian scholars, the Institute managed to publish a remarkable number of works during the past decade. It was closed forcibly in 1996, its building was taken over, and its facilities pillaged. In the summer of 1999 it reopened.

Enti i Tekseve dhe i Mjetere mesimore i Kosovës (Office of Textbooks). Enti i tekseve published school texts and materials for all levels of Albanian education in Kosova. In general the quality of high school texts, particularly in literature, has been high. It also published important monographs for Kosova.

Instituti i historisë (The Historical Institute) and Galleria e arteve (The Gallery of Art) were also State-sponsored publishers that published in history and art, respectively.

Drita (The Light). Located in the city of Ferizaj (Uroševac), Drita published Roman Catholic missals and Bibles in Albanian. It also published a handsome photograph- and commentary-filled book on the life of Mother Teresa, *Lule për nënën*, in 1985. Not only was Mother Teresa Albanian, but both her parents were from Prizren, making her a Kosovar. It is not known if Drita has reopened since the fighting of 1999.

ÉMIGRÉ PUBLISHING

It is mostly Albanians from Albania, forced to leave their country because of the regime of Enver Hoxha, who engaged in significant émigré publishing. They have published from Italy (Rome, Milan, Trieste), France (Paris), various cities in Germany, and the United States (New York, Boston, and Harper Woods, Michigan). Beginning in the 1980s their newspapers and periodicals included news of Kosova and interviews with Kosovar intellectuals. (See below for émigré newspapers and periodicals.)

Émigré publishing by Kosovar Albanians has been more limited and recent. Kosovar Albanians did not emigrate westward in significant numbers until the 1980s. They have published from countries that were republics in former Yugoslavia, especially Zagreb in Croatia, Skopje in Macedonia, as well as from Tirana in Albania. In the rest of Europe their main publication center was Zurich, Switzerland. In America it has been New York.

One example of an émigré publisher in New York that has come out with books most relevant to Kosova is Gjonlekaj. In 1989 it published *Kanuni i Lekë Dukagjinit = The Code of Lekë Dukagjinit*, translated into English by linguist Leonard Fox. The *Kanun* is a compilation of centuries-old customary law that long regulated life among the northern Albanian clans in Albania, Montenegro, and Kosova. It is published in Albanian and English and is a work of considerable scholarship as well as aesthetic appeal. Another recent publication of Gjonlekaj is *Skekulli 21: Mendime dhe Opinione* (Century 21: Thoughts and Opinions), published in 1996. It is a collection of studies edited by Naum Prifti and Dino Asanaj, including contributions by the Albanian intellectual elite from all communities (Kadare, Qosja, Liolin, Ajeti, and Demiraj, among others).

Among the main émigré newspapers with special focus on Kosova is *Zëri i Kosovës*, a weekly political and informative newspaper published in Switzerland in Albanian with information in English and German. It was formerly a monthly periodical of the movement for the Kosova Republic of Yugoslavia.

Zëri i Kosovës
Buchhandlung, Badhausstr. 35
2502 Biel-Bienne, Switzerland
http://www.zik.com/

Another important émigré newspaper with much coverage of Kosova is *Illyria*. It has become the main Albanian-American newspaper, with approximately twenty-one pages per issue. It is published twice weekly in Albanian and in English. It was founded by Hajdar Bajraktari in the Bronx in 1991; its current editor is Ekrem Bardha.

Illyria
2321 Hughes Avenue
Bronx, New York 10458-8120
IllyriaNWS@aol.com

NOTABLE CURRENT PUBLICATIONS (SERIALS)

National Bibliography

Political conditions have not favored the development of an official bibliography for Albanian Kosovar writings and media. The closest approximation to such a bibliography is the bibliography at the end of Robert Elsie's *Kosovo: In the Heart of the Powder Keg.*[1]

Main Newspapers and News Magazines

Rilindja (Rebirth or Renaissance). The oldest Kosovar Albanian daily newspaper, *Rilindja* was published in Prishtina from 1945 until it was closed by Serb authorities in 1990. In the mid-1990s until 1998 it was published in Zurich, Switzerland. In July 1999 it resumed publication in Prishtina under editor Berat Luzha, a former political prisoner who headed Kosovapress (founded by the Kosova Liberation Army) through the spring of 1999 during the NATO air strikes. Rilindja has long included not just news, but also essays on Albanian history and interviews with prominent Albanian intellectuals. E-mail: rilindja@ swix.ch. Web: http://www.rilindja.com/page-main.html

Koha Ditore (Daily Times). Today this newspaper has the largest circulation of any newspaper in Kosova and is well known for its political courage. It was first founded as a weekly in 1990 and became a daily in 1997. By the mid-1990s it had become the main independent Kosovar Albanian newspaper. It was founded by Veton Surroi, a signatory of the Rambouillet Agreement, who remained in hiding in

Prishtina throughout the spring fighting. *Koha Ditore* was closed by the Serb government in March 1999. One of its editors, Baton Haxhiu, escaped along with other staff to Tetovo, Macedonia, where they began printing again in April 1999. *Koha Ditore* has since returned to publishing in Prishtina where its editor-in-chief, Veton Surroi, is a member of the Kosova Transitional Council. It has also been published on the Internet, though it stopped updating its Web site after August 15, 1999.

Kosova Sot (Kosova Today). A daily newspaper, it was founded by Ruzhdi Kadriu, a longtime executive of Rilindja. It began publishing in September 1998 and quickly grew. It was heavily fined in March 1999 and had its bank account blocked by Serb authorities. It continued printing until its papers were all confiscated by the Serb police on March 17, 1999. In the early days of the NATO air strikes, its premises were destroyed by Serb forces. It has since resumed publication. Contact person: Margarita Kadriu, editor. E-mail: inpres@eunet.yu

Zëri (The Voice). This publication was scheduled to become a daily newspaper in November 1999. See below for its history as a periodical.

Periodicals

Current Events and History, Religion and Social Conditions

Koha (The Times) was the most prominent independent political weekly in Kosova, published from September 1990 until 1991. It opened again in 1994, printed by a private publisher in Pejë. It was critical of the Serbian regime, as well as Albanian political parties, and was distributed both in Kosova and in the Albanian diaspora. Its digest in English was distributed in Western Europe. Its founder, Veton Surroi, was also the founding editor of the newspaper. *Koha Ditore*, where he remains on the editorial board.

Zëri (The Voice). An independent weekly magazine of Kosova, *Zëri* was originally published in 1945 as an official publication of the League of Socialist Youth of Kosovo and Metohija. It was transformed into a political weekly in 1990 and was closed in 1992. It opened again in 1993 and was largely independent, although it tended to support Rugova and his party (the LDK, or Democratic League of Kosova). Its editor-in-chief, Blerim Shala, is well respected in Kosova. Like Surroi, Shala was a signatory of the Rambouillet Agreement and is a member of the Kosova Transitional Council. *Zëri* was scheduled to become a daily newspaper in November, 1999. Available at http//www.dds.nl/~pressnow/zeri/

Gazete Shqiptare, a biweekly, published by the same board as *Kosova Sot*, the newspaper. Its editor is Bajrus Morina. Other biweeklies include *Kombi* (The Nation) and *Fjala Jonë* (Our Words).

History (Single Focus)

Gjurmime Albanologjike: Seria Historike (published 1971-1989).

Belles Lettres; Literary Criticism

Jeta e re (New Life), the leading literary journal, was founded in 1949. Many major Kosovar Albanian writers were first published in its pages.

Revista MM. A mixed quarterly review for theory and literature, published quarterly by MM Society and Dukagjini Publishing House. Web: http://www.albaniana.com/Dukagjini/mm.html

Fjala (The Word) is also a literary review.

Other

Kosovarja is a weekly magazine for women, which features articles relating to women's health, education, home crafts and special interests, as well as interviews with prominent Kosovar women. Its editor was sentenced to sixty days in prison in the mid-1990s for calling for an end to police terror.

Shkendja is a periodical for educational issues. It, too, managed to keep publishing well into the 1990s.

Diturija Islame (Islamic Knowledge) is a monthly Islamic journal.

Books

Publishing in Albanian in Kosovo came relatively late for political reasons. It is only since the 1960s that there have been significant numbers of books. An interesting feature of this publishing is the important place of poetry. In Albanian culture in general poetry is highly valued. Indeed, forty percent of publications in Albania are poetry. In Kosovo before the early 1990s seventy percent were poetry.[2]

The following are the major writers of twentieth century Kosova, with an emphasis on their most recent work or the work for which they are especially well known. They are presented here by publisher. Especially well-regarded books and authors are starred.

Rilindja, the Main Publishing House for Works in Albanian in Kosova Since World War II

Social Science, Literary Theory, Folklore, Linguistics

- Cetta, Anton.
  - *Nga folklori ynë* (From our folklore). Prishtinë, 1983.
  - *Balada dhe legjenda* (Ballads and legends). Prishtinë, 1974.*
- Demaci, Adem.
  - *Libër për vet mohimin* (A Book on Self Denial). 1994.
  - *Gjarpinjt e gjakut* (The Serpents of Blood). ca. 1955.*
    Demaci spent twenty-seven years in Serbian jails, and was awarded the Sakharov Prize for Peace in 1991.
- Berisha, Anton.
  - *Antologji e përrallës shqipe* (Anthology of Albanian tales). Prishtinë, 1982.
- Bobi, Gani.*
  - *Sprovimet e modernitetit* (Challenges of Modernity). 1982.*
- Ismajli, Rexhep.*
  - *Gramatika e parë e gjuhës shqipe* (The First Grammar of the Albanian Language). Prishtinë, 1983.
- Qosja, Rexhep.*
  - *Historia e letërsisë shqipe* (The History of Albanian Literature). 2 vols. Prishtinë, 1984.*
  - *Kritika letrare* (Literary Criticism). Prishtinë, 1969.
- Rugova, Ibrahim.
  - *Pavarësia dhe demokracia, intervista dhe artikuj* (Independence and Democracy: Interviews and Articles). Prishtinë: Fjala, 1991.*
  - *Strategjia e kuptimit* (The Strategy of Meaning). Prishtinë, 1980.
  - *Kah teoria* (Towards Theory). Prishtinë, 1978.

Poetry, Short Story, Novel, Drama

- Gajtani, Adem.
  - *Ti kangë, ti zog i largët* (Thou Song, Thou Distant Bird). Prishtinë, 1974.
- Hamiti, Sabri.
  - *ABC*. Prishtinë, 199?
  - *Trungu ilin* (Illyrian Heritage). Prishtinë, 1983.*
  - *Një kind vjet vetmi* (A Hundred Years of Solitude). Prishtinë, 1976.
- Gunga, Fahredin.
  - *Gramatika e gjëllimit* (The Grammar of Living). Prishtinë, 199?
- Kelmendi, Ramiz.
  - *Shtegtimet e mia* (My Wanderings). Prishtinë, 1982.
  - *Letra prej Ulcini* (Letters from Ulcinj). Prishtinë, 1966.*
- Mehmeti, Din.
  - *Fatin tim nuk e nënshkruaj* (I Do Not Seal My Fate). Prishtinë, 1984.*
- Mekulli, Esad.
  - *Për ty* (For You). Prishtinë, 1955.
- Podrimja, Ali.*
  - *Ishulli albania* (Island Albania). 1998.*
  - *Drejtpeshimi* (Balance). Prishtinë, 1981.*
  - *Hija e tokës* (The Shadow of the Land). Prishtinë, 1971.*
- Shkrelli, Azem.*
  - *Zogj dhe gurë* (Birds and Stones). Prishtinë, 199?*
  - *Varri i qypes* (The Cuckoo's Grave). Prishtinë, 1983.
  - Lotët e maleve (Tears of the Mountain). Prishtinë, 1974.*
- Shkrelli, Ymer.
  - *Pikëpjekja* (The Meeting). Prishtinë, 1982.
  - *Poezia të zgjedhura* (Selected Poetry). Prishtinë, 1983.
- Vinca, Agim.
  - *Populli i pandalur* (Unrestrained People). Prishtinë: Zëri i Rinisë, 1992.*
  - *Kohë e keqe për lirikë* (Bad Times for Lyrics). Prishtinë, 1997.*

Dukagjini, the Recent High-Quality Publisher From Pejë.

Social Science, Literary Theory, Linguistics, "Fryma" Series

- Agani, Fehmi.*

- *Demokracia, kombi, vetëvendosja* (Democracy, Nation, Self-Determination). Pejë, 1994.*
- Berishaj, Anton Kolë.
  - *Ndërrimi i etnive/Familja malësore ndërmjet vendlindjes: Pluralizimit kulturor dhe melting-potit amerikan* (Change of Ethnicities/ Highlander Family Between Birthplace(s?): Cultural Pluralism and American Melting Pot). Pejë, 1998.
- Bobi, Gani.
  - *Konteksti i vetëkulturës* (The Context of Self-Culture). Pejë, 1994.*
    Note: The works of Gani Bobi (5 vols.) are also listed under Special Editions.
- Islami, Hivzi.
  - *Rrjedha demografike shqiptare* (Albanian Demographic Trends). Pejë, 1994.*
- Ismajli, Rexhep.
  - *"Në gjuhë" dhe "për gjuhë": Rrjedhat e planifikimit të shqipes në Kosovë,* 1945-1968 ("In the Language" and "For the Language": Trends of the Planning of the Albanian Language in Kosova, 1945-1968). Pejë, 1998.
  - *Etni e modernitet* (Ethnicity and Modernity). Pejë, 1994.*
- Kullashi, Muhamedin.
  - *Ese filozofiko-politike* (Philosophical and Political Essays). Pejë, 1994.*
- Maliqi, Shkelzen.
  - *Estetika e arealit bizantin 1* (Esthetics of the Byzantine Area 1). Pejë, 1998.*
  - *Shqiptarët dhe Evropa* (Albanians and Europe). Pejë, 1994.*
- Qosja, Rexhep.
  - *Ceshtja shqiptare: Historia dhe politika* (The Albanian National Question: History and Politics). Pejë, 1994.
- Rexhepagiqi, Jashar.
  - *Sektat dhe teqetë në Kosovë, në Sanxhak dhe në rajonet e tjera përreth në të kaluarën dhe sot* (Dervishes, Sects and Tekkes in Kosova, in the Sandjak and in Other Surrounding Regions of the Past and Today). Pejë, 1998.
- Shala, Blerim.
  - *Strehimore letre* (The Paper Shelter). Pejë, 1995.*

- Shukriu, Edi.
- *Dardania paraurbane: Studime arkeologjike të Kosovës* (Pre-Urban Dardania: Archaeological Studies of Kosova). Pejë, 1996. This book was awarded the Gani Bobi Prize for the best scientific and humanitarian book published in any Albanian-speaking land in 1996.

Poetry, Short Story, Novel, Drama, "Rozafa" Series

- Basha, Eqrem.
- *Marshi i kërmillit* (The March of the Snail). Pejë, 1994.*
  This book was awarded a prize for best prose book of the year by Kosovar Writers' Association. Basha was born in Macedonia, but spent his working life in Kosova until he was expelled.*
- Demolli, Arif.
- *Shkulësit e përjetshëm* (Eternal Snatchers). Pejë, 1997.
- Hamiti, Sabri.
- *Letra shqipe: Sprova për një poetikë 5* (Albanian Letters: Temptation for Poetics 5). Pejë, 1996.*
- Podrimja, Ali.
- *Buzëqeshje në kafaz* (Smile in the Cage). Pejë, 1994.*
- Ramadani, Musa.
- *Vrapuesja e Prizrenit* (The Racer of Prizren). Pejë, 1995.*

Gjon Buzuku, One of the First Private Publishers in Kosova

Novels, Plays, Novellas and Short Stories, Translations

- Berisha, Ibrahim.
- *Origjina e rinjohjes.* Prishtinë, 1997.
- Camaj, Martin.
- *Djella.* Prishtinë, 1994.
- *Pishtarët e natës.* Prishtinë, 1991.
- Dërvishi, Teki.
- *Zhvarrimi i Pjetër Bogdanit.* Prishtinë, 1990.*
- Elsie, Robert.
- *Një fund dhe një fillim: Vëzhgime mbi letërsine dhe kulturën shqiptare.* Translated by Abdyrrahim Myftiu. Prishtinë, 1995.
- Kaçinari, Gjergj.
- *Margaritarët e këngëve të vjetra popullore* (Pearls of Old Traditional Songs). Prishtinë, 1995.*

- Krahja, Mehmet.
  - *Portat e qiellit.* Prishtinë, 1997.
- Ramadani, Musa.
  - *Antiprocesioni.* Prishtinë, 1997.

Instituti Albanologjik (Institute for Albanology)

Albanology Series

- *Gjurmimi Albanologjike* 20-25 (1990-1995).
  - Seria e shkencave filologjike.
  - Seria e shkencave historike.
  - Folklore dhe etnologji.
- *Gjuha shqipe* 1 (1990, 1997, 1998).

Special Publications

- Doçi, Rexhep.
  - *Antroponomia e shqiptarëve të Kosovë,* 1. Prishtinë, 1990.*
- Murati, Qemal.
  - *Elementet e shqipes në gjuhët sllave jugore* (Elements of Albanian Language in Southern Slavic Languages). Prishtinë, 1990.
- Sedaj, Engjëll.
  - *Etnonimi arbë-shqiptar: kontributi për autoktoninë e shqiptarëve,* (Arberesh-Albanian Ethnonym: Contribution for the Autochthony of the Albanians). Prishtinë, 1996.
  - *Tridhjetë vjet të Institutit Albanologjik,* 1967-1997 (Thirty Years of the Institute of Albanology, 1967-1997). Prishtinë, 1997.

Folklore

- Cetta, Anton et al.
  - *Kënë Kreshnike III.* Prishtinë, 1993.
- Cetta, Anton.
  - *Nga folklori ynë* 3 (From Our Folkore). Prishtinë, 1995.
  - *Pleqni dhe tregimi etnografike* (Old Age and Ethnographic Narratives). Prishtinë, 199?.*

- Fetiu, Sefedin.
  - *Alternative e kuptimit.* Prishtinë.
- Kabashi, Emin.
  - *Kadare-mendësia shqiptare.* Prishtinë, 1997.*
  - *Lasgush Poradeci-jeta dhe vepra.* Prishtinë, 1997.
  - *Poetikë e poemave të Jeronim de Radës.* Prishtinë, 1994.
- Krasniqi, Bajram.
  - *Intelegjenica, letërsia dhe realiteti.* Prishtinë, 1996.*
- Qosja, Rexhep.
  - *Ligjërata paravajtëse.* Prishtinë, 1996.
  - *Cështja shqiptare-historia dhe politika.* Prishtinë, 1994.*

Ethnology

- Hadri, Flamur.
  - *Gjergj Kastriot Skënderbeu.* Prishtinë, 1995.
- Pirraku, Muhamet.
  - *Kalvari i shqiptarisë së Kosovës-Tivari 1945.* Prishtinë, 1993.
- Ternava, Muhamet.
  - *Popullsia e Kosovës gjatë shekujve XIV-XVI.* Prishtinë, 1995.*
- Uka, Sabit.
  - *Vendosja dhe pozita e shqiptarëve në Kosovë 1878-1912.* Prishtinë, 1994.*

Enti i Teksteve

A current list of monographs is not available, apart from the following work:

- Goçi, Rexhep.
  - *Gjerqj Kastrioti-Skenderbeu në antet figurative.* (George Kastrioti-Skenderbeg in Figurative Art). Prishtinë, 1998.*

  Skenderbeg is the Albanian national hero.

Galeria e Arteve

- *Arti bashkohor i Kosovës* (Contemporary Art of Kosova). Prishtinë, 1998.*

Kosova Information Center (Prishtina)

This was the official publisher of the LDK, the Democratic League of Kosova, led by Ibrahim Rugova. It published books on the current situation in Kosova and the historical background of the crisis.

Web/Internet

- http://www.albanian.com/ (Note: it is "albanian," not "albania" so as to encompass Albanians who live in different countries): a general information site on Albanians, their history and culture in Albania, Kosova, Macedonia and Montenegro.
- http://www.alb-net.com/: an important site for Albanian media on the Internet, it includes parallel Albanian and English sites, with a comprehensive section on world international sites, including the BBC, CNN, Radio Free Europe, but also Deutsche Welle in German and some Italian media.
- http://www.kosovacrisiscenter.com/: an important site during the fighting in 1999, it includes monthly archives beginning in December 1998 and continuing through June 1999, of events involving Kosovar Albanians and Serb military and police, with updates several times per month through October 1999. It is principally directed to Kosovar Albanians and offers ways for people to find their missing relatives.
- http://www.come.to/albatrosi/: this site is meant to appeal to young Albanians around the world, with information for students about culture and music and e-mail listings and Web sites of Albanian students worldwide. It is sponsored by Albanian students in Hannover, Germany and includes their student publication *Bashkimi*.
- bota-letrare@eGroups.com: an e-mail listserv for discussion of literary works in Albanian.

PRESERVATION CONCERNS
AND LEADING RESEARCH COLLECTIONS

The main preservation concern in the 1990s has been the lives and well-being of Albanian Kosovar writers and journalists. Intellectuals were especially targeted by the Serb authorities (Fehmi Agani was killed in May 1999, and Adem Demaci spent twenty-eight years in Serbian jails). There is a strong tradition of intellectuals being respected by the society at large and of their taking active leadership roles in the society. Rugova, Demaci and Qosja are examples of intellectuals who are also writers/professors and who are politically active and still alive.

There has also been major concern with preservation of Albanian books. It is estimated that 100,000 Albanian books from the National and University Library were taken to paper mills by Serbian authorities and destroyed in the 1990s. Other libraries and historical museums lost their materials to Serbian authorities during the decade. In particular, the documents at the Museum of the League of Prizren were taken away by Serbian authorities, as were the State Archives.

At the National and University Library the newly reinstated head librarian, Mehmet Gerguri, is concerned with the condition of the remaining volumes. The Yugoslav Army used the library as its headquarters during the time of bombing in 1999. Even before that, beginning in 1995, the library was used to house Serbian colonists from Croatia. The Library will need major assistance to rebuild its collections and try to preserve what survived.

Some Major Libraries with Significant Albanian Collections

British Library. The Albanian holdings do not have a separate catalog, but there are about 1,200 titles in Albanian in the current online catalog, which covers items acquired since 1975. The holdings of early Albanian literature include seventeenth-century works in Latin (Barletius' history of Scanderbeg) and other seventeenth-century works (Budi's Christian Doctrine, an early dictionary from 1635, many works by Blanchus and Bogdani). From the nineteenth century there are works by DeRada and Frashëri. From the years of Hoxha, there is a good collection of Albanian Socialist Realist literature. In the 1990s there is a focus on materials on political developments during the time of transition. Contact: Magda Szkuta, e-mail: magda.szkut@ mail.bl.uk.

U.S. Library of Congress. One of the largest collections of materials on Albania and Albanians in North America is found at the Library of Congress. A subject search on Albania, of materials published from 1975 to 1999, yielded 1,889 titles. (Information related to Kosovo is much more likely to be found in publications after 1960.) The collection of belles lettres, both in the vernacular and in translation, consists of about 775 volumes. The Library of Congress has a total of 315 titles focusing specifically on Kosovo. Of these, 299 were published from 1975 to 1999, and 59 are in the Albanian language. Contact: Grant Harris, e-mail: grha@ loc.gov.

Bayerische Staatsbibliothek in Munich. Since 1950 the Bavarian State Library has maintained albanica materials within the specialized field of Eastern Europe for the German Research Council. This means that the Library purchases relevant scholarly writings, as extensively as possible, especially in the fields of history, including economic and social history; politics; sociology; cultural geography and area studies. Until 1997 this national collection contained as well the fields of language, literature and ethnology. (Now the Thuringian University and Regional Library of Jena are responsible for these latter fields.) The albanica collection, which includes approximately 3,500 titles, can be found through the general catalog of the Bavarian State Library. The largest part of these materials, mainly literature published before 1840, and from 1953 to today, can be accessed through the Internet (http://www.bsb.badw-muenchen.de). The older works are not numerous due to the burning of historical and ethnographic albanica during the Second World War. Among these were works of Delavardi, Funccius, and a part of the sixteenth-century edition of Barletius. Among the writings of the post-war period, historical literature as well as belles lettres are well represented. These include not just the works of contemporary writers like Spasse, Jakova, Gjata, Xoxa, and Kadare, or the immigrant Camaj, who lived in Munich. Rather, there are also reprinted works of the older authors like Budi and Bogdani. Political writings dominate the literature of the 1990s. Contact: Hannelore Gonschior, e-mail: gonschior@bsb.bade-muenchen.de.

Columbia University. One of three libraries in the United States with an independent press collection from Eastern Europe at the time of the collapse of communism, Columbia University's Butler Library also has a general collection of books on Albanians and in Albanian. Since 1981 it has acquired 223 works in the Albanian language. Contact: Jared Ingersoll, Russian and East European Studies Librarian; tel. 212-854-4701; e-mail: slavic@libraries.cul. columbia.edu

Modes of Acquisition

In general, requests for works should be addressed to the editor or director of the press.

1. Rilindja
Nazmi Rrahmani, Editor
[name of specific series]
Pallati i Shtypit
38000 Prishtinë, Kosova[3]
phone: + 381-38-28-547

Rilindja (newspaper)
Berat Luzha, Editor-in-Chief
Pallati i Shtypit
38000 Prishtinë, Kosova

Zëri
Blerim Shala, Editor-in-Chief
Pallati i Shtypit
38000 Prishtinë, Kosova
e-mail: blerimsh@Eunet.yu

2. Shtëpia Botuese Dukagjini
Agim Lluka, Director/Publisher
P.O. Box 147
39000 Pejë, Kosova
http://www.albanian.com/dukagjini
fax: + 381-39-31-601
32-025
34-025
e-mail: dukagjini@albanian.com

Dukagjini
Eqrem Basha, Editor-in-Chief
Prishtinë, Kosova
phone/fax: + 381-38-48-634

3. Ndërmarrja Botuese Gjon Buzuku
Abdullah Zeneli, Publisher/Editor
(Hana Zeneli, President)
Rr. Taslixhe 1-42
Prishtinë, Kosova
phone/fax: + 381-38-53-08-73
e-mail: samik@kohaditore.com

Representative in Switzerland:

Enver Robelli
Buzuku Verlag
Postfach 22
J. Schweizerische Bankgesellschaft
Ch-8806 Bach, Switzerland
phone/fax: + 41-1-785-01-26
e-mail: robelli@bluewin.ch

4. Instituti Albanologjik
Director: Sadri Fetiu
38000 Prishtinë, Kosova

5. Gjonlekaj Publishing Company
118-21 Queens Boulevard
Suite 608
Forest Hills, New York 11375 USA

6. *Illyria*
2321 Hughes Avenue
Bronx, New York 10458-8120 USA
e-mail: illyriaNWS@aol.com

RECOMMENDED ACADEMIC WORKS ON KOSOVO IN ENGLISH

There are several scholars whose writings in English should be included in any collection on Kosova. Canadian Albanologist Robert Elsie is responsible for excellent works on broader Albanian studies, both fiction and non-fiction, including specialized bibliographical studies on Kosovar Albanian authors. Historian Noel Malcolm is also highly recommended.

Highly Recommended

Elsie, Robert, ed. *Kosovo: In the Heart of the Powder Keg*. East European Monographs, no. 478. Boulder: East European Monographs, 1997. Includes important twentieth century historical texts (Vasa Čubrilović, Edith Durham, Leo Freundlich, Ivo Andrić) commentaries on the political situation in Kosovo by Albanian writers (Ismail Kadare) and Kosovar Albanian leaders (Rexhep Qosja, Adem Demaci, Ibrahim Rugova, Nuhi Vinca), all well translated into English.

_____ . *Studies in Modern Albanian Literature and Culture*. East European Monographs, no. 455. Boulder: East European Monographs, 1996.

_____ . "Albanian literature in Kosovo." In *History of Albanian Literature*, vol. 2, 632-653. East European Monographs, no. 379. Boulder: East European Monographs, 1995.

Fox, Leonard, trans. *Kanuni i Lekë Dukagjinit = The Code of Lekë Dukagjinit*. New York: Gjonlekaj, 1989.

Human Rights Watch/Helsinki. *Week of Terror: Drenica in Humanitarian Law Violations in Kosovo*. New York: Human Rights Watch, 1999.

_____ . *Human Rights Abuses in Kosovo*. New York: Human Rights Watch, 1998.

_____ . *Human Rights Abuses in Kosovo*. New York: Human Rights Watch, 1993.

Malcolm, Noel. *Kosovo: A Short History*. New York: New York University Press, 1998. Revised ed., 1999.

Mead, Alice. *Adem's Cross*. New York: Bantam Doubleday of Dell, 1998.

Mertus, Julie. *Kosovo: How Myths and Truths Started a War*. Berkeley: University of California Press, 1999.

_____ . *Open Wounds: Human Rights Abuses in Kosova*. New York: Human Rights Watch, 1993.

Pipa, Arshi, and Sami Repishti. *Studies on Kosova*. East European Monographs, no. 155. New York: Columbia University Press, 1984.

Reineck, Janet. "The Past as Refuge: Gender, Migration and Ideology Among the Kosova Albanians." Ph.D. diss., University of California, Berkeley, 1991.

Skendi, Stavro. *Albanian National Awakening, 1878-1912*. Princeton: Princeton University Press, 1967.

Vickers, Miranda. *Between Albanian and Serb: A Study of Kosovo.* London: Hurst & Co., 1998.

Young, Antonia. *Albania.* Rev. ed. World Bibliographical Series, vol. 94. Santa Barbara, Cal.: Clio Press, 1997.

Recommended

Berisha, Ibrahim et al. *Serbian Colonization and Ethnic Cleansing in Kosova: Documents & Evidence.* Prishtina: Kosova Information Center, 1993.

Biberaj, Elez. *Kosova: The Balkan Powderkeg.* London: Research Institute for the Study of Conflict and Terrorism, 1993.

Campbell, Greg. *The Road to Kosovo: A Balkan Diary.* Boulder, Col.: Westview Press, 1999.

De Vries, Franklin, ed. *Kosovo: The Conflict Between the Serbs and the Albanians and the Role of the International Community.* Antwerp: IPIS, 1995.

Durham, Mary Edith. *High Albania.* 1909. Reprint. New York: Arno Press, 1971.

_____ . *Twenty Years of Balkan Tangle.* London: George Allen & Unwin, 1920.

Grothusen, Klaus-Detlev, ed. *Albanien.* Südosteuropa-Handbuch, 7. Göttingen: Vandenhoeck & Ruprecht, 1993.

Hall, Derek. *Albania and the Albanians.* New York: St. Martin's Press, 1994.

Kadare, Ismail. (Note: Kadare is the foremost Albanian writer, from Albania, but respected in Kosova.) Many of his books have been translated into English; recent ones include:

The File on H. New York: Arcade; distributed by Little, Brown and Co., 1998.

The Three-Arched Bridge. New York: Arcade; distributed by Little, Brown and Co., 1997.

Albanian Spring: The Anatomy of Tyranny. London: Saqi Books, 1995.

The General of the Dead Army. New York: New Amsterdam, 1991.

Broken April. New York: New Amsterdam Books, 1990.

Doruntine. New York: New Amsterdam Books, 1988.

Chronicle in Stone. New York: The Meredith Press, 1987.

Kekezi, Harillaq, and Rexhep Hida. *What the Kosovars Say and Demand: Collection of Studies, Articles, Interviews and Commentaries.* 2 vols. Tirana: 8 Nëndori Publishing House, 1990.
Ismail, Rexhep. *Kosova and the Albanians in Former Yugoslavia.* Prishtina: Kosova Information Center, 1992.

NOTES

1. Robert Elsie, *Kosovo: In the Heart of the Powder Keg* (Boulder: East European Monographs, distributed by Columbia University Press, 1997), 516-553 (for western European languages), 554-586 (for Balkan languages).

2. Robert Elsie, *History of Albanian Literature* (Boulder: East European Monographs, 1995), 2: 632-653.

3. Much as many of its citizens would like it to be otherwise, Kosova is still part of Serbia/Yugoslavia as of February 2000. Post offices may or may not deliver mail without *Serbia* and/or *Yugoslavia*. –Ed. (KR)

MACEDONIA

MAP 7. Macedonia

Source: *The Balkans*. Scale 1:2,500,000. Washington DC: Central Intelligence
Agency, 1993

Publishing in Macedonia

George Mitrevski

SUMMARY. After a brief history of Macedonia and the Macedonian language, the author discusses the general publishing scene from 1949 to 1998. He then lists important publishers, along with their contact information and profiles. The final part consists of a list of current serial publications (daily newspapers, news magazines and periodicals), with their publishers and a description of their contents. *[Article copies available for a fee from The Haworth Document Delivery Service: 1-800-342-9678. E-mail address: <getinfo@ haworthpressinc.com> Website: <http://www.HaworthPress.com> © 2000 by The Haworth Press, Inc. All rights reserved.]*

KEYWORDS. Macedonia, FYROM, publishers and publishing

Macedonia is the last country to be formed from the disintegration of the former Yugoslav republics (1991), and the Macedonian literary language, the youngest European literary language, is the last to be constituted (in 1944) from the group of Slavic languages. One would thus assume that publishing in Macedonia must have a very short history. In fact, the geographical region of Macedonia, which currently is divided among Greece, Bulgaria and the Republic of Macedonia, is the birthplace of the Cyrillic alphabet, which is the basis for the alphabets of most Slavic languages. This region is also the birthplace of the earliest writers of literature written in a Slavic language.

George Mitrevski, PhD, is Associate Professor of Russian Language and Literature, 6030 Haley Center, Auburn University, Auburn, AL 36849-5204 (E-mail: mitrege@auburn.edu).

[Haworth co-indexing entry note]: "Publishing in Macedonia." Mitrevski, George. Co-published simultaneously in *Slavic & East European Information Resources* (The Haworth Information Press, an imprint of The Haworth Press, Inc.) Vol. 1, No. 2/3, 2000, pp. 187-209; and: *Publishing in Yugoslavia's Successor States* (ed: Michael Biggins, and Janet Crayne) The Haworth Information Press, an imprint of The Haworth Press, Inc., 2000, pp. 187-209. Single or multiple copies of this article are available for a fee from The Haworth Document Delivery Service [1-800-342-9678, 9:00 a.m. - 5:00 p.m. (EST). E-mail address: getinfo@haworthpressinc.com].

After the split of the Slavic languages into the Eastern, Western and South Slavic groups, the dialect spoken in the region of Macedonia was closely related to that in Bulgaria, and for several centuries the two regions shared the same history and culture. The gradual development of the local Macedonian and Bulgarian dialects into standard literary languages was closely tied to the changing political situation in the region. During the first four centuries of Turkish occupation of the Balkans, written literature was restricted to production of books for use by the church. These were written in Church Slavonic, a language that was quite distinct from the local vernacular. The relatively late development of a standard literary language in this region is attributed to the lack of voluminous literature in the vernacular. This lack of a literary standard also allowed for the gradual differentiation between the eastern (Bulgarian) and western (Macedonian) dialects. By the beginning of the 19th century in Macedonia there is already limited production of written scholarly literature, and voluminous popular literature in the local western and central dialects. By the end of the 19th century the central and western Macedonian dialects differed from standard Bulgarian to such an extent that Bulgarian no longer served effectively as the language of daily communication. This period was also the beginning of the development of a distinct Macedonian national consciousness that was separate from the Bulgarian, as well as the formation of numerous revolutionary organizations that fought for establishing a separate Macedonian state that would encompass the entire region of Macedonia.

During most of the 19th century the extent of book publishing in Macedonia was closely tied to the needs of the local schools. The first schools were organized and administered by the church. Since the intent of these schools was to train students in copying and writing literature necessary for church services, the language of instruction was Church Slavonic. In the secular world, Turkish and Greek were the languages of business, politics and trade. With the spread of trade and industrialization outside of the larger cities, there was increased need for communication in the local dialects. We find many examples of agreements, notes and correspondences in the local dialects, though many of these were written in the Greek alphabet.

The first secular schools in Macedonia were organized in the middle of the 19th century. The first teachers were Serbian, the language of instruction was Serbian, using Serbian textbooks. In the sixties and seventies the Serbian ministry of foreign affairs established a special fund for printing textbooks for schools in Macedonia. The objective of this effort was to counter Bulgarian attempts to organize schools in Bulgarian with Bulgarian teachers and textbooks. Bulgaria began organizing schools, sending teachers and textbooks into Macedonia in the sixties. The Macedonian-Bulgarian Friendship Society in Salonika was responsible for sending financial assistance to schools throughout Macedonia.

Teodosie Sinaitski, the Macedonian owner of a printing press in Salonika, is considered to be the first Macedonian publisher. Among his first publications in a local Macedonian dialect were a prayer book and a short dictionary. The first primers written in a Macedonian dialect by Macedonian teachers appeared in the 1830s, and from 1857 to 1875 there were 15 primers published by Macedonians. Macedonian teachers, such as Partenija Zografski, Kuzman Shapkarev, Dimitar V. Makedonski and Gorgi Pulevski, who were educated mostly in Bulgarian and Greek schools, were among the first to write and publish primers and textbooks in Macedonian. Although many of these were quite short, some no longer than a dozen pages, they had a profound influence on the further development of a distinct Macedonian language and culture.

The educated class in Macedonia in the last century was quite small, and since education was almost exclusively in Bulgarian, Serbian and Greek schools, the demand for literature in Macedonian was also quite small. Some Macedonian intellectuals, including Partenija Zografski and Kuzman Shapkarev, proposed the idea of restructuring standard Bulgarian grammar to create a "general" Bulgarian language, which would include features of some central and western Macedonian dialects. This idea of a single common Bulgaro-Macedonian literary language was supported by a number of intellectuals of the period. Bulgarians did not accept this idea, but favored the use of Bulgarian as the standard language for Macedonia. Beginning in the 1870s there was immense competition among Bulgaria, Serbia, and Greece for schools and school teachers in Macedonia, accompanied by an equally intense effort to stamp out the Macedonian national consciousness through their schools. Meanwhile, the term "Macedonia," which originally referred to a geographical region, was used among Macedonian intellectuals to express the desire for a separate Macedonian nation and language. A new group of teachers and knowledgeable men, led by Gorgi Pulevski, gathered to discuss the possibility of codifying a separate Macedonian language, and to plan the writing of a new Macedonian grammar.

At the beginning of the twentieth century Macedonia's neighbors (Serbia, Bulgaria, Greece and Turkey) fought two wars (First and Second Balkan Wars) over Macedonia, at the end of which the region was divided into three entities: the eastern part went to Bulgaria, the southern part to Greece, and the western part to the Kingdom of Serbia (subsequently Yugoslavia). In the years between the two world wars each of these countries made a concerted effort to eliminate Macedonian cultural and linguistic differences, including schools in the Macedonian language. In Aegean Macedonia the Greek government published a primer to be used in schools for the Macedonian minority, but it was never put to use. Eventually a law was passed that made the speaking of Macedonian illegal, and publication in Macedonian during this period was understandably quite limited. In the years immediately before World War II several Macedonian writers had some of their poetry published in Macedonian by publishers in Sofia and in Zagreb. In Macedonia itself, the journal *Luch* (1937-38) and the underground paper of the Communist Party *Nasha rech* (1939-1941) also published some poetry and prose in Macedonian. In 1939 the newspaper *Juzhna stvarnost* was published in Skopje, but it had a very short life. Macedonian was also used in the literature of the Macedonian branch of the Yugoslav Communist Party, specifically in underground newspapers, resolutions, fliers and propaganda literature. The process of unifying the various Macedonian dialects into a standardized language was steady through the war years, particularly in Partisan war communications, pamphlets and newspapers. During the same period there was also concerted resistance to speaking Bulgarian, which was considered the language of the occupiers. Some Macedonian writers who had originally written literary works in Bulgarian or Serbian, began to translate them, out of a sense of patriotic duty, into their local Macedonian dialect.

Contemporary standard literary Macedonian used in the Republic of Macedonia was based on the central Macedonian dialects. Recognition of Macedonian as the language of the Macedonian state took place on August 2, 1944 during the first meeting of the first Macedonian government at the Prohor Pchinski monastery. The resolution simply states:

Resolution of the first session of ASNOM for the introduction of the Macedonian language as an official language in the Macedonian state.

Article 1

The national Macedonian language is introduced in the Macedonian state as the official language.

The government newspaper, *Nova Makedonija*, in number 104 for May 5, 6 and 7, 1945, published the order of the Macedonian government that declared Macedonian as the official language of the state. It listed the letters of the Macedonian alphabet (31) both in printed and script form.

The first phase in post-war Macedonian literature begins with the publication of *Nov den* (1949-1950), the first Macedonian literary magazine written in the modern Macedonian literary language. The magazine published poetry and prose, as well as articles on Macedonia's past literary history, particularly about 19th century Macedonian revivalists. Its other major contribution was in promoting the newly codified Macedonian literary language. *Idnina* (1945-1950), the second post-war literary magazine to be published in Macedonia, was edited by the younger generation of post-war Macedonian writers. Its aim was to "strengthen the socialist patriotism. . . to develop the image of the new socialist man." The fifties were a boom period in the publication of journals and newspapers in the field of literature. Between 1951 and 1956 the magazines *Sovremenost, Mlada literatura, Razgledi, Stremež, Literaturen zbor, Horizont,* and *Kulturen život* were established. *Sovremenost* came out in 1951 as a replacement for *Nov den. Mlada literatura* came out as an official publication of the Young Writers Club at Skopje University, and was edited by the second generation of Macedonian writers. The fifties were also the period when many government publishing houses were established. They were charged with publishing primers and textbooks in the new literary language. From the sixties through the mid-eighties the publishing industry relied exclusively on government subsidies, which were always forthcoming for the publication of works by writers whose ideology was acceptable to the government. As a result of the country's general economic decline in the mid-eighties, government subsidies to publishers began to decline rapidly in the mid-eighties as well. Publication runs rarely exceeded three thousand copies, and three hundred was often the norm for scholarly publications by research institutes. Translations of literary works from foreign languages also declined. In bookstores, books in Serbo-Croatian, especially translations of foreign literature, competed for shelf space against books in Macedonian. Serbo-Croatian was a required language for study in all schools in Macedonia, and it was a second language for most Macedonians. Macedonian publishers had no economic incentive to translate and publish books that were already available in Serbo-Croatian.

Since Macedonia's independence in 1991 the publishing industry has experienced a steady growth of new, private publishers who can compete with government publishers. One of the most active new, private publishers in the early 1990s was Templum. Its publishing program, book design, and its magazine, *Margina*, were all aimed at readers who favored alternative art and culture. In the mid-nineties Kultura was the most vital among all government publishers and the most distinguished in publishing books in the area of humanities. A steady decline in government subsidies, has resulted in the decline of new publications issued by government publishers. Government and private publishers now have to compete for a limited readership. Given the poor economic condition of the country, very few people can afford the luxury of buying a book. The price of a typical novel in the late nineties was equivalent to approximately the average wage for one day's work.

In the nineties, as under Titoist Yugoslavia, the Ministries of Culture, Education and Science were the main sources for funding book publishing, especially of scholarly books. The role of the Ministry of Culture has not lessened at all. The office of the Minister of Culture is one of the more powerful positions in the Macedonian government. The Minister makes appointments to all cultural organizations that receive financial support from the Ministry, and often subsidizes the publication of expensive, extravagant books as a reward for an author who supports the ruling political party. Such books have practically no readership, but they are purchased and distributed for free to libraries and government institutions. In 1998 the Ministry refused to provide a subsidy for *Stožer*, the magazine of the Macedonian Writers Union, because the majority of its members supported the opposition party. In 1999 the Minister also refused to provide a subsidy of $15,000 for a conference of European P.E.N. centers that was to be hosted by the

Macedonian P.E.N. According to published reports, the conflict between the Ministry and the Macedonian P.E.N. arose after a declaration by the P.E.N. center, calling upon all Macedonians to "defend the identity of the Macedonian people, language and literature from the representatives of our own government." P.E.N. members claimed that the current government, and specifically the Minister of Culture, was attempting to "Bulgarize" Macedonian language and culture. This same claim was also voiced by members of the Writers Union. This argument arose out of debates among Macedonian intellectuals regarding the historical development of Macedonian culture in relation to the cultures of its neighbors.

One steadily growing source for publishing subsidies in Macedonia is private industry. Many small, successful private companies underwrite the publication of one or several books each year. Another institution that has provided considerable support for publishing in the nineties is the Open Society Institute (OSI) in Macedonia, funded by Hungarian-American financier George Soros. In 1993 OSI began providing financial assistance to recently established small publishers by covering printing expenses. The grants are used primarily to cover part of the printing costs of the titles of both original Macedonian works and translations from foreign languages. The OSI Macedonia also supports publications in the language of ethnic minorities living in Macedonia, as well as books in Macedonian that reveal and represent the cultures and traditions of those minorities. It provides support for the publishing programs of local publishers, in particular those working on translations of important works in the area of philosophy and sociology. Several journals, including cultural journals, journals on social theory and criticism, and journals in the languages of the ethnic minorities were given permanent financial support, with grants to cover around thirty percent of their total costs. This kind of help is meant to enable them to be published regularly. In 1993 the total amount of support for publishing from OSI was around $100,000.

In the second half of the nineties OSI contributed to the effort of Macedonian publishers to present important works of world intellectual history in the Macedonian language. To promote inter-ethnic dialogue and communication, Albanian-Macedonian and Macedonian-Roma dictionaries were supported with grants to cover printing costs. The presentation of Macedonian publishing at the Frankfurt Book Fair was supported by covering the costs for printing a special book fair catalog. In 1997 one hundred publishers asked for support to publish four hundred titles, of which sixty were awarded partial subsidies; twenty of these were in the languages of the nationalities. Fifteen periodical magazines received support, four of them in the Albanian language. The magazine *Lettre Internationale*, founded by OSI in 1995, was given over for management to the publishing house Gurga. OSI, in cooperation with the Ministry of Education and the World Bank, initiated a project for writing and publishing new textbooks, to encourage the development of the textbook sector and to support educational reforms in the Republic of Macedonia. It provided a credit line of $120,000 for publishers, which was intended for issuing short-term working capital loans. It was targeted at small publishing companies that had at least two years' profitable working experience, and whose main activity was publishing. The Macedonian Business Resource Center provided cost-free training to publishing houses on the preparation of business plans. This program has continued through 1999, when the amount allocated to publishing and media was increased to approximately $300,000, and the maximum loan amount was limited to $10,000 with a one-year repayment period.

IMPORTANT PUBLISHERS

National and University Library (Bul. Goce Delčev 6, 91000 Skopje, tel.: 115-177). Prepares and publishes current and retrospective bibliographies of Macedonia, specialized bibliographies, printed catalogs of library holdings, union catalog of the Republic of Macedonia, handbooks for librarians.

Misirkov (29 Noemvri 12, 97000 Bitola, tel.: 222-951). Publishes titles in Macedonian and world literature. Specializes in books on the history of the Macedonian people and the history of literature and folklore.

Grigor Prličev (Bul. Sv. Kliment Ohridski 13/1-1, 91000 Skopje, tel.: 119-696). Publishes works by contemporary Macedonian writers, textbooks for secondary schools, books on literary theory, historiography and translations of foreign literature.

Menora (Bul. Jane Sandanski 35/4-13, 91000 Skopje, tel.: 128-370). Publishes books with scientific, scholarly and popular content. Also serves as printer of books, journals, catalogs for other publishing houses, museums, educational and scientific institutions.

Kinoteka (Goce Delčev bb., p.f. 161, Skopje, tel.: 228-064). Publishes the magazine *Kinopis*, and is the only publisher in Macedonia that publishes books in the field of history and theory of film.

Gurga (11 Oktomvri 2/6-2, 91000 Skopje, tel.: 228-076). Claims to be the first independent publishing house in Macedonia. Publishes several magazines, such as *World Press Izbor*, a biweekly of selected articles from the foreign press, and *Lettre Internationale*, the Macedonian edition of the international magazine of the same title. The publisher maintains a literary and art salon in Skopje, with a large bookstore and antique shop and a reading room with foreign newspapers. It publishes a series of books on fine arts from around the world.

Zumpres (Ul. Venjamin Mačukovski 6, P. fah 363, 91000 Skopje, tel.: 421-175). Publishes books in several significant series: Historia Macedonica, Universum, Litera Viva, Poetica Viva, Magica, Touch, Thalia, Light, Scientific Treasury, Foundations, Great Men. These collections include selected titles in the field of belle-lettres, philosophy, history and psychology. It established a competition for short novels, and the best novel is published under the designation "Novel of the Year of Zumpres."

Archives of Macedonia (Ul. Grigor Prličev 3, P. fah 496, 91000 Skopje, tel.: 116-571). Publishes scholarly books based on archival material preserved in the Archives of Macedonia, as well as materials in other Macedonian institutions and throughout the world that deal with the history of Macedonia. The most significant publications are based on Turkish, British, French, Austrian and other documents on the history of the Macedonian people. Recently it started publishing books on the diplomatic history of Macedonia.

Studentski zbor (Pirinska bb., baraka 5, P. fah 484, 91000 Skopje, tel.: 365-836). This is a publishing organization within the University of Skopje. It publishes the review *Studentski zbor* and the journal *Dijalog*, as well as textbooks and other learning aids for students at universities in Macedonia. It also prepares exhibitions, photo editions and other documentary materials. As of 1998 it had published over 750 titles.

Birlik (Mito Hadživasilev-Jasmin bb., 91000 Skopje, tel.: 111-146). This publisher is part of the Nova Makedonija publishing firm. It publishes titles in Turkish. Its primary activity is the publication of the newspaper *Birlik*. It also publishes the magazines for children, *Sevnik* and *Tomurcuk*, as well as the culture magazine *Sesler*, and books in the field of literature for all ages.

Flaka e Vellarezimit (Mito Hadživasilev-Jasmin bb., 91000 Skopje, tel.: 228-632). This publisher is part of the Nova Makedonija publishing house. It publishes belles lettres in Albanian by Albanian, Macedonian and world writers. It publishes books in several collections: Gezimi (children's literature), Valet (poetry for adults), Jehona (prose for adults), Flaka (criticism, aesthetics, science).

Matica Makedonska (Ul. Marshal Tito 43/1-6, 91000 Skopje, tel.: 232-435). This is one of the largest publishers in Macedonia, which publishes in the fields of Macedonian history, lexicography, science and fiction. It also publishes in conjunction with the Australian publisher AEA Publishers. Its mission is to promote awareness of Macedonian culture throughout the world. It publishes books and albums on Macedonia's cultural heritage. Genres and types of materials include anthologies, parallel editions (Macedonian-English), interpretations, selected works, arts and criticism, contemporary prose, dictionaries and practical language guides.

Krste Misirkov Macedonian Language Institute (Bul. Grigor Prličev 5, 91000 Skopje, tel.: 114-733). Publishes the scholarly journals *Makedonski jazik* and *Makedonistika*, special editions, medieval texts and dictionaries.

Makedonska kniga (11 Oktomvri bb., 91000 Skopje, tel.: 235-524). One of the oldest publishing houses in Macedonia. Its series include: Vine, Modern Macedonian Poetry, Jubilee editions, Special editions, Interpretations, Poetry selections, Translations, Monographs, The Past–The Present, Dictionaries.

Prosvetno Delo (Ul. Veljko Vlahovič 15, Gradski dzid, blok 4, 91000 Skopje, tel.: 117-255). Publishes mainly textbooks, handbooks and other learning aids for pre-school, elementary, secondary and university students. It claims to have published 7000 titles and 70 million copies during its fifty-year existence. Publishes textbooks in minority languages–Albanian, Turkish, Serbian, Romany, Vlakh–as well as translations of foreign-language works.

Misla (Bul. Partizanski odredi 1, 91000 Skopje, tel.: 116-759). Publishes Macedonian belles lettres and works on culture, history, foreign literature and history; as well as hit novels from around the world, classical literature, special editions, classics for young readers, children's literature, literature readers.

Kultura (Bul. Sveti Kliment Ohridski 68-a, 91000 Skopje, tel.: 111-332). Publishes a large range of editions in the fields of literature, science, philosophy, history and lexicography. In addition to literature by Macedonian writers, Kultura also publishes masterpieces by world authors, modern world novels, as well as philosophical, anthropological, sociological and aesthetic works. Kultura also publishes school readers jointly with other publishers. Its series include: Biographies, Meridian, Picture Books, Dictionaries, The Past, Reminiscences, Special Editions, Criticism and Essays, Modern Macedonian Poetry and Modern Macedonian Prose.

Detska radost (Mito Hadživasilev-Jasmin bb., 91000 Skopje, tel.: 112-394). This publisher is part of the publishing firm Nova Makedonija, and is one of the oldest publishing houses in Macedonia. It specializes in children's and youth literature and magazines. It publishes approximately one hundred titles per year in Macedonian, Turkish, Romany, Serbian, Croatian, Albanian, English and Slovak. Its series include Contemporary Balkan Poetry, Worlds (presenting Macedonian literature and eminent writers in English), Dictionaries, History of Macedonian Literature, Monographs, Irises (contemporary Macedonian prose), Critiques and Essays (by eminent Macedonian essayists and critics), and Fables from Around the World (picture books).

DAILY NEWSPAPERS

- *Nova Makedonija*, 1944- .
  Skopje: NIP "Nova Makedonija"

- *Večer*, 1963- .
  Skopje : NIP "Nova Makedonija"

- *Dnevnik*, 1996- .
  Skopje : NIP "Krug" d.o.o.

- *Makedonija Denes*, 1998- .
  Skopje : NIK Denes

- *Bitolski vesnik*, 1964- .
  Opštinski odbor na SSRNM

NEWS MAGAZINES

Denes

Covers people and events, letters to the editor, interviews, editorials, political and economic issues, political cartoons, short news items from around the world, culture (art, literature), interviews, film, fiction, sports, WWW and related issues.

Lettre Internationale
Macedonian P.E.N., 1973- .
Skopje : Macedonian P.E.N. Center

European review of culture, Macedonian edition. Comes out twice yearly.

Loza
Skopje: Filozofski fakultet

Monthly news magazine. Interviews with professors, topics from various departments in the Faculty of Philology. News events, book promotions, lectures, practical information (e.g., how to write a research paper), essays. Buy-sell books. Stories and poems by students, some in Albanian. Literary dictionary: explanation of terms used in literary criticism.

Zbor, 1991- .
Skopje: Redakcija "Zbor"
e-mail: zbor@unet.com.mk

Claims to be the first, independent news magazine in Macedonia. Covers topics in politics, economics and culture. Comes out every two weeks. Book reviews, theater reviews, film reviews, music, review of Internet sites that deal with cultural issues. Page of aphorisms and political cartoons, editorials, letters to the editor.

Makedonsko vreme/Macedonian Times, 1994- .
Skopje: "MI-AN" d.o.o.
http://www.mian.com.mk/

The *Macedonian Times* is the first independent newsmagazine in Macedonia that is printed both in English and in Macedonian. Comes out once a month. Items that deal with political, economic, social, cultural and historical issues in Macedonia.

Makedonsko delo
e-mail: delo@unet.com.mk, makedonskodelo@usa.net

Publishes on political issues, investigative reports, interviews, memoirs, popular interest stories, poetry.

Makedonsko sonce, 1994- .
Skopje : Makedonski svetski kongres
http://www.makedonskosonce.com/

Published by the émigré organization World Macedonian Congress. Publishes articles critical of government, editorials, human interest stories, letters to the editor, religion (Orthodoxy), book reviews, sports, advice column, recipes.

Puls, 1991- .
Skopje: NIP "Nova Makedonija"
e-mail: puls@simt.com.mk

This is one of the more popular and less biased independent news weeklies. Publishes articles dealing mainly with internal and foreign political issues and economics. Strong focus on events in the Balkans. Also covers theater, film, music, economy, interviews with important individuals.

Start
http://www.start.com.mk/

Primary focus on politics and the economy. Includes sections on culture and events around the world. Maintains an excellent Web site with archives of earlier issues.

Fokus, 1995- .
Skopje: PNID "Step"

PERIODICALS

Visual Arts

Golemoto staklo, 1995- .
Skopje: Muzej na sovremenata umetnost

Magazine with focus on the visual arts. Review of art exhibits in Macedonia and abroad, critical studies, interviews with artists, book reviews, list of exhibits; uses color and black and white photographs extensively. Issue 4, 1996 contains a listing of all the public and private galleries in Skopje, with addresses and phone numbers.

Kinopis, 1989- .
Skopje: Kinoteka na SR Makedonija

Focuses on the history and theory of film. Essays dealing with world film, information on world film festivals, film reviews, interviews, bibliographies. Also publishes articles on photography, video and cartoons.

Teatarski glasnik, 1978- .
Skopje: Internacionalen teatarski centar

History of theater in Macedonia, reports on theater festivals around the world. Published irregularly, each issue lists all plays performed in the previous season in Macedonia. Publishes memoirs, essays, book reviews, theater reviews.

Children's Literature

Magazines published by Detska radost publishing house:

- *Rosica*. Monthly magazine for preschoolers. Each issue contains a 16 page coloring book.
- *Drugarče*. Aimed at second and third graders. Very well illustrated.
- *Razvigor*. Literary magazine for older youth, edited by well known Macedonian writers. Publishes translations of world literature. Well illustrated.
- *Naš svet*. Aimed at young readers age 10-15, covers topics on literature, every day life, music, sports, geography, history and art.

Economics and Finance

Bilten, 1995- .
Skopje: Ministerstvo za finansii

Bulletin of the Ministry of Finance.

Economy Press, 1993- .
Skopje : NIP "Leidi L"

Ekonomija i biznis, 1998- .
Skopje: "Euro-Mak-Kompani"

Focus on theory and practice in economics and business. Published monthly; independent; economic theory and practice, macroeconomic policy in the Republic of Macedonia, successful development strategy, interviews, essays, book reviews; in Macedonian with abstracts in English.

Ekonomski glasnik, 1994- .
Skopje: Sojuz na smetkovoditeli finansisti i revizori na Republika Makedonija

Ekonomski magazin, 1993- .
Skopje: PIPD (Pretprijatie za izdavačka i publicisticka dejnost "Biznis medium"

Ekonomsko praven sovetnik, 1992- .
Skopje: Centar za ekonomsko-praven konsalting V&F

Informator, 1995- .
Skopje: Agencija za ekonomsko pravna podrska, procenka i revizija "Pro Agens"

Perspektivi, 1996- .
Skopje: Agencija na Republika Makedonija za transformacija na pretprijatijata so opštestven kapital, 1996- .

Focus on social reforms in Macedonia.

Fakti za privatizacijata

Bulletin of the Agency for Reconstruction. Published six times each year. Each issue maintains a list of companies that have received permission for transformation, and those that are for sale.

Education

Prosveten, 1953- .
Skopje: Ministerstvo za obrazovanie

Published by the Ministry of Education, comes out every two weeks except 1 July and August. Includes short news items, editorials, news and announcements from the Ministry of Education, announcements of meetings (past and future), essays, practical advice on teaching, pedagogy, excerpts from school newspapers, book reviews.

Prosvetno delo, 1949- .
Skopje: Ministerstvo za prosveta na Narodna Republika Makedonija

Organ of the Ministry of Education. Publishes research and methodology on K-12 education, history of education, teaching methods, role of the family in education, educational psychology, technology in education. Contents page is translated into English.

Učitel, 1998- .
Bitola: Fakultet za učiteli i vospituvači

Published by the Teachers Faculty in Bitola.

Studentski zbor: vesnik na Sojuzot na studentite od Skopskiot univerzitet, 1954- .
Skopje: UO na Sojuzot na studentite
http://www.szbor.org.mk/

Published by the Student Union of Skopje University. Includes essays on politics, issues dealing with the university, culture, sports, interviews, short news items, review of art, literature, film, music.

Folklore

Makedonski folklor
Skopje: Institut za folklor

Geography

Geografski razgledi, 1962- .
Skopje: Sojuz na geografskite združenija na Republika Makedonija

Published by the Geographic Association of Macedonia. Includes articles dealing mainly with Macedonian geography. Includes literature review and statistical information; abstracts in English.

History

Glasnik, 1971- .
Skopje: Institut za nacionalna istorija

Research essays, abstracts in English, materials and papers, book reviews, articles on special topics.

Ziva, 1951- .
Skopje: Filozofski fakultet, Seminar za klasična filologija
Years: 1951-1986, 1989, 1991, 1993-1998

Published by the Society for Classical and Ancient Studies, Faculty of Philology, Skopje. Articles published in Macedonian, English, German, French or Serbian/Croatian with abstracts in several languages; includes book reviews and bibliographies. Authors are Macedonian and foreign.

Istorija
Skopje: Institut za instorija

Published by the Institute of History. Table of contents translated into English. Includes research articles, articles on how to teach history, materials and resources, book reviews, bibliographies, announcements, new book promotions.

Philosophy

Etički tetratki, 1998- .
Skopje: Filozofski fakultet, Institut za filozofija

Philology

Jazikot vo praktikata, 1996- .
Skopje: Združenie za primena na makedonskiot literaturen jazik vo službenata i vo javnata komunikacija

Focus on usage of literary Macedonian in official and public communication. Includes sections on syntax, style, lexicon, word formation, phonetics, spelling, accent, answers to questions from readers, language in the media (TV, radio, print).

Law

Makedonska revija za Kazneno pravo i kriminologija, 1994- .
Skopje: Združenie za krivično pravo i kriminologija na Makedonija

Pravnik, 1992- .
Skopje: Združenie na pravnicite od stopanstvoto na Makedonija

Published by the Association of Macedonian Business Lawyers. Table of contents translated into English. Focus is on corporate law, privatization law; includes information on legislative changes that have taken place, are about to take place. Includes supplement titled "Judicial practice." Information is very useful to foreign missions, embassies and consulates in Macedonia. Comes out ten times each year.

Priračnik za ekonomsko pravni raboti, 1996- .
Skopje: "Ekonomski sovetnik"

Sudiska Revija, 1995- .
Skopje: Združenie na sudiite na Republika Makedonija

Table of contents is translated into English and French. Publishes reports of meetings of the Judges Association, views and opinions; includes a section on court practice and procedures. Provides abstracts in English and French.

Library Science

Bibliotekarski informator, 1994- .
Skopje: Narodna i univerzitetska biblioteka "Kliment Ohridski"

Bibliotekarski informativen bilten, 1966- .
Skopje: Narodna i univerzitetksa biblioteka

Makedonika. 2. serija: Stranski publikacii za Makedonija, 1975/1976- .
Skopje: Narodna i univerzitetska biblioteka "Kliment Ohridski"

Publications on Macedonia published outside Macedonia.

Literature

Literaturen zbor, 1954- .
Skopje: Društvo za makedonski jazik i literatura

Naše pismo, 1995- .
Skopje: Nezavisni pisateli na Makedonija

Published by the Independent Writers Union. Comes out six times each year. Includes critical essays, poetry, short stories, translations, theoretical essays by younger writers, book reviews, reviews contents of literary and art journals and of art exhibits.

Oko, 1992- .
Skopje: "Detska radost"

Contents are in Macedonian and English. One of the best literary magazines dealing with contemporary Macedonian literature. Publishes poetry, criticism, interviews, essays on important trends in world literature and literary texts by foreign authors. Its main function is to promote the publisher's own book titles.

Razgledi, 1954- .
Skopje: Razgledi

Comes out six times each year, publishes poetry, short stories, critical essays, essays on literary theory and book reviews.

Sovremenost, 1951- .
Skopje: "Kočo Racin"

Comes out five times each year. Focuses mainly on Macedonian literature; includes critical essays on theater and art, and book and art reviews. One of the earliest literary and art journals. Its editors have been some of the best-known and most influential Macedonian writers and critics. Includes poetry and stories by contemporary Macedonian writers.

Spektar, 1983- .
Skopje: Institut za literatura

Publishes articles on literary theory, myth, folklore and contemporary Macedonian literature, with abstracts in English, book reviews and short notes.

Stremez, 1954- .
Prilep: Klub na mladite pisateli

Publishes short stories, poetry, translations, essays and book reviews.

Stozer, 1996- .
Skopje: Društvo na pisatelite na Makedonija

Journal of the Macedonian Writers Union. Publishes poems, short stories, interviews. Some numbers focus on a specific theme; includes letters to the editor.

Struga, 1984- .
Struga: Struga Poetry Evenings

International review of poetry, published by the Struga Poetry Evenings organization. Includes works of poets participating in the yearly poetry competition in Struga.

Media

Makedonski mediumski bilten, 1996- .
Skopje: Evropski institut za mediumi

Published by the European Media Institute. Includes information on media law, interviews, letters to the editor, state of the media in Macedonia, statistical information on viewers or listeners, new technology, new projects, announcements of meetings and conferences, politics and the media, media in other countries, media and elections.

Music and Dance

Muzika, 1997- .
Skopje: Sojuz na kompozitorite na Makedonija

Politics and the Military

Glas na VMRO-DPMNE, 1991- .
Skopje: VMRO-DPMNE

Voice of the VMRO-DPMNE political party.

Demokratija: vesnik na Socijaldemokratskiot sojuz na Makedonija, 1993- .
Skopje: Socijaldemokratski sojuz

Published by the Social-Democratic Union of Macedonia. Includes interviews, political cartoons, political and economic issues. Includes a section titled "Demonstrant" that deals with youth issues.

Odbrana, 1992- .
Skopje: Ministerstvo za odbrana na Republika Makedonija

Published by the Ministry of Defence. Short news items, analysis of current issues dealing with the military, description of weapons and training, world military news, arms technology around the world, traditions and history of the Macedonian army, collectible weapons, book reviews. Includes "At Ease" comedy section and military-related cartoons.

Religion

Vesnik, 1959- .
Skopje: Makedonska pravoslavna crkva

Official paper of the Macedonian Orthodox Church.

Vistina, 1991- .
Bitola: NIRDOP "Centar za pečat i radio"

Published by the Prespa-Pelagonija Eparchy of the Macedonian Orthodox Church

Voskresenie, 1981- .
Skopje: Makedonska pravoslavna crkva

Published by the Macedonian Orthodox Church; focuses on religious education.

Domostroj, 1993- .
Strumica: Pravoslaven sobor Sveti Naum Ohridski

Focuses on Orthodox spiritual culture.

11-ti mart '43, 1997- .
Skopje: Evrejska zaednica

Bulletin of the Jewish Society of Macedonia.

Pelagonitisa, 1996- .
Bitola: Prespansko-pelagoniska eparhija

Published by the Prespa-Pelagonija Eparchy of the Orthodox Church. Includes essays on religion and philosophy, works by the church fathers, art, esthetics, as well as translations of articles from other languages.

Crkoven život, 1996- .
Skopje: Makedonska arhiepiskopija

Social Issues

Perspektivi, 1996- .
Skopje: Agencija na Republika Makedonija za transformacija na pret-prijatijata so opštestven kapital

Sociološka revija, 1995- .
Skopje: Združenie na sociolozite

Published by the Macedonian Sociological Association. Table of contents translated into English. Essays in Macedonian with abstracts in English. Includes book reviews, research reports, announcements.

Filozofska tribina

Official organ of the Macedonian Philosophical Society. Publishes articles on epistemology, ethics, esthetics, political philosophy, metaphysics, history of philosophy, logic, philosophy of knowledge, philosophy of the spirit, etc. Each issue has a section dedicated to an individual philosopher or idea.

Statistics

Osnovni ekonomski podatoci za Republika Makedonija, 1993- .
Skopje: Republički zavod za statistika

Macedonia Basic Economic Data. English and Macedonian parallel texts. Area, major cities, counties, climate, population, foreign trade, prices, GNP, wages, etc.

Statistički pregled, 1980- .
Skopje: Republički zavod za statistika

Popular Culture

Kotelec, 1979- .
Skopje: OOZT "Večer"

Kulturen život, 1956- .
Skopje: Kulturno prosvetna zaednica na Makedonija
e-mail: kulziv@soros.org.mk

Well-designed and illustrated. Best all-around popular culture magazine. Includes essays on literary theory and criticism, literary research, art, theater, special topics, ballet, music, book reviews, fiction, drama, poetry. Includes some translations of works in other languages.

Žena, 1990- .
Skopje: Prosvetena zena

Monthly magazine for women. Interviews, essays on style, short news items of interest to women, Orthodox holidays for the month, explanations, reviews of books, video and music. Section titled "You and Your Home," health advice, recipes, garden section, horoscope, fiction.

Kulturno nasledstvo, 1982- .
Skopje: Republički zavod za zaštita na spomenicite na kulturata, 1984- .

Focus on Macedonia's cultural heritage. Topics include church architecture, frescoes, folk traditions and archeology. Provides abstracts in English.

Macedonian Review, 1971- .
Skopje: Kulturen život

Published in English. Contains translations of articles that appeared in other journals and magazines. Includes essays on history, literature, arts, as well as notes and commentaries. Main focus is the promotion of Macedonian literature, art and culture abroad.

Index

A Theory of Justice, 138
Acta Analytica: Philosophy and
  Psychology: International
  Periodical for Philosophy in
  Analytical Tradition, 33
Acta carsologica, 35
Acta ecclesiastica Sloveniae, 28
Acta Histriae, 29
Acta neophilologica, 32
Adem, D., 170
Adem, G., 171
Ademović, F., 79
Advent News: religiski informativnni
  vijesnik, 72
Agency for Women's Policy, 21
Agim, V., 171
Agriculture publications, in Bosnia
  and Herzegovina, 62
Ahmetspahić, J., 61
AIM. See Alternativna Informativna
  Mreža (AIM)
AIM Review, 56
Akademija nauka i umjetnosti Bosne i
  Hercegovine, 48
Akordi: avazova muzička revija, 68
Aladin: poučno-zabavni dječji list, 65
Albahari, D., 124
Albanian collections, libraries with,
  177-178
Albanology Series, in Kosova/Kosovo,
  174
Alem: list za kulturui društvena
  pitanja KDM "Preporod,"
  63
Alergološko imunološki časopis:
  stručno medicinski časopis,
  68
Ali, P., 171,173
Alić, S., 56

Almanah: časopis za proučavanje,
  zaštitu i prezentaciju
  kultunoistorijske baštine
  Muslimana-Bošnjaka, 153
Alternativna Informativna Mreža
  (AIM), 55-56
Amalietti, 11
Anali, 66
Andrić, I., 119
Annales: anali Koprskega primorja in
  bližnjih pokrajin, 29
Antologija savremene književnosti
  bošnjaka iz Sandžaka, 78
Anton, B., 170
Anton, C., 170,174
Anton Kolë, B., 172
Apel: bosanskohercegovačko glasilo
  Saveza ratnih vojnih invalida
  BiH, 74
Archaeology publications, in Bosnia
  and Hercegovina, 62-63
Archival publications
  in Bosnia and Hercegovina, 66-67
  in Macedonia, 195
  in Montenegro, 154
Arheoloski veštnik, 29
Arhiv grada Kotora, 147
Arhivi, 29
Arif, D., 173
Arsenijevič, V., 125
Art publications
  in Montenegro, 155
  in Slovenia, 30-31
Arts Libri, 125
AS: nezavisna informativno-politička
  revija, 58
Asanaj, D., 166
ASNOM, 191
Association of Librarians of
  Montenegro, 151